HENRY FORD CENTENNIAL LIBRARY

MAR 0 7 200

D0560898

B
HITCHCOC
K

Chandler, Charlotte.

It's only a movie.

$26.00

DATE			

WITHDRAWN

BAKER & TAYLOR

ALSO BY CHARLOTTE CHANDLER

Nobody's Perfect: Billy Wilder—A Personal Biography

I, Fellini

The Ultimate Seduction

Hello, I Must be Going: Groucho and His Friends

It's Only a Movie

ALFRED HITCHCOCK:

A PERSONAL BIOGRAPHY

CHARLOTTE CHANDLER

Simon & Schuster

New York London Toronto Sydney

SIMON & SCHUSTER
Rockefeller Center
1230 Avenue of the Americas
New York, NY 10020

Copyright © 2005 by Charlotte Chandler
All rights reserved,
including the right of reproduction
in whole or in part in any form.

SIMON & SCHUSTER and colophon are registered trademarks
of Simon & Schuster, Inc.

For information about special discounts for bulk purchases,
please contact Simon & Schuster Special Sales at
1-800-456-6798 or business@simonandschuster.com

Book design by Ellen R. Sasahara

Manufactured in the United States of America

1 3 5 7 9 10 8 6 4 2

Library of Congress Cataloging-in-Publication Data
Chandler, Charlotte.
It's only a movie : Alfred Hitchcock, a personal biography / Charlotte Chandler.
p. cm.
Includes index
Filmography: p.
1. Hitchcock, Alfred, 1899–1980. 2. Chandler, Charlotte. 3. Motion picture producers and
directors—Great Britain—Biography. I. Title.
PN1998.3.H58 C53 2005
791.4302'33'092—dc22   2004052559

ISBN 0-7432-4508-3

ACKNOWLEDGMENTS

With special appreciation

Pat Hitchcock-O'Connell, Alma Reville Hitchcock, Chuck Adams, and Bob Bender.

With appreciation

Michael Accordino, Jan Anderson, Judith Anderson, Claudio Angelini, Enrica Antonioni, Michelangelo Antonioni, Amelia Antonucci, Dennis Aspland, Linda Ayton, Diane Baker, Roy Ward Baker, Charles Bennett, Marcella Berger, Ingrid Bergman, Sidney Bernstein, Robert Boyle, David Brown, Kevin Brownlow, Henry Bumstead, Bob Calhoun, Jack Cardiff, Fred Chase, Larry Cohen, Herbert Coleman, Wilkie Cooper, Rusty Coppleman, Warren Cowan, Henri-Georges Clouzot, Hume Cronyn, George Cukor, Tony Curtis, Georgine Darcy, Marlene Dietrich, Karin Dor, Mitch Douglas, Lisa Drew, Jean-Louis Dumas, Laura Elliott, C. O. "Doc" Erikson, Ray Evans, Douglas Fairbanks, Jr., Rudi Fehr, Jean Firstenberg, Henry Fonda, Joan Fontaine, Barry Foster, Joe Franklin, John Emmanuel Gartmann, Bob Gazzale, Anthony Gentile, John Gielgud, Lillian Gish, Milton Goldman, Elliott Gould, Farley Granger, Cary Grant, Hilton Green, Dick Guttman, Dolly Haas, Robert Haller, Peter Handford, Curtis Harrington, Robert A. Harris, Harry Haun, Edith Head, Tippi Hedren, Audrey Hepburn, Bernard Herrmann, Arthur Hiller, Thurn Hoffman, John Houseman, Evan Hunter, Peter Johnson, James Katz, Howard G. Kazanjian, Fay Kanin, Grace Kelly, Theodore Kheel, Alexander Kordonsky, Martin Landau, John

Landis, Ted Landry, Fritz Lang, Bryan Langley, Henri Langlois, Robert Lantz, Arthur Laurents, Ernest Lehman, Johanna Li, Janet Leigh, Norman Lloyd, Joshua Logan, Sirio Maccioni, Shirley MacLaine, Karl Malden, Groucho Marx, James Mason, Mary Merson, Ray Milland, Ruth Anna Millman, Laurent Momméja, Thom Mount, Dieter Mueller, Reggie Nalder, Ronald Neame, Paul Newman, Arthur Novell, Eileen O'Casey, Maureen O'Hara, Laurence Olivier, Robert Osborne, Jerry Pam, Gregory Peck, Anthony Perkins, Vlada Petric, Jay Presson Allen, Dan Price, Michael Redgrave, Claude Reininger, Robert Rosen, David Rosenthal, Eva Marie Saint, Sandra Seacat, Daniel Selznick, Peter Shaffer, Sidney Sheldon, Sylvia Sidney, Martin E. Segal, Walter Slezak, John Springer, June Springer, Jeff Stafford, Michael Starr, Gary Stevens, James Stewart, Roy Thinnes, Richard Todd, François Truffaut, John Vernon, King Vidor, Lew Wasserman, Cheryl Weinstein, Billy Wilder, Emlyn Williams, Paul Wilson, Teresa Wright, Jane Wyman.

The Academy of Motion Picture Arts and Sciences, the American Film Institute, Anthology Film Archives, the British Film Institute, the Cinémathèque Française, Film Forum (New York), The Film Society of Lincoln Center, the Italian Cultural Institute, New York, The Leytonstone Alfred Hitchcock Society, the Museum of Modern Art, The New York Public Library for the Performing Arts, the Plaza Athénée Hotel (Paris), The Potsdam Museum, The Royal Lancaster Hotel (London), the Savoy Hotel (London), Turner Classic Movies, UCLA Department of Theater, Film, and Television.

To Hitch

CONTENTS

It's Only a Movie

PROLOGUE

I REMEMBER INGRID BERGMAN coming up to me in a terrible state," Alfred Hitchcock told me. "Worried, miserable, high-strung, romantic, idealistic, sensitive, emotional. Dear Ingrid. She took life very seriously, and fiction even more seriously. She said, her voice pregnant with feeling, almost trembling, 'Hitch, there's something I must ask you about my part. I don't feel it. I can't find my motivation . . .'

"I said to her, 'Ingrid, fake it. It's only a movie.'

"That seemed to satisfy her, but then, a few weeks later, Ingrid was back standing to the side, shyly waiting for me to be free. I turned to beckon her over. It was interesting, because Ingrid is many things, but shy isn't one of them. I asked her what was bothering her.

"'Oh, Hitch, I've been thinking . . .'

"I thought, 'Oh, dear.' I said, 'Please go on.'

"She did. I couldn't have stopped her.

"'I've been feeling that what I do isn't worthwhile. Movies. Being an actress. I'm not doing enough to help people. Of all the worth-while things you can do with your life, I feel I should be doing some-thing more.'

"'Well, Ingrid,' I said, 'have you thought about going to a hospital and emptying bedpans?'

"When the actors were taking themselves too seriously," Hitchcock told me, "I hoped the light touch would give them some perspective. I found it rather successful. There was only one person on whom my little diversionary technique didn't work.

"Whenever I found myself getting overwrought over problems with one of my films, I would say to myself, 'Remember, it's only a movie.' It never worked. I was never able to convince myself."

INTRODUCTION

M Y DEAREST DREAM," Alfred Hitchcock said to me, "would be to walk into an ordinary men's store on the street and buy a suit, off the rack.

"There are, I suppose, many men who would envy me having the finest tailors to make my bespoke suits of the best material, but my own dream would be to buy a suit—on sale.

"Now, I have pretty much given up my hope of losing enough weight, which I don't think will ever happen, but that is not the problem. The real problem is not my size, but my shape.

"Even sex is embarrassing for a person who looks the way I do. There weren't enough light bulbs to turn off.

"If I had been given the choice in life, I would have looked like Cary Grant on whom everything looked good, and I would have indulged some fashion fantasies, a *39 Steps* raincoat, tossed on, a beige cashmere cardigan thrown casually around my shoulders, or better yet, tied around my waist—if I had one.

"Some writers say that Cary Grant was my fantasy alter ego. Silliness. When I look into my mirror, I don't see Cary Grant. I look into my mirror as little as possible, because the person who looks back at me has always seemed something of a stranger who doesn't look at all the way I feel. But, somehow, he kept getting into my mirror."

When Alfred Hitchcock showed me his home on Bellagio Road in Bel Air, California, in the mid-1970s, I had the opportunity to see his astounding wardrobe. Most remarkable was not the quantity of suits, nor the quality, all of the finest fabric, but that they seemed to be the same suit, repeated many times.

At second glance, however, it was obvious that there were numerous subtle distinctions. Among the black suits, there were shades of black.

Hitchcock's suits were famous, and it was widely assumed that he invariably wore the *same* black suit. James Stewart remembered, "Hitch in Marrakech, 110 in the shade, scarcely ever taking off his dark jacket or even loosening his tie." Director Ronald Neame recalled that even as far back as 1928 when Hitchcock was directing *Blackmail,* he wore a dark suit, white shirt, dark tie, black shoes and socks, in spite of the intense heat from the klieg lights, before air-conditioning.

Many of these suits actually were navy blue. "It is called French blue," Hitchcock told me, a blue so dark that it seems black. Every suit appeared new, in keeping with the reputation of the director for being meticulous.

Another noteworthy aspect of the collection was that there were many different sizes. "Those suits are all in my sizes," he said.

"If my weight changes, up or down, I'm prepared."

I asked him how he kept so many suits paired, together with their mates. He explained that they were all keyed, the trousers with their jackets, the sizes with labels sewn in and dated. Inside the waistband of each pair of trousers was a large number in black, and in each coat was a number. "I don't enjoy any suspense about finding my clothes."

Continuing in a more serious tone, he said, "I never achieved the body I wanted, but I am proud of my body of work. It is tall and thin and handsome."

Henri Langlois, the founder and secretary general of the Ciné-mathèque Française, introduced me to Alfred Hitchcock and his wife, Alma Reville, at the Plaza Athénée hotel in Paris. Some years before, Langlois's dismissal by the French government from his post as curator of the Cinémathèque had provoked demonstrations that escalated into the 1968 riots, effectively shutting down Paris. Throughout dinner, Hitchcock and Langlois talked about Hitchcock's films, those that existed, and a few that existed only in Hitchcock's mind.

"I once had an idea," Hitchcock told us, "that I would like to use to open a film. We are at Covent Garden or La Scala. Maria Callas is onstage. She is singing an aria, and her head is tilted upwards. She sees, in a box high up, a man approach another man who is seated there. He stabs him. She is just reaching a high note, and the high note turns into a scream. It is the highest note she has ever sung, and she receives a tremendous ovation."

Hitchcock seemed to have finished the story.

"And then? What happens next?" Langlois would have leaned forward on the edge of his chair, except that because of his substantial girth, he already *was* on the edge of his chair.

Hitchcock turned and indicated his wife, Alma, who had worked with him officially and unofficially for more than fifty years. He said to Langlois, "Ask the Madame. She does continuity."

"I've retired," Alma said.

"The closest I ever came to doing this opera vignette," Hitchcock continued, "was in *The Man Who Knew Too Much*.

"I've always wanted to do a murder among the tulips, too. When I saw the vast fields of tulips in Holland, I knew right away it was a setting I wanted to use, especially in color with blood on the tulips.

"There's another scene waiting for a story that I've thought about, involving an automobile assembly line in Detroit. The cars are moving along, and the workers are talking about their lives, an argument with the wife, lunch, and other mundane matters. A car rolls off the assembly line, and when the door is opened, a body falls out. That's as far as I got.

"Some years ago, I was in New York for *Rope,* and the publicist took me to my first baseball game. We watched from the broadcast booth, and I made a few drawings. I asked him how many people were watching the game, and he said sixty thousand. I thought, what a perfect spot for a murder! A murder on a baseball field. One of the players is shot, and there are sixty thousand suspects.

"Then, it actually happened a few years later."

"Sometimes your films seem like nightmares that are really happening," Langlois said.

"I consider them frightmares," Hitchcock explained. "Frightmares are my specialty. I have never been interested in nightmares per se. Frightmares have a great deal of reality. A far-fetched story must be plausibly told, so your nonsense isn't showing.

"Fear of the dark is natural, we all have it, but fear in the sunlight, perhaps fear in this very restaurant, where it is so unexpected, mind you, *that* is interesting.

"Fear isn't so difficult to understand. After all, weren't we all frightened as children? Nothing has changed since Little Red Riding Hood faced the big bad wolf. What frightens us today is exactly the same sort of thing that frightened us yesterday. It's just a different wolf. This fright complex is rooted in every individual.

"It's what you don't see that frightens you, what your mind fills in, the implicit usually being more terrifying than the explicit. The unexpected is so important. I've never liked heavy-handed creaking-door suspense and other clichés. I like to do a 'cozy.' Something menacing happens in a serene setting. The cozy setting is a wonderful opportunity for danger and suspense.

"I, personally, have always been interested in rounding up the *un*usual suspects.

"Eventually everything becomes avoiding the cliché. Your own cliché as well as everyone else's. It's not just what *you've* done. It's what everyone else has done and done and done. I pity the poor people in the future."

Hitchcock was interested in Langlois's activities on behalf of film preservation during the World War II German occupation of Paris. The French film lover had broken the law of the occupation, risking his life to personally save hundreds of films that might have been destroyed or lost.

Hitchcock asked, "How did you choose which ones to save?"

Langlois answered, "Those which came to me and said, 'Save me!' I didn't have the possibility to see them—only to save them."

"It was very brave of you," Hitchcock commented. "You could have been put into a concentration camp."

"I didn't do anything brave," Langlois continued. "I just hid the films in my bathtub and the bathtubs of my friends. We didn't take so many baths."

"Not taking those baths was a great service to the world," Hitchcock said. "At the end of the war, I made a film to show the reality of the concentration camps, you know. Horrible. It was more horrible than any fantasy horror. Then, nobody wanted to see it. It was too unbearable. But it has stayed in my mind all of these years.

"I don't think many people actually *want* reality, whether it's in the theater or in films. It must only *look* real, because reality's something none of us can stand for too long. Reality can be more terrible than anything you can imagine.

"I, myself, was not old enough for World War I until near the end, when I was rejected. I was too old for World War II, but I like to believe I would have been brave."

"Trying to make films you *want* to make requires some bravery, too," Alma said.

"I have heard of a film," Langlois said, "that you have wanted to make for years, but . . ."

"Mary Rose," Alma said. "It would be a wonderful picture, but they have typecast him as a director who doesn't make that kind of picture. But we're not giving up.

"My husband is very sensitive to criticism," Alma added. "But when people don't like what he does or won't let him do something he believes in, I'm twice as hurt. I'm hurt for myself, and I'm hurt for him."

"*Mary Rose,*" Hitchcock explained, "was a play by James M. Barrie which I saw in London in the early 1920s. It impressed me very much. In brief, it is the story of a twelve-year-old girl who is taken on an excursion to an island by her parents. She disappears and, weeks later, reappears, with no explanation. As a young woman, she returns to the island with her husband, and disappears again. She is gone many years. Then, when she reappears, her son is a grown man, her husband is middle-aged, but she hasn't changed at all. In the end, she has to go back, but to where?

"I have never forgotten it. I'm trying to attack it now from a science fiction angle, because the public will want to know where Mary Rose went when she disappeared for twenty-five years and then came back as young as she was when she disappeared.

"There was another story I always wanted to do. It was a true story, on which *So Long at the Fair* was based. A woman searches for her mother who has disappeared without a trace at the Paris Exposition of 1889. The missing person has contracted the plague, and the facts have been covered over to protect the city from panic. It is a story like *Death in Venice,* also a very good film. I would like to have made both of those.

"And *Diabolique;* I'd like to have made that one, too, but [Henri-Georges] Clouzot beat me to it. For many years, I thought I would do a John Buchan book, *Three Hostages.* It's not as good as his *39 Steps,* but it's a good story. And, oh, something of Wilkie Collins. What a writer that man was! I admired Dickens, and I'd like to have done something of Poe.

"I was always an avid reader of the newspaper from the time I was a boy. As I became interested in the world of film, I became more alert to stories, especially crime stories that could be the basis for a film. There was one I read somewhere, I don't know where, which has never left my mind. It's not one I could ever use because it's too horrible to show, except in a horror film, and even in a horror film, it would be too shocking and probably would provoke a release of tension resulting in a few gasps, some giggles, and then laughter.

"There was a report of a Chinese executioner who did heads. He was so good at his job that people requested him when they were sentenced to have their heads chopped off. You can imagine how painful botched and sloppy work could be, especially if the whole procedure were dragged out.

"One poor fellow who had resigned himself to his fate, stepped up, and this super-executioner deftly dealt the death blow with the greatest precision, but nothing happened.

"The man said, 'Please don't keep me waiting.'

"The executioner said, 'Please nod.'

"The man did, and his head fell off. What imagery!

"I don't know if the story was true or not," Hitchcock said, "but it's so far-fetched, that maybe it was."

Our conversation was a mix of movies and food, the two passionate interests of which neither Hitchcock nor Langlois ever tired. Langlois was even stouter than Hitchcock.

"I believe that there is a perfect relationship between love of food and a healthy libido," Hitchcock said. "People who like to eat have a stronger libido, a greater interest in sex.

"I was very innocent and sexually repressed in my youth. I was a virgin when I married, you know."

He hesitated momentarily, having noted the disapproving frown on his wife's face, and then continued. "I think that too much sex while you are working goes against the work and that repressed sex is more constructive for the creative person. It must get out, and so it goes into the work. I think it helped create a sense of sex in my work.

"The experiencing of passion, as with fear, makes you feel alive. In the film, you can experience these very extreme feelings without paying the bill."

Before dinner, Hitchcock had enjoyed his then-favorite drink, a Mimosa. Both Hitchcock and Langlois ate rapidly. Since both of them seemed to enjoy food and be so interested in it, I would have expected them to savor the experience more and make it last.

A waiter brought out a splendid multi-layered cake, frosted in butter cream, with pink and yellow flowers and the message *Bienvenue* spelled out on top. The chef came out, too, wearing his toque blanche and an impeccable white apron. He was glowing as he told Hitchcock that the cake was being presented with the compliments of the Plaza Athénée, and then, in a sort of aside to Hitchcock in French, he whispered that he was a great fan of his films and that it had been such an honor to work on this cake for him. As if embarrassed by his own audacity in daring to speak for himself to the great director, the chef rushed off. As he left, Hitchcock, who spoke French rather well, called out after him, thanking him for the beautiful *torte*.

The captain then ceremoniously carried the cake away. After a few minutes, the waiter returned with four slices of chocolate cake and a slice was served to each of us.

Hitchcock turned to Langlois and said, "My films, you know, aren't slices of life, but slices of cake."

He said he was reminded of the first film he was supposed to have directed in Hollywood, *Titanic*. It was to have been his first American project for David O. Selznick.

"My favorite scene was in the ship's great kitchen where the pastry chef is decorating an extraordinary cake. It has many layers, and with a flourish of his pastry bag, he is putting the final petals on a butter cream rose of which the cake has many. Then, the pastry chef writes out *Happy Birthday*.

"The chef is smiling slightly with pride as he works. He is *so* pleased with his creation. He is tasting it in his mind.

"But we all know everything he's doing is for nothing. Nobody will ever eat the cake. The cake is going to a watery grave and maybe the people who were supposed to be eating it, too. Maybe also the chef we have come to know.

"The audience is thinking, 'It's no use.' They want to scream out, 'Stop! Run to the lifeboats!'"

The maître d' asked Hitchcock if he would like to have the rest of the cake kept for him for the next day. Hitchcock declined, telling us that the waiters and the people in the kitchen, the chef included, would be disappointed if they didn't have the chance to taste the cake.

"I want to ask you," Langlois said, "what was it like going from working in London to suddenly working in Hollywood?"

"It wasn't as different as I had expected it to be," Hitchcock explained. "The technical possibilities, because of the bigger budgets and better equipment, were dazzling. On the other hand, everything in America seemed a bit less spontaneous and, of course, more complex *because* of the bigger budgets and the need for more careful planning."

"In America, were you conscious of making films for a different audience?"

"No. When we make films in America, we are automatically making them for the world, because America is full of people from everywhere.

"Selznick had wanted to buy an old American merchant ship that was being scrapped to play the title role. He was going to sink it in Santa Monica harbor, but we burned down Manderley instead."

"I am glad," Langlois said, "because *Rebecca* is one of my favorite films. It was brilliant never to show *Rebecca* except as a painting. She was so beautiful there was no *actrice* who could have played the part. There could not have been a Rebecca."

"But there *was* an actress to play Rebecca," Hitchcock said. "A perfect Rebecca. And she even wanted to be in the film, only she wanted to play the wrong part, that of the cringing, meek girl with rounded shoulders who was totally lacking in self-confidence.

"The actress was Vivien Leigh, who was born to be Rebecca, as she was to be Scarlett O'Hara. Scarlett shared many characteristics with

Rebecca. Vivien Leigh had the requisite beauty. She and Rebecca were both uniquely strong women who knew what they wanted and how to get it, if not how to enjoy it. They were not girls; they were women.

"Vivien Leigh was absolutely right to play Rebecca, but Rebecca never appears in the film, so neither does Vivien. And for people who knew about the real-life affair between Olivier and Leigh, that would have intruded on any illusion.

"Joan Fontaine was rather outside the little clique of British actors on the set, and that worked well for her character, who was supposed to be alone and apart."

As we were served coffee, Hitchcock suggested *"a divertissement."*

"Let's play a little game of Murder," he said. "We'll choose a victim, and then try to find the murderer."

He looked around and chose as victim the fattest man in the room, saying he could best identify with him. "Now we need a villain." Looking around again, he selected a good-looking man with blond hair and blue eyes. In a room full of well-dressed people, this man stood out as *exceedingly* well dressed. "A villain cannot look villainous or no one would let him into their house," Hitchcock told us.

A man and a woman sitting at a table near us who were deep in conversation caught Hitchcock's attention. Her earrings were next to her plate. Observing the couple, Alfred Hitchcock pointed out that they knew each other well. "You can tell she is comfortable with him or she wouldn't have taken off her earrings, which were bothering her.

"See that man? He's wearing very expensive shoes. You can tell a great deal about a man by his shoes," Hitchcock said. Langlois pulled his feet farther back under the table.

Hitchcock then asked Langlois to choose a victim for our little game of Murder. He selected a very thin man at a nearby table who was enjoying a chocolate mousse, saying, "Look at the chocolate mousse he's eating and see how thin he is. That is enough reason for me to hate him."

Hitchcock accepted that as logical. "I understand. I am an expert on losing weight. I have lost hundreds of pounds in my lifetime, and I represent the survival of the fattest."

His weight was unearned, Hitchcock claimed, since he ate so little. "Journalists often ask how much I weigh. I tell them, 'Only once a day, before breakfast.' The number of pounds, though, must remain a mystery."

"Can you believe," Langlois said, "that when I was young I was so thin, women were always trying to *force* me to eat, my mother, my nurse. I ate chocolates and cake and an entire jar of marmalade in the afternoon. I thought it would *always* be that way. At that time, I never walked up stairs. I ran up."

"Me, too," Hitchcock said. "I was always heavy, but I was agile. I think the reason that I've never received an Oscar is that I don't look like an artist. I don't look like I've starved in a garret.

"But the real reason is that the suspense genre is not so highly esteemed. It's treated like a switchback railway in an amusement park, just for thrills. Villains and heroes, hisses and kisses."

"You should receive many Oscars," Langlois said. "There is time."

There wasn't, however, much time remaining, and Hitchcock never did receive an Oscar as a director. He had been nominated as best director five times; for *Rebecca, Lifeboat, Spellbound, Rear Window,* and *Psycho.* It was Langlois who was awarded a special Oscar, for his contribution to film preservation.

Langlois asked Hitchcock if he liked mysteries and melodrama best.

"Yes, I do. But I like to feel that I don't do mysteries. I do mystifyings. That's my brand of melodrama."

"What is most difficult about melodrama?" Langlois asked.

"Casting. In melodrama, you lay out the plot, and only after you have the story, do you put in the characters. For that reason, I believe in typecasting.

"If you do it right, casting, you don't need to do much direction of actors. The really good ones find their way, and you only need recognize if they are going astray.

"Stars do have an advantage when you are casting. When something is happening to a star, a Cary Grant or a James Stewart, the public feels it more."

"Or Ingrid Bergman or Grace Kelly," Alma added.

"Yes," Hitchcock agreed. "There has been a lot of talk about the Hitchcock blondes and my heroines, you know. There was one very important factor in my selection of leading ladies, which isn't mentioned. The heroine must please women. Women not only represent half of the audience for my films, but very often the man wants to please and impress a woman, and he asks her, 'What film would you like to see?' So *she* chooses."

"Madeleine Carroll was *my* choice for *The 39 Steps*," Alma said. "I saw her first, and told Hitch about her."

As we spoke, Alma was quiet and reserved, a tiny person, pleasant, not eating very much. Hitchcock often looked at her for her reaction to what he had said.

"Do you know the proof of her love for me?" Hitchcock asked, indicating Alma. "She diets with me. She doesn't have to, but to make it easier for me, she eats only what I eat. Then she loses the weight and I don't. I couldn't afford to stay too long on a diet, or the Madame might disappear entirely."

"You are a fortunate man," Langlois said.

"We were so lucky," Alma said. "Our two imaginations met."

"She'd been working in films when I met her," Hitchcock continued, "and she knew more about it than I did. She taught me. I don't know why she married me."

Alma laughed. "Because I liked older men."

"I was born on August 13, 1899," Hitchcock said, "and she was born on August 14, 1899, so I am one day older."

"That is *formidable*," Langlois said.

Hitchcock agreed. "Yes, it is unusual."

"No, what I mean is, it is the very same thing that is true of Mary and me." Mary Merson was his close associate at the Cinémathèque Française.

"Our birthdays, Mary and me, are only a day apart. I was born on November 12, and she was born on November 13. We are Scorpios. And you are Leos."

"You're like Marlene Dietrich," Hitchcock said. "She wouldn't do anything on *Stage Fright* until she consulted her astrologer. He should have received a credit."

Langlois asked Hitchcock if he would like to have any of his past films screened for him at the Cinémathèque while he was in Paris.

"Thank you, we don't have time. If we had time, I would rather see someone else's film, Fellini or Antonioni, one of those Italian fellows.

"I have a visual mind, and my past films are all storyboarded in my mind, if I choose to recall them. I do not, however, choose to resee my films in a theater, nor to rerun them in my mind."

"I have heard," Langlois said, "that after you see the script, you can visualize the entire film."

"Yes. Definitely."

"Could you do this when you began to make silent films in the early 1920s?"

"Yes. I believe it's intuitive to visualize, but as we grow up, we lose that intuition. My mind works more like a baby's mind does, thinking in pictures. I have vague memories of my infancy, all visual, none verbal. I can't be certain, but I believe they are true memories."

"I learned to do that from him," Alma added. "Now I can't read a book without dramatizing every scene, every camera angle, every word of dialogue. It takes me forever to read a book."

Hitchcock said, "My life and the Madame's are films. If that were not true, what would we have talked about all these years?"

I asked Hitchcock if it was true that he didn't look into the camera when he was directing.

"I don't have to," he answered, "and I'll tell you why.

"About 1923, before we worked together, young Miss Alma Reville asked me if I would mind shooting some inserts for a picture she was editing. Since it was lunchtime, I walked on the stage and just as I was looking through the viewfinder of a camera, a voice behind me said, 'That's my job. You stick to what's in front of it.' It was Jack Cox, who later became my cameraman on *Blackmail* and a lot of other pictures. From that moment on, I learned everything I could about cameras and lenses, what they did in terms of angle and perspective. I trained myself to see like a camera, so I never needed to look through a lens again. Now all I need to know is the focal length of the lens, and I know exactly what the cameraman is seeing."

Langlois asked about Hitchcock's often repeated quote that "actors are cattle."

"I have been accused of saying that," Hitchcock answered, "but I believe what I said is, 'Actors should be *treated* like cattle.' Of course, I was joking, but it seems I was taken seriously. If I had been speaking seriously, I would have said, 'Actors are children.'

"I have always been available to my actors for reasonable help. 'Reasonable' is an actor who, when he walks through the door, does not ask me 'why?' but 'how?'"

As we spoke, someone approached Hitchcock for an autograph, and he drew his famous sketch of himself. After the person left, Langlois apologized. "I'm sorry they disturb you here in Paris, even while you are eating."

"They never disturb me," Hitchcock said. "They are the ones who make it all possible. The public."

It brought him great pleasure that audiences in New York, Los Angeles, London, Paris, Berlin, Tokyo, and Buenos Aires could look at his pictures and feel the same emotions.

"Emotions are universal, and art is emotion. Therefore, putting film together and making it have an effect on an audience is for me the main function of film. Otherwise, it is just a record of events.

"In the distant future, they will have what I call 'the Tickles.' People will go into a big darkened auditorium and they will be mass-hypnotized. Instead of identifying themselves with the characters on the screen, they will *be* that character, and when they buy their ticket, they will be able to choose which character they want to be. They will suffer all of the agonies and enjoy the romance with a beautiful woman or handsome man. I call them 'the Tickles,' because when a character is tickled, the audience will feel it. Then, the lights come up, and it's all over." Hitchcock paused reflectively.

"And it's a good way to dispense with real actors. Walt Disney has the right answer. If he doesn't like his actors, he tears them up!"

"Were there any actors you would like to have worked with?" Langlois asked.

"Of course. Claudette Colbert. Did you know she was French? I would like to have made a Lubitsch-style picture with her. I also would like to have worked with William Holden. *Sunset Boulevard* was a wonderful film, one of the greatest. And I would like to have worked with Miss Hepburn. Audrey, not Katharine. Katharine Hepburn wouldn't have fit into my films, but I wanted Audrey, and I almost worked with her, but it didn't happen."

"Would Miss Hepburn, Audrey not Katharine, have been a blonde?" Langlois asked.

Hitchcock shook his head. "No. Definitely not."

I mentioned that Claudette Colbert, William Holden, and Audrey Hepburn were all in Billy Wilder films.

"I envy him," Hitchcock said. "A great director, Wilder. He knew how I felt about those actors in his film. I told him, and he said the actor *he* most wanted to work with was Cary Grant. So there you are.

"I believe directing actors is really only a matter of getting good actors in the first place. Then, you have a chat with them."

As we finished our meal, Langlois said, "You have a career to be very proud of, Mr. Hitchcock."

"Not *Mr.* Hitchcock. Hitch. Call me Hitch. I am proud, but I've been lucky. Getting the opportunity is the most important part.

"A few times, it looked like I might fail. There is that thin line between success and failure. I managed to survive the tightrope, even though I don't think I'm built for tightrope walking."

As we left the restaurant, Alma said to me, "In all the years we've been together, my husband has never bored me. There aren't many wives who can say that."

I MET HITCHCOCK several times while I was writing about Groucho Marx. Groucho's favorite restaurant in Los Angeles was Chasen's, which was also the favorite of Hitchcock and his wife.

Groucho's preferred night at Chasen's was Thursday, and Thursday night dinner at Chasen's was a ritual for the Hitchcocks, who frequently came to dinner with Lew and Edie Wasserman, and Gregory and Veronique Peck.

Erin Fleming, Groucho's friend, was frequently with us. Groucho and Hitchcock would greet each other. Each had one of the few tables in the small front room of the restaurant.

Groucho's favorite part of the meal was a specialty of Chasen's, banana shortcake. He would say he ate the dinner "to get to the shortcake."

One night, as we finished our banana shortcakes, Groucho said he wished that he could have a second portion of the dessert. The captain heard him and rushed back with some. Groucho wouldn't accept it, because even in his eighties, he had a great deal of discipline. He said if he had one slice, he could enjoy the memory without feeling guilty.

Summoning the captain, Groucho said, "When they get to dessert, send over a round of banana shortcakes to Mr. Hitchcock and his friends, and be sure to put it on my check and not on his. And see what the boys in the back room will have."

We left and didn't see what happened afterward.

At his home, months later, Hitchcock finished the banana short-cake story.

"Everyone at our table that night was on a diet except the Madame and Peck. The Madame doesn't eat much when I'm on a diet, and I'm always on a diet. So Peck got all six of the shortcakes."

Hitchcock indicated the green, grassy view from the window of his Bel Air home. "I own all of that," he said in a mock serious tone.

The huge expanse of property was actually a golf course.

Hitchcock began our meeting by telling me, "To interview me, you would have to interview my films."

"I already have," I said, "and they told me many of their secrets—but not all."

No visit to the Hitchcock home would have been complete without seeing the kitchen, the most important room in the house for Hitchcock and his wife. It had taken him many years to remake the kitchen and create the wine cellar, all exactly to their specifications.

He showed me the giant refrigerator, of which he was justifiably proud. As I looked in, he stood behind me and put his hand on my shoulder, as if to push me in.

"Just joking," he said.

No matter. It was so full of food, there wouldn't have been room for me.

"This food is our luxury," he said. "We don't have a swimming pool or a tennis court. We don't live to impress anyone else."

"We fly in fish and meat weekly from England," he said. "Dover sole, beef, and lamb."

The lamb reminded him of one of his favorite stories, "Lamb to the Slaughter," by Roald Dahl, done on *Alfred Hitchcock Presents,* an episode he directed in 1958.

"A woman, played by Barbara Bel Geddes," he said, "learns from her unsympathetic husband of many years that he is leaving her. She kills him with a frozen leg of lamb, the most perfect murder weapon of my entire career. Then she cooks that leg of lamb while policemen are searching for the murder weapon, and she serves them the delicious leg of lamb. That's one murder weapon they will never find. I call that my 'ticking lamb' story, which is a variation on my 'ticking bomb' theory.

"The idea is that you want to let the audience in on everything so they know that a ticking bomb is there while the characters don't know it. That is the suspense, waiting for the bomb to explode, only they are waiting for the leg of lamb to be discovered as the murder weapon."

He said that he never ate leg of lamb without thinking of that story.

"Are you able to distinguish between English Dover sole and French Dover sole?" he asked me.

I'd never given it any thought. I considered that the question might be what Hitchcock referred to as "a leg pull."

I answered, "Only if I saw the fish's passport."

"I only eat Dover sole caught by a net, not by a hook," he said. "Have you ever seen a fish with a hook in its mouth?" He squeezed his lips together and twisted his face like a fish with a hook in its mouth. I assumed he was referring to the pain inflicted on the fish, but I wondered, how did he know if the fish was *really* caught in a net?

Hitchcock was extremely proud of his wine cellar. He enjoyed the acquisition of great wine and brandy, some of it bought to drink, and some of it to have and hold with the instinct of the passionate collector.

He told me that he had "authentic Napoleonic brandy, bottles of wine from the nineteenth century, and dazzling vintages from the 1920s."

"Do you drink these?" I asked.

"Oh, no," he said, "I could never do that. Those bottles are really irreplaceable. The responsibility for drinking one is too great. It might be the last bottle in the world of its kind. Then, there is the possibility that the actual taste would not live up to the taste buds in my mind. And then, too, perhaps I don't feel I deserve it."

I was shown around the rest of the house, a lovely home, but considered modest by Bel Air standards. I recognized Liberty of London fabrics. "We don't have to move to a bigger house," Hitchcock said. "I do not enjoy the process of moving. I find it like enduring a sickness.

"It's the work that's important. I've made films people enjoyed, and I didn't wish to prove myself with a bigger house. I like to use words such as cozy and snug when I describe my home."

Hitchcock's art collection was impressive, including paintings by artists who hung not only in the Hitchcock home, but also in the great museums of the world. His favorite artist was Klee, and Alma's, Utrillo. His favorite sculptor was Rodin, and he was proud to own a work of his. Hitchcock's own drawings bore a certain resemblance to those of Klee.

During his teens and early twenties, Hitchcock had eagerly visited art museums. At first he went to museums as an art school assignment, but very quickly these visits became one of his favorite pastimes on a Sunday or whenever he had a few hours free. "They also sent us to a railway terminal to sketch people, which I liked even better."

Hitchcock said that if he had become an artist rather than having gone into films, he would have been an abstract painter only because he didn't feel he would have been able to master the technique required by representational art. Ideally, he would have liked to have been a sculptor, like Rodin.

Being interested in dream and fantasy in art, he was fascinated by the idea of having Salvador Dali create a fantasy dream sequence in *Spellbound*. As it turned out, most of Dali's work was not used in the film.

"Very early, I was immensely struck by the Symbolists. For a time, I had Symbolist dreams."

Hitchcock said he felt privileged to be able to afford the work of Rouault, Dufy, Vlaminck, Rodin, Klee, de Chirico, and other famous twentieth-century artists, but he selected only pictures he enjoyed living with, the kind about which he could make up stories. "Klee could have made good storyboards, you know.

"Mrs. H. and I never acquired a painting unless it was liked by both of us." For a time, they had a mystery drawing hanging on their wall. "It was much admired. There was no signature. It was the work of our daughter, Pat, when she was a child."

As a young man standing in long queues to see a painting, he never dreamed that one day he would simply look up in his own home and enjoy a glance at a great painting. "They become a part of you."

Along with the paintings, there were first editions by George Bernard Shaw and James Barrie, the complete works of William Shakespeare and of Somerset Maugham. He prized an edition of *Juno and the Paycock,* which had been given to him by Sean O'Casey when Hitchcock was making a film version of the play.

He showed me some dishes.

"Do you remember these?"

I did, because I also had admired the dishes at the Plaza Athénée hotel when we had dinner there.

"I asked at the hotel if I could buy some of the dishes from them," Hitchcock continued. "I had in mind a demitasse or two. A few weeks after we returned home, several cartons arrived from Paris. They had sent a whole set, and no bill. They said it was their gift to us."

When my taxi arrived, Hitchcock walked with me to the door, where the driver was waiting. Raising his voice so the driver could hear, Hitchcock said, "Don't worry about the blood. I'll wash off what's left, and then I'll get rid of the knife. Don't worry about the body. I'll see that it's discreetly disposed of. But do check your clothes for bloodstains. Blood spattered on the wall like catsup on a hamburger bun."

The driver showed no concern. I wondered if he recognized Alfred Hitchcock.

When the taxi dropped me off, I gave the driver the fare and a tip. He returned the tip. I said, "That's for you!" When there was no response, I realized that Hitchcock's performance had been wasted. The driver wasn't really English-speaking.

"EVERY DAY IS A GIFT, which is why we call it the present."

Alfred Hitchcock said this to director King Vidor and me just before the March 7, 1979, American Film Institute gala honoring Hitchcock. We had stopped to speak with him as he waited to enter the Beverly Hilton ballroom for his tribute evening.

Vidor and I sat down next to Hitchcock, who apologized for not rising, because he couldn't. "Please accept that I have risen in spirit," he said.

"It's *your* night, Hitch," Vidor said. "You ought to be feeling great."

"Knees. It's all about knees. My knees aren't what they used to be—even what they were yesterday.

"The problem is, I had to bring along a friend. Well, not exactly a friend, more of a constant companion. Arthur Ritis."

Besides the pain, Hitchcock was apprehensive about his entrance, afraid his knees would fail him at the moment he had to walk through the audience to his table, that he would fall and be mortified. "Worse than dying," he said. "Worse even than forgetting to button your fly. I shouldn't have accepted. It's like *Jamaica Inn*. Walking the plank, you know."

"But if you felt this way, why *did* you accept?" Vidor asked.

"I didn't feel like this on the day I accepted. I did it for Alma. I wanted her to see all of these people here because of our films. I wanted to go home with her afterwards and see the look in her eyes. That was what I most looked forward to. The best part of the evening will be when we are back at home together and all of this is behind us. We'll sit and talk about it in the old way, sharing. Another memory for our old age.

"I want to tell everyone how important she has been, not only in my life, but to the Hitchcock films. They are hers, too. And I thought it might be the last time Alma and I could go together to an event like this, my last opportunity to pay public tribute to her."

"You're lucky to have had that kind of marriage," Vidor said. "It didn't work out that way for me."

"I hope I won't embarrass the Madame by not being able to stand up."

"I wish they'd do it for me, an evening like this," Vidor said, trying to cheer Hitchcock, and also telling the truth.

"I hope they do it for you while you're still able to enjoy it."

"They'd better hurry!" Vidor, though in better health, was even older than Hitchcock. "Well, at least you'll get a good dinner."

"I could never eat at a time like this, with everyone watching me. I had a ground steak earlier at home with Mrs. H."

"It's my favorite meal," Vidor said. "Do you know where you can get the best hamburger in town?"

"My house," Hitchcock answered.

"I'd like to invite you for lunch, Hitch, at my favorite restaurant, Hamburger Hamlet. And they have a good roll and French fries."

"I'd like to invite you to my house for the greatest beef you ever tasted, but Alma hasn't been well. When she feels better, we can go to Chasen's. That's *our* favorite restaurant."

Alma was seated with Cary Grant at the honoree's table as Hitchcock entered. Grant was there to assist Hitchcock, should it be necessary. Everyone in the ballroom rose except Alma, who was so small, she could scarcely be seen. Her hair and makeup artfully done, she had hoped to wear high heels, but needed the support of heavier shoes.

Weakened after a series of strokes, it was only with great force of will that she had succeeded in being there at all. Unlike her nervous husband, she had looked forward with enthusiasm to the evening. She watched intently as he entered and inched his way toward her through an audience that included some of the most famous and powerful names in Hollywood. It was as if she were taking every step with him, so great was her empathy.

John Houseman introduced Ingrid Bergman, who was the mistress of ceremonies for the evening. Speaking from the stage were Anthony Perkins, Janet Leigh, James Stewart, and François Truffaut, and from the audience, Teresa Wright, Pat Hitchcock O'Connell, Norman Lloyd, Sidney Bernstein, Victor Saville, Jane Wyman, Edith Head, Rod Taylor, Vera Miles, Ernest Lehman, Tippi Hedren, Sean Connery, Judith Anderson, and Cary Grant.

During the program, some of the tension Hitchcock had been feeling seemed to lift, and he and Alma appeared to enjoy the evening, especially as the end drew near. The strain of the intense scrutiny was nearly over.

Ingrid Bergman came onstage and spoke directly to Hitchcock. "Now, there's just one little thing I'd like to add before we finish this evening. Do you remember that agonizing shot when you had built some kind of elevator? It was a basket or something with you and the cameraman, and you were shooting this vast party in *Notorious*, and you came zooming down with your elevator and your poor pull-focus man, all the way down, into my hand, where you saw the key in a close-up. So, that was from an extreme long shot to close-up, just the key that we saw. You know what? Cary stole that key after the scene, and then he kept it for about ten years. And one day, he put it in my hand, and he said, 'I've kept this long enough. Now, it's for you for good luck.' I have kept it for twenty years, and in this very same hand, there is the key.

"It has given me a lot of good luck and quite a few good movies, too. And now, I'm going to give it to you with a prayer that it will open some very good doors for you, too. God bless you, dear Hitch. I'm coming to give you the key."

Bergman left the stage and walked past the tables to where Hitchcock was seated. When she reached him, he rose, unassisted, though not without difficulty. He accepted the key, and they embraced tenderly in what was an emotional moment for both.

Ingrid Bergman was also ill, and there was only a little time remaining for them to be together.

After the show ended, I was standing near Ingrid Bergman and Cary Grant as they chatted. "Was that *really* the same key we used in the film?" I heard her ask him.

Grant smiled and shrugged.

HILTON GREEN, longtime professional associate of Hitchcock, was there with his wife. Although Green had worked on *Alfred Hitchcock Presents, Psycho,* and *Marnie,* his wife had never met the great director.

"I kept my family away," Green told me. "I thought that was the right thing to do. But the AFI function was all over, and my wife said, 'I want to meet him.'

"I said, 'No, this is not the appropriate time.' Mr. H. was at a table, ringside, down there with Mr. and Mrs. Wasserman, and Cary Grant, and Alma. They were all at the same table, and I said, 'You're not going down there with *that* group.'

"She said, 'I'm going to go and meet him.' I didn't know what to do.

"I'll never forget. Cary Grant was in the middle of telling a story. Hitchcock was seated and I walked up behind him, and all I did was put my hand on his shoulder. He turned and looked up, and he interrupted Cary Grant, and said, 'Hilton.'

"I said, 'I don't want to interrupt,' and he said, 'Please, please.' I said, 'No, I just want you to meet my wife.'

"And he said, 'The Madame is here? Ah! you've kept me away from her for so long!' And he struggled to get up, with a great effort.

"I said, 'Don't get up, don't get up.'

"He said, 'Of course I'm going to get up.' And he did. He turned and kissed my wife's hand and said it was a wonderful pleasure to finally meet the Madame."

THE LUNCH WITH KING VIDOR at Hamburger Hamlet never happened.

The AFI event was the last time I saw Alfred Hitchcock.

I.

THE EARLY YEARS

HITCH

"**A**LFRED HITCHCOCK turned a small boy's fear into that incredible body of work," Robert Boyle, colleague and friend of Alfred Hitchcock said.

That small boy, Alfred Joseph Hitchcock, was born at the very end of Queen Victoria's reign, and he grew up during the Edwardian era. He would bring to the motion picture screen his own personal sensibilities and intelligence, shaped by a time we can only envision in faded photographs and flickering films.

The third and last child of William and Emma Jane Whelan Hitchcock, Alfred, was born on August 13, 1899, a Sunday, in Leytonstone, at the edge of London's East End. Hitchcock told me that it was remembered in his family that the day was a Sunday, "because it was one of the only Sundays in my mother's life that she missed church." The family's store is gone, but Hitchcock's early life in Leytonstone is commemorated by a mosaic picture of him as a child and scenes from his films on the walls of the local tube station.

The Hitchcocks' first son, William, had been born in 1892, three years after their marriage, and their daughter, Ellen Kathleen, called "Nellie," in 1896. "I was told," Hitchcock said, "that as a baby and small child I never cried. Even then, I didn't engage in the negative waste of energy. I have always looked upon that kind of behavior in public as a loss of control, not to mention dignity.

"Since my brother and sister were so much older, they didn't have much interest in me when I was growing up, so I had myself almost entirely to myself. I used my freedom to draw pictures and to watch life pass in front of my father's store."

Very early, young Alfred became fascinated by the traffic on the High Road, at that time, mainly horse-drawn vehicles. "There was quite a horsey smell, in fact, you might say an overwhelming stench. There was also a lot of noise from the horse's hooves and carriage wheels. I think it was the beginning of my lifelong interest in travel.

"As a boy, I knew I wanted to travel just as soon as I could. If you are lucky enough to travel when you're young, everything you see becomes a part of you on which you can draw all through life."

Early in the twentieth century, the horse-drawn streetcars that passed through Leytonstone were replaced by new electric trams. "I remember their tracks and sparking trolley wire, before they put it underground, coming from somewhere and going to somewhere else, rapidly transporting people to places I could only imagine. And the street smelled better.

"When I was no more than six years of age, perhaps younger, I did something that my father considered worthy of reprimand. I don't recall the particular transgression, but at that tender age, it could hardly have been such a serious offense.

"My father sent me to the local constabulary with a note. The police officer on duty read it and then led me down a long corridor to a jail cell where he locked me in for what seemed hours, which was probably five minutes. He said, 'This is what we do to naughty boys.'

"I have never forgotten those words. I have, ever since, gone to any length to avoid a repetition of that kind of experience, loss of control to authority. I have never enjoyed surprises, even good ones, because they make me feel out of control.

"I can still hear the clanging of the cell door behind me.

"I've always said I didn't remember why I was punished, but I think it was because earlier that day, late in the afternoon, I'd followed the tram tracks. I hadn't gone very far when it started to get dark, and I lost my way. Realizing I would be late for dinner, I hurried home. My father had been forced to wait for his dinner, although I certainly would have been happier for him to have gone ahead without me. In later years, I considered perhaps he was angry because he was worried about me.

"Even before that, I was never a little boy who wanted to grow up and be a policeman. Indeed, policemen have always frightened me, the British bobby being the most frightening. That may come from my youthful trauma, or perhaps it's simply because British policemen were the first I saw when I was young, and thus they seem more *policemen* than the rest. I think they seem more sinister because they are *so* polite, all those good manners!"

The Hitchcocks were Catholics, a minority in Leytonstone, as in England. "Just being Catholic," Hitchcock said, "meant you were eccentric." The ceremony of the weekly Sunday mass impressed young Alfred, though in later life he described himself as "neglectfully religious." His mother was of Irish descent. His father was descended from a long line of English Catholics.

William Hitchcock was a wholesale and retail greengrocer and fruiterer who had a store in Leytonstone and who dealt with the market at Covent Garden. "When I was shooting exteriors for *Frenzy* in London," Hitchcock said, "a very old man came up to me who told me he remembered my father when he bought and sold vegetables at Covent Garden.

"Some of my happiest memories were on the rare occasions when my father took me with him to the countryside. He would buy a whole field of cabbages and that sort of thing.

"My parents didn't require me to work in the store, as my older brother and sister did. Perhaps I disappointed my father because I never showed any interest in his business and no inclination to follow him into it. I could not imagine how a wilted lettuce leaf could be of such concern to him.

"Though my father made a comfortable living as a greengrocer, dealing in perishables contributed to a certain feeling of insecurity in our family. My father had a conservative nature, but his occupation put him in the position of being a speculator. In a way, it's not so different from my own field. Though I am in no way a gambler by nature, the endeavor I have chosen as my life's work has put me in a position not so different from that of my father—a speculator in perishables. But no one in our family ever went hungry. That's the advantage of being the child of a vegetable and fruit dealer.

"My mother was a homemaker, as they say. It was her full-time career, as was the accepted custom in those days. I don't remember ever coming home and not finding her there.

"Our house was always perfectly kept. Immaculate. I took it for granted. My mother was meticulous about our home and her person. She never left the house without presenting herself at her best, her posture, her demeanor, her dress, her shoes, perfectly polished, a well-kept handbag, inside as well as outside, and gloves whenever possible. I have always admired a lady who wears gloves.

"Ingrid [Bergman] wore gloves, and I thought it very sexy, the way she took them off. I always thought it was more sexy if a woman revealed her secrets gradually, rather than indulging in overexposure.

"My mother was well groomed and properly attired, even when she was cleaning our home. She would put on a big white apron that was spotless and had a starched ruffle, covering everything but her sleeves.

"She was not a complainer. I never heard her complain. She was also not a gossip. I never heard her speak badly about anyone. Her concern was entirely for her family. She did not have women friends dropping over. At the time that did not seem unusual to me. I observed the same thing about my wife. They had full lives and did not need more.

"My mother was a good cook. My father brought home the best greens and even some imported luxury fruit he might have spotted on his visit to the Covent Garden Market. Fresh milk was delivered to our house.

"I liked to shop with my mother on the High Road and especially to visit the bakery where I was always given a free cookie or two. The bakery had the most wonderful aromas. Like perfume. Lemon Cake Number 5. Guerlain Ginger Biscuit.

"My mother liked to cook, but she didn't care about baking, so our kitchen did not have the same delightful scents as the High Road bakery. I was able to fully enjoy the experience because it was before I ever heard the word 'diet.' Plumpness in very small children was considered 'cute' and even a sign of good health. It reflected well on the parents and their prosperity, and showed they were taking good care of their child.

"I remember my father going to work in a dark suit with a very white starched shirt and a dark tie. I never saw him when he wasn't clean-shaven. It wasn't for the cabbages. It was a matter of self-respect.

"My parents loved the theater and took me with them, whenever my father could be free, and that very much influenced my life. I could feel how much they enjoyed it. I did, too, and I never forgot those green-lit villains in the melodramas, accompanied by sinister music. The heroine always had rosy-pink light to help her to be more beautiful and pure."

Very early, other children made fun of the way young Alfred looked, one of them telling him he was "funny-looking." He went home and looked in the mirror. He turned to check his profile. His mother saw him doing it.

"Do you think I look funny?" he asked her.

"You'll outgrow it," she said. It wasn't the answer he was hoping to hear. "I didn't outgrow it," Hitchcock said. "I just outgrew. No one wants to be fat. That's a universal. With a small u."

His pudgy, overweight appearance, his lack of interest in the games the other children played, and little athletic ability, isolated him and led to his development of more solitary interior interests. As a boy, "I led an active inner life. The other boys judged everyone on their outer lives. I may not have been athletic, but I was well coordinated." Hitchcock said that he rather came to enjoy not having to participate in games he considered a waste of time. In those first years, his mother was his best and only companion.

"My mother was so consistently there for me, I took her presence for granted, which is a very good thing for a child. I felt I was her favorite.

"I wasn't a popular type, so I was forced to live in my imagination, and I believe that helped me to develop my creative resources. I don't need much stimulation from the outside world.

"There are internal people and external people. External people are more likely to spend or waste their creative resources. They are constantly faced with temptations that did not come my way. It was an advantage that the homely, less popular child has. I was forced to develop my interior self, not be dependent on the others. Then my work brought me a kind of appreciation, even love, you might say, that I never expected. Perhaps that made it all sweeter, the cream on the bun.

"My private person, the real me, is a very shy person, not at all the public impression," he told me. "The man is not different from the boy. To understand me, you have to accept that I'm really, truly shy, you know, and I have been so all of my life. When you start out that way as a child, it's rare that you lose it. I certainly didn't. As a child, I found solace in my mother's company, and in my own."

A childhood passion he could pursue alone was collecting anything to do with travel, especially tram and omnibus maps. "I kept my collections of maps, timetables, schedules, tickets, and transfers in an orderly, careful way. I liked to see each thing in its place and in perfect condition."

He imagined himself traveling every route, and then he set out to do just that. This interest was then extended to other cities. "I'd never been on the New York subway," he said, "but the first time I visited New York, I felt I could have traveled anywhere in the city because I had memorized every line."

He collected maritime schedules. "The magical moment in any journey," he told me, "is that first moment the ship or the train departs. It's as if you're already a thousand miles away from where you started. I never get the same feeling with air travel."

Hitchcock disliked the names Alfred and Joseph, and was soon known as "Hitch" to his classmates. Later in life, he was known to say to people he met, though not to women, "Call me Hitch, without a cock."

Hitchcock's education in Catholic schools left a lasting impression on him, particularly the Jesuit school, St. Ignatius. "What did I learn in Jesuit school? A consciousness of good and evil, that both are always with me. They taught me control, organization, discipline, and that I did not like to get a tanning, which was something I didn't need to go to school to learn.

"The threat of corporal punishment was worse than the actual experience. I couldn't escape the threat of it no matter how careful I was."

Hitchcock speculated that having this fear of punishment always hanging over him may have contributed to his "ticking bomb" theory of suspense in cinema, that it wasn't the explosion, but the threat of the explosion that created the suspense. He also learned that a sense of the forbidden and of sin makes everything more fascinating.

"My childhood was not an unhappy one, nor was it happy. At that time, I didn't have a strongly defined sense of happiness. I was more aware of good and evil, of right and wrong."

Reading was one of Hitchcock's favorite activities during his childhood, and books continued to influence him throughout his life. "I was much impressed by Edgar Allan Poe, G. K. Chesterton, and by the English 'shockers,' such as John Buchan. I became acquainted with Conan Doyle, Wilkie Collins, and Dickens when I was very young. My favorite Dickens was *Great Expectations*. In Collins's and Dickens's Victorian world, to murder someone was an unspeakable crime, an attitude which stayed with me. Even in murder mysteries, it is important not to waste human life. People cannot just be thrown away.

"I learned from Poe that you could experience all of the emotions and physical sensations of being afraid without yourself being in any physical danger, though after reading him, I didn't like to go immediately into the dark.

"I don't know if a night in my early childhood when I woke up alone in the blackness was the start of my childhood fear of the dark, or if I already had it.

"I called out, but no one came. The entire house was dark and I couldn't find my parents.

"Then they returned. It seemed that on a warm summer evening, my parents had gone for a short walk. There was a maid somewhere about, but I didn't know that. I suppose I was about four. My dislike of the dark has stayed with me. It represented the unknown, while my preference has always been for the familiar. One never knows what could be lurking in the darkness. One does not wish to know."

Not all of Hitchcock's fears were physical. "One of my greatest fears has always been that of making a fool of myself in public. An embarrassing moment. I think of it as open-fly phobia. What I consider to be my greatest fear of all is—to know the future."

Joining with his three brothers, who were fishmongers, William Hitchcock was able to expand his business. The Hitchcocks were comfortable, but there was always lingering tension about money, about future security, which the young Hitchcock couldn't understand. "Only later, I realized what great pressure there was on my father. He worked those very long hours and didn't show the strain, until one day he died."

On December 14, 1914, William Hitchcock died of a heart attack at age fifty-two. "My father was always away," Hitchcock said, "except for his Sunday morning attendance at church and our visits to the theater. It was only after he died that I realized he was never home, because he was out there working hard for us, his family.

"My father never seemed carefree, except at the theater. I think he worried a lot. Selling produce that can spoil in a day must be nerve-wracking."

The death of his father forced Hitchcock to find a career. His older brother took over the family business, and Alfred was asked what he would like to be. "I said maybe I would like to be an engineer, so I was sent to a school of engineering and navigation. I took courses in mechanical drawing, electricity, and other aspects of engineering, and I gained a great deal of practical knowledge in the shop courses that helped me later in film work. It was quite a program they had. I could have become a blacksmith, but I think I made a better choice for myself. It was the draftsman training that eventually got me a job as an art director.

"I'd always liked to draw, and I took evening art classes at the University of London. It was suggested that we students visit museums, and I found the museums wonderful."

Hitchcock went to work at the W. T. Henley Telegraph and Cable Company where he was at first employed in a clerical position. He got the job because he knew something about electricity, and also because during World War I, there was a labor shortage. He quickly tired of ohms and volts, and began visiting the advertising department where the supervisor let him do some layouts for ads. They liked what he did, so he began designing ads and brochures. He helped design Henley's employee magazine, and even wrote for it.

Hitchcock's short story, "Gas," appeared in the first issue of the *Henley Social Club Magazine*. Hitchcock described it as being "about an unfortunate young Englishwoman who goes to Paris and is kidnapped by a gang of cutthroats, robbed, and then tossed into the

Seine. At the end of the story, we learn that she dreamed it all under anesthetic at the dentist's office."

Hitchcock already had some idea of who he was, who he wanted to be, and how he wanted to live. While a few of his thriftier co-workers carried lunch pails or bagged lunches, most preferred a communal break at the local pub. Standing up while eating never appealed to Hitchcock, who selected a restaurant which not only served good food but, as he recalled, "had very clean fine linen napkins." He had a lifelong appreciation of table linen, china, crystal, and silver. After lunch, he would smoke one cigar, the best he could afford, considering the straitened circumstances at home after his father's death and the need for him to contribute part of his salary.

He did not remember feeling lonely at that time, and he never minded eating alone. "Besides, I didn't earn enough money to pay for two."

Hitchcock wanted to fit in with his co-workers while not really sharing their interests. "I had too much to do, my solitary pursuits, which were of much greater interest to me."

He chose to protect himself from rejection. "I have always been uncommonly unattractive. Worse yet, I have always known it. The feeling has been with me so long, I cannot imagine what it would be like not to feel that way."

Hitchcock was too young to fight in the Great War until it was nearly over, but as soon as he was eighteen, he immediately went to take his physical. He was rejected, which he said was a blow.

"It shouldn't have been such a shock. They didn't say what was wrong with me, but I think they just didn't like the way I looked. I'm an upside-down cake. I was very healthy, but I believe they thought I would have been a disgrace to the uniform.

"They would have had to make my uniform to order because they didn't have any that came in my shape. My legs are too small for my body. I suppose they thought I wouldn't have been able to charge into battle, or even out of it."

He joined the volunteer corps of the Royal Engineers, which didn't require a uniform, and which met to practice home defense.

"I was deeply interested in movies from childhood, well before I became involved with them. Deeply interested. They were a passion of mine. I didn't read fan magazines. Stars were of no interest to me. Later, I understood better why. I read the trade papers and technical journals.

"I saw films that looked like someone had set up a camera in front of a stage, especially the British films. I'd be over the moon with the Frenchman Georges Méliès. I was thrilled by the movies of D. W. Griffith and the early French director Alice Guy."

In 1919, Hitchcock read in the trade papers about a Hollywood company—Famous Players-Lasky, which eventually became Paramount—setting up a branch in London at the Islington Studios. "It was important in my life," Hitchcock said, "both as Famous Players-Lasky and later as Paramount."

He applied for a position at the studio with an elaborate portfolio he had put together while at Henley. "Someone I knew, knew someone who knew what their first film was going to be. Actually, at the time, the plan was only tentative, but fortunately, I didn't have that excess of information to hinder me. It was an occasion where what I *didn't* know was as important as what I *did* know. I rushed out and bought *The Sorrows of Satan,* a Victorian novel, and stayed up much of the night for several nights, not something I ever liked to do.

"It was rather unfair to Henley because I was pretty tired on the job, but I did all of my work. I was utterly conscientious. When I completed all the main titles, I called Famous Players-Lasky for an appointment. Another thing I didn't think about, due to my youth, lack of experience, and perhaps stupidity, was that I didn't know the script or the scenes, and what I was offering would only be useful if they let it shape their film. It was presumptuous of me, but I didn't even know it.

"'You can have these free,' I said. My enthusiasm was taken in the best spirit. My drawings, which I knew were good, were praised, and the confirmation of what they said was they offered me a part-time job. So, my first job in the film world was as a writer and designer of titles for silent films."

The movies, then being silent, required full-screen titles, called intertitles, whenever there was dialogue, and Hitchcock's job was to adorn the titles with artwork as well as to select the type. Hitchcock was so fascinated by the film studio, he volunteered to do other jobs as well, becoming what he described as "a kind of third assistant at a time when they didn't have third assistants."

He was spending so much time there, they thought he was a full-time employee. When they realized he wasn't, they asked him if he would consider leaving his job and coming to work for them full-time. It didn't take much persuasion. He quit his job at Henley and went to work at Famous Players-Lasky. Later, Hitchcock always said proudly, "I was American-trained in film, you know," because he had worked first for an American company in England. "I got a pittance, but I didn't know it, so I was very happy."

From 1920 until 1922, he designed intertitles for films, as well as doing other tasks. "I was the first to pick up a piece of paper from the floor and deposit it in a wastebasket, even though officially I was employed in the editorial department. I did whatever odd job had to be done around the office, while spending as much time as I could in the studio watching the films being shot, sometimes even doing the work of an assistant director without benefit of title. I was very happy in my work.

"At that time, the American scriptwriters were all women, and I learned screenplay writing from them. There were many opportunities at that time for women to work in films. This kind of sedentary work was considered appropriate for women, like sewing. When films became more important, these positions were no longer readily available to women."

By 1922, the American company had become discouraged with their British venture, and decided to phase it out, renting the Islington Studios to independent producers. One of them, Seymour Hicks, a well-known actor-playwright, rented the studio to film his own successful stage play, *Always Tell Your Wife*. In the middle of shooting, Hicks had an argument with his director, Hugh Croise, and fired him, intending to direct the rest of the picture himself. As his assistant, he hired Hitchcock.

During this period, Hitchcock directed part of his first film, which was never finished.

"Paramount's head of publicity liked me and asked if I would want to direct a two-reel comedy called *Number 13,* which she had written and for which she had some backing. She had worked with Chaplin, so everybody took her quite seriously. We started, but the film was never finished.

"The money ran out, and it may have been just as well. We were saved from disgrace and from having that piece of film floating around forever."

In 1922, the Islington Studios were leased and eventually sold to a new British company, Gainsborough Pictures, which had been created by Michael Balcon, with Victor Saville. Balcon had been a salesman and Saville a film distributor. They were soon joined by Graham Cutts, an exhibitor who wanted to direct.

Hitchcock applied for a job on their first picture, *Woman to Woman*, and was hired.

"On my own time," Hitchcock said, "I practiced my hand at writing a script from a novel. When the job at Gainsborough came up, they hired me as the assistant director. Then, they said in a panic, 'Who's going to write our script?' I said, 'I'll do it.' They read it, and liked it. I was twenty-three.

"I had a friend who was going to be the art director on the picture, and he found he couldn't work on it. *Woman to Woman* was a big, important picture. It featured a Hollywood star, Betty Compson. I said, 'I'll do the art direction, I'll design the sets,' and so forth. They believed me, and I did some drawings to show them. So, I became art director as well."

Hitchcock chose as his assistant on *Woman to Woman* an attractive young film editor who had begun working at Islington in 1916. Her name was Alma Reville.

HITCH AND ALMA

H ELLO, MISS REVILLE. My name is Alfred Hitchcock
and I have just been appointed assistant director on a
new film. I wonder if you would consider the position
of cutter on this film?"

Thus Hitch and Alma began their relationship. Hitchcock had
noticed the petite young redhead from the moment he started work
at Famous Players-Lasky, but had been too shy and too conscious of
his own lower professional status to make an approach until he at
least felt equal in rank.

"I was surprised to hear from him," Alma told me, "and very
grateful. I'd been out of a job ever since Paramount left Islington."

She became Hitchcock's assistant. The job involved editing film
and being the script girl, which was an important position on the
silents. "I began by admiring her from afar," Hitchcock told me. "I
much preferred admiring her from a-near."

Fifty-seven years later, nobody expressed better the relationship
between Hitch and Alma than Hitchcock himself in his acceptance
speech at the American Film Institute's 1979 Lifetime Achievement
Award Tribute to him:

"Among those many people who have contributed to my life, I ask
permission to mention by name only four people who have given me

the most affection, appreciation, and encouragement, and constant collaboration.

"The first of the four is a film editor.

"The second is a scriptwriter.

"The third is the mother of my daughter, Pat.

"And the fourth is as fine a cook as ever performed miracles in a domestic kitchen.

"And their names are Alma Reville.

"Had the beautiful young Miss Reville not accepted a lifetime contract without options as Mrs. Alfred Hitchcock some fifty-three years ago, Mr. Alfred Hitchcock might be in this room tonight, not at this table, but as one of the slower waiters on the floor. I share my award, as I have my life, with her."

There has been much discussion of the glamorous, mysterious blondes who were predominantly the heroines of Hitchcock's films, though there were brunettes, too. The most important woman for Hitchcock, however, was the heroine of his private life, a mysterious redhead. She was Alma Reville, who became Alma Hitchcock.

Hitchcock had always acknowledged privately Alma's contribution to his films, and for some of them she had been credited onscreen, but her full contribution to the cinema of Alfred Hitchcock was never declared so publicly until the American Film Institute dinner, during the last year of their life together. That was the way Alma had wanted it. As Hitchcock was the public person, his wife was a totally private person. While Hitchcock was nourished by recognition and praise, it made Alma blush.

"Alma, you know," he told me, "was the only person I could lose my dignity with, and dignity was a heavy burden to always carry."

A satisfied Alma told me, "He gave me a life I never imagined."

Norman Lloyd, actor, producer, and long-time friend of the Hitchcocks, said, "He was the eye, she was the ear."

•   •   •

ALMA LUCY REVILLE was born on August 14, 1899, in Nottingham, a lace-making center 120 miles north of London. Alma's father, Matthew Reville, was the London representative of a Nottingham lace firm. Shortly afterward, her family moved to Twickenham, west of London.

She was educated at a private girls school where she was a good student until forced to drop out for two years when she contracted chorea, commonly called Saint Vitus' dance. Being a semi-invalid for so long changed her aspirations and the direction of her life. An advanced education had become even less a possibility, and Alma began looking for a vocation.

Since her mother loved to attend the cinema, she took her young daughter with her over the objections of an aunt who, according to Hitchcock, warned Alma's mother, "'You mustn't take young Alma to the cinema, because she will only pick up fleas.' Well, she did get involved in the cinema, and after a while, she picked me up. But I'm certainly no flea."

With lace going out of style, especially during the economic and social changes of the Great War, Alma's father had gone to work at the London Film Company in the costume department. It was housed in a converted power station in Islington, only a few blocks from the Reville home, and Alma often rode her bicycle there to see her father and to watch the actors. Noticing his daughter's interest, and preferring that she work close to home, he arranged for her to be employed there, making Alma a second-generation film person. "I was hired as a tea girl, the only job possible for an untrained sixteen-year-old," Alma remembered.

She made the tea for the morning break and then again for afternoon tea, as well as all during the day for anyone who wanted it. Even in that task, Alma immediately wanted to excel. She not only learned all of the refinements of tea making, rinsing the cups with scalding water so they would retain the heat longer, allowing the leaves to steep the right amount of time, but she learned all of the preferences of each of the tea drinkers, such as pouring the cold milk in first before the bath of hot tea. Such enterprise and good spirit did not go unnoticed. Despite her extreme youth, even for that time, she was quickly in line for rapid promotion.

Her employers noticed how bright and energetic she was, and being in need of a cutter at the lowest possible salary, they promoted her. She was thrilled. She wanted to learn everything about the business she already loved. At that time, a cutter assisted the director, who was expected to edit his own movies. She was also a script girl and secretarial assistant to the director. On occasion, she appeared in a film, briefly inspiring in her some ambition to become an actress. Director Maurice Elvey asked her to step in to play young Megan Lloyd George in the 1918 film, *The Life Story of David Lloyd George*. This film, considered lost for eighty years, was recently found by Kevin Brownlow, noted British filmmaker and historian.

Alma understood the filmmaking process from the development of the screenplay to the development of the film stock. There wasn't anything she hadn't done except star in a film. She had all but one of the qualifications to be a director at a time when women had some opportunity in this field. "I'm too small," Alma told me. "Not just short, but small. I could never project the image of authority a director has to project. A director has to be able to play the role of a director."

"Would you have liked to have become a director if you hadn't met Alfred Hitchcock?" I asked.

"I don't know. The people I worked for said I might become an assistant director at the time. I never really thought about it. I loved my work, and I would have just wanted to go on with it. I liked writing, and I liked best working with a small group of people, like a stock company. As everything got so big, you were no longer part of a team, but part of an organization. Later, sometimes I thought I might like to write a novel because you can do that alone."

In 1919, when the London Film Company closed down, and the

studio at Islington was sold to Famous Players-Lasky, Alma was invited to stay on as a continuity girl.

"It sounded very nice," she told me. "In truth, I hadn't the faintest idea what a continuity girl did. I think it's *because* I hadn't a clue to what it involved and didn't know any better that I said yes. I didn't hesitate. I figured I always had time later to say no, and then I never wanted to."

At that time, Alma was rare because she worked both as a cutter *and* a script girl. For her first job in both capacities, she was assigned a costume film. "When I saw the picture I had put together, I was horrified. I had made *so* many mistakes! All these years later, it makes me blush to remember it. A girl comes into a hallway with mittens on and goes into another room where she doesn't have them on, and then she leaves with the mittens back on. It's a wonder I wasn't made redundant immediately. Everybody laughed. Well, it was better than losing my job, but I didn't enjoy being laughed at, either."

It was while Alma was working on Donald Crisp's *Appearances* that she met the young man who had come to work for Famous Players-Lasky in 1919 as an intertitles artist, Alfred Hitchcock. At that moment in time, Alma was far ahead of him in her knowledge of filmmaking.

She noticed him immediately, but as she remembered, he didn't seem to be aware of her, being completely absorbed by his work. This surprised her, since she was accustomed to being noticed by young men, who liked her perky style.

"I regarded myself as a very attractive girl, prettier perhaps than I really was, but I was outgoing and social. You might say I had good self-esteem. I enjoyed pretty clothes. I loved movies and I loved what I was doing. I was an optimistic type, and I saw a rosy future."

Like her future husband, Alma always believed in the importance of first impressions.

"I remember a young man coming in with a large package under his arm, wearing a dingy gray topcoat." She giggled at the memory, seeming to relive it in her mind. Hitchcock told me that Alma's giggle was the first thing he had noticed about her.

Although immediately attracted to her, Hitchcock didn't feel he could properly court her yet because he and Alma inhabited a world not far into the twentieth century, and each lived within a nineteenth-century family. The prevalent values were still those of a Victorian world. Only when Hitchcock graduated to assistant director did he feel he could pursue his courtship. Being shy, he approached Alma by telephone, offering her a job. "It wasn't very romantic," Hitchcock remembered.

Alma was different from any girl he had ever met. "Until then," he told me, "I never understood what women wanted. I only knew it wasn't me."

When Famous Players-Lasky gave up on the English market and leased the Islington Studios to independent producers, Alma went to work for one of those independents, Gainsborough. Hitchcock, who had been kept on as the property master by the American company, soon joined Gainsborough, too.

Working together for Gainsborough provided the opportunity for them to know each other better. They spent most of their courtship talking about movies, according to Alma. "Still do," she added. "We wrote letters to each other, but they weren't love letters. They were letters about filmmaking." They enjoyed meetings of the London Film Society. A young actor named John Gielgud was also a member and film enthusiast. Many years later, he told me, "It was where we went to see the highbrow movies." One of the founders was Sidney Bernstein, a distributor who immediately noticed and liked Alfred Hitchcock. This was the best opportunity to see what was going on throughout the world in film. The Russian cinema was important to Hitchcock, who particularly noted its use of montage.

Hitchcock was an enthusiastic, committed theatergoer. Many of the actors he saw on the stage at that time would later appear, sometimes more than once, in his films. Among them were Tallulah Bankhead, Edmund Gwenn, Leo G. Carroll, Gladys Cooper, Sara Allgood, Isabel Jeans, Ian Hunter, Miles Mander, John Williams, and Ivor Novello.

Woman to Woman was the first of five films on which Hitchcock and Alma worked together. It was a joyful time for them, although, as Alma added, "It was somewhat marred because director Graham Cutts was not our cup of tea. He didn't appreciate Hitch, he knew very little, and actually we carried him. Then, he resented it. He was jealous of Hitch, who was intuitive and perfectly understood everything technical. Cutts was ready to depend on others, but not to share credit."

The film was a great success, encouraging Gainsborough to follow it with *The Passionate Adventure* and *The White Shadow,* again with Hitchcock as assistant director, though uncredited, and art director of *The White Shadow.* Hitchcock also adapted the stage play and, with Alma, wrote the screenplay, again uncredited. The film was unsuccessful, and Cutts complained to producer Michael Balcon that Hitchcock was undermining his authority on the set. Balcon, however, was impressed by the young man, who seemed to be saving him money by doing so many jobs so well.

After the success of *Woman to Woman,* Balcon made a low offer in a bid to purchase the Islington facilities, not expecting Paramount to accept, but they did. Balcon had the idea that the only way to run a successful film company in England was to own the studio facilities.

In 1924, Hitchcock was sent by Balcon to Berlin as assistant director on *The Prude's Fall,* an Anglo-German production again directed by Cutts. Alma was sent as Hitchcock's assistant.

At UFA (Universum-Film Aktien Gesellschaft), the great German studio founded by Universal in Neubabelsberg, they were able to watch F. W. Murnau directing *The Last Laugh* (*Der letzte Mann*), as well as Fritz Lang, G. W. Pabst, and other important German directors. Hitchcock learned from the German technicians as they worked.

At that time, UFA was more artistically and technically advanced in filmmaking than England, and was challenging Hollywood. Murnau was generous to Hitchcock, answering whatever questions he asked, explaining what he was doing, inviting him to watch the filming, and encouraging him in his career. Murnau's influence on Hitchcock would last a lifetime, according to Hitchcock: "From Murnau, I learned how to tell a story without words."

Aboard the ship returning from Germany where they had been scouting locations for *The Prude's Fall*, Hitchcock had determined he would ask Alma to marry him "before our feet touched English soil." He hoped that she would still feel somewhat carried away by their odyssey. His plan was complicated by her bout of seasickness. It was almost continuous from the moment they boarded the ship, which made Hitchcock hesitate. Even if the situation was not as romantic as he might have wished, he wondered if her weakened condition might help his cause, lowering her resistance. He could not imagine his future life without Alma. He had never before felt so comfortable with a woman. He realized that she was socially graceful, as he believed he could never be, and he felt that she could have anyone in the world she wanted. It was a daunting prospect, but Hitchcock was never one to say no to himself.

He planned his words and pondered scenarios. The end of the voyage, however, drew close, with Alma's seasickness, which she believed was terminal, showing no sign of abating.

As Alma, "looking green," lay in agony on her bunk, Hitchcock remembered paying her a visit and blurting out his proposal. It didn't come out as he had rehearsed it, but she didn't say no. She only burped, which Hitchcock took as yes.

Alma told me, "I was too weak to say yes, or I would have said it."

• • •

WHEN THE ISLINGTON STUDIOS were offered for sale, and Balcon bought them for Gainsborough Pictures, it was for a fraction of the asking price, to be paid out over a period of seven years. Balcon was on his way to becoming one of Britain's most important producers.

The next Cutts-directed Gainsborough picture to be shot in Germany was *The Blackguard,* for which Hitchcock was able to incorporate into his set designs some of the ideas of forced perspective he had been observing at UFA. He was also able to save a great deal of money by using suggestion rather than showing everything.

"One of the important things I learned at UFA was that you are only responsible for what is in the frame. If you want to give the impression of a great European cathedral, all you have to do is show an important detail. The audience will see the whole cathedral in its mind."

When Cutts said that he did not want to work with Hitchcock again, Balcon decided it was time to give the younger man a chance to prove himself. In 1925, Hitchcock was assigned to direct another Anglo-German production, *The Pleasure Garden,* to be shot in Munich and Italy. Alma would be his assistant director.

"Someone told me," Hitchcock recalled, "that Cutts said to Balcon, 'I don't want to work anymore with that know-it-all son-of-a-bitch, Hitchcock.'

"Well, Cutts not wanting me could have ruined my career, but instead, it was the making of it. It gave me the opportunity I didn't even know yet I wanted. I was to be a director."

II.

THE BRITISH FILMS

CUB DIRECTOR

❧

The Pleasure Garden to *The Lodger*

W HEN I WAS STARTING OUT in films," Hitchcock told me, "I was a cub director. But I didn't want anyone to know it.

"Nita Naldi was my first murder. I'd never killed anyone before—in a picture I directed, that is. In *The Pleasure Garden,* she's drowned by the villain, though it was actually her stand-in who was murdered, since Miss Naldi hadn't arrived in Italy yet.

"Someone said that I didn't personally direct that murder, but I am guilty of every one of my screen murders. It's how I've earned my blood money."

Balcon preferred that Hitchcock prove himself as a director away from England, so he was sent to Munich, where he and Alma would work with a German company. For the American market, Balcon had contracted Nita Naldi, Virginia Valli, and Carmelita Geraghty, well-known Hollywood actors, as the stars. Naldi had just starred with Rudolph Valentino in *Blood and Sand.* The actual filming would be done at the Emelka Studios in Munich, as well as on location in Italy.

After preparations in Munich, Alma went to Cherbourg to meet

Valli and Geraghty, while Hitchcock went to Genoa to shoot the departure of a ship. Accompanying him were actor Miles Mander, who was also to be in the film, and the cameraman, the Baron Gaetano di Ventimiglia.

At the Italian border, their film stock was confiscated. In Genoa, after Hitchcock had sent for more film, the confiscated film arrived with an unexpected duty imposed. As other unexpected expenses accrued, Hitchcock's money was stolen from his hotel room, and he had to borrow from Mander and Ventimiglia in order to shoot the scene.

When he returned to Munich already over-budget, Hitchcock found that the Hollywood stars had demanded first-class accommodations from Cherbourg to Munich. At the end of shooting, in late summer of 1925, they were left "virtually pfennig-less," said Hitchcock. "Until a check arrived from London, we were dependent on the hospitality of our German friends, who saw to it that we lost no weight, unfortunately. Looking back at some snaps Alma took of me at the time, a bit of hunger might have done me some good."

Alma told me that during the years of World War II, she and Hitch thought many times about these people who had been so kind to them, and the Hitchcocks worried about their fate.

Titles and credits share the screen with a 1920s chorus girl who appears on one side, looking almost like a dancing doll. Then, other chorus girls scamper down the backstage spiral staircase of the Paradise Garden Theatre.

Jill Cheyne (Carmelita Geraghty), applying for a job as a dancer, is befriended by chorus girl Patsy Brand (Virginia Valli), who invites her to stay with her. Patsy persuades the theater manager (Georg Schnell) to give Jill a chance, and the audacious young woman dances so well, he hires her instantly.

Jill is soon star of the show. Though engaged, she becomes the girlfriend of an older Russian prince (Karl Falkenberg).

Jill's fiancé, Hugh Fielding (John Stuart), arrives with his friend, Levett (Miles Mander). Hugh then leaves for the Far East to seek his fortune.

Patsy, charmed by Levett, marries him. Levett tires of Patsy and leaves to join Hugh. Though heartbroken, when she learns he is sick, Patsy goes to nurse Levett.

Arriving at the island, she finds him living with a native girl (Nita Naldi). Feverish and drunk, he throws the girl out and demands that Patsy stay, but she leaves. An English doctor asks Patsy if she will help nurse another "sick white man."

Levett drowns the native girl in the sea.

The "sick white man" is Hugh. He imagines Patsy is Jill. Levett returns, making threats. To protect Hugh, Patsy goes with Levett to his bungalow.

Imagining he sees the ghost of the native girl, Levett attacks Patsy with a sword. The doctor arrives and shoots Levett.

Patsy and Hugh return to London—together.

Balcon was so pleased with *The Pleasure Garden,* he assigned Hitchcock to his second Anglo-German film at Emelka, *The Mountain Eagle,* also starring Nita Naldi. *The Pleasure Garden* would, however, have to wait for two years to be released because a powerful backer of Gainsborough, the financier and distributor C. M. Woolf, did not think it was suitable for English audiences.

The Mountain Eagle was shot in the Tyrolean Alps in late 1925.

Beatrice (Nita Naldi), the schoolteacher in a Kentucky town, angers Pettigrew (Bernard Goetzke), the justice of the peace and owner of the town's general store. He believes she has encouraged the attentions of his crippled son, Edward (John Hamilton), who is taking evening classes with her. When she rebuffs the elder Pettigrew's own attentions, he proclaims her as wanton, and she is driven out of town.

> A hermit, John "Fear o' God" Fulton (Malcolm Keen), takes her in. He offers marriage with the promise she can divorce him whenever she wants. Pettigrew, still angry, performs the ceremony.
>
> Beatrice is happy with Fear o' God. They have a child.
>
> When Edward disappears, Pettigrew blames Fear o' God, and has him arrested for murder. He is tried, found guilty, and imprisoned. He escapes from jail and hides with his wife and child in the hills.
>
> The child falls ill, and Fear o' God goes into town for a doctor. He and Pettigrew have a fight, but Edward returns safe.
>
> The child recovers, Fear o' God is exonerated, and Beatrice's respectability is restored.

After being distributed in England, Germany, and America, all prints and the negative of the film disappeared. Much of the script has also disappeared, leaving only a few production photos. The synopsis is based on Peter Noble's reconstruction for the British Film Institute.

Woolf again disapproved of Hitchcock's finished film, so *The Mountain Eagle* was held and released only after the huge success of his third film, *The Lodger.*

Mrs. Marie Belloc Lowndes wrote *The Lodger* first in 1911 as a magazine short story, and then as a novel in 1913. It was based on the 1888 serial killings of young women in London's East End slums, the notorious Jack the Ripper murders. In the novel, the landlady never finds out if her lodger is indeed the infamous killer.

Hitchcock, with writer Eliot Stannard, emphasized that part of the novel which dealt with the fear and uncertainty the family feels about their lodger.

> A new boarder (Ivor Novello) arouses the suspicion of his landlady (Marie Ault), and her husband (Arthur Chesney), but their

fashion model daughter, Daisy Bunting (June Tripp), is attracted to him. Daisy's boyfriend, police detective Joe Betts (Malcolm Keen), becomes jealous.

When Mrs. Bunting hears the lodger leaving late at night, she fears he may be the notorious murderer of young women, the Avenger. She tells Betts, who obtains a warrant to search his rooms.

Police find a pistol, a map indicating past murders, and a picture of the first victim. Though the lodger claims the girl in the picture is his sister, and says that he is looking for her killer, he is arrested.

He escapes, and Daisy helps him. His handcuffs are noticed at a pub, and he is pursued by an angry mob and finally cornered. At the last moment, he is saved by news that the real killer has just been arrested.

The lodger is really a wealthy gentleman. He marries Daisy, and the Buntings adjust to their new station in life.

Hitchcock said that the ending he would have preferred was to have the lodger really turn out to be Jack the Ripper, who goes free at the end, thought to be innocent, "while the audience knows he's going to go on about his dirty business. At the very least, there might have been some doubt left as to whether he had done the nefarious deeds or not. But it would have been unacceptable to cast a leading man like Ivor Novello as a villain. I had the same problem later with Cary Grant in *Suspicion*."

A memorable image in *The Lodger* is an overhead shot of a stairwell, with the lodger slowly descending the stairs, shown only by his gloved hand on the guard railing as the hand slides down.

"This was a substitute for sound," Hitchcock said. "Nowadays, we wouldn't do that.

"Later on, I show how he paces up and down in his room. I have the faces of the people below, looking up to the ceiling. So I dissolved the ceiling away to show this agitated man. I had a one-inch-thick plate glass floor made so his feet showed through. This was instead of sound."

The Lodger was the first film in which Hitchcock had a cameo appearance. He is in the newsroom at the beginning and in the crowd pursuing Novello near the end. "Two actors didn't show up. In those days you used to be able to hop in and do a bit if necessary," he recalled.

Balcon brought in a young editor, Ivor Montagu, to work with Hitchcock. They recognized each other as fellow members of the London Film Society, and they were immediately compatible.

"When *The Lodger* was ready," Hitchcock said, "the distributors screened the film and said it was dreadful. C. M. Woolf particularly objected to the transparent ceiling. He wanted to give the story to another director to reshoot.

"I was at a pretty low ebb in my career. *The Lodger* was shelved for several months, and then they decided to show it after all. They had an investment, and wanted their money back. It was shown, and acclaimed as the greatest British picture ever made. So, there, you see, is that thin line between failure and success.

"If I'd made the story again as a talker," Hitchcock told me, "I would have wanted to do something different. Perhaps *Jacqueline the Ripper.*"

"My father always referred to *The Lodger* as the first true Hitchcock picture," Pat Hitchcock told me. With this film, Hitchcock led the emergence of the British cinema.

GREAT BRITISH HOPE

꧁

Downhill to *Waltzes from Vienna*

O
N DECEMBER 2, 1926, Hitch and Alma were married in a small Roman Catholic ceremony. Alma converted to Catholicism.

They spent their honeymoon in Paris and at the Palace Hotel in St. Moritz, Switzerland. The Palace perfectly suited the young Hitchcocks' dreams and their reality. Afterward, they celebrated their anniversary there whenever they could.

Back in London, they moved into their new flat, decorated with fabrics and furniture from Liberty's Department Store. It was a top-story flat, something that never bothered them, although Pat Hitchcock told me that she remembered in 1936, at the age of eight, counting ninety-six steps from the ground floor to their flat. It was where they were to live until they left for America.

When the Hitchcocks married, their future seemed far from secure. During 1927, however, all three of the films he had directed were finally released. Four more were finished that year, and Hitchcock was becoming the most famous British director.

Downhill, Hitchcock's next film, was based on a play by Ivor

Novello and Constance Collier, writing under the pseudonym Robert LeStrange.

School sports captain Roddy Berwick (Ivor Novello), accused of fathering a waitress's child, doesn't expose the true seducer, his best friend, Tim Wakely (Robin Irvine). Roddy is expelled from school, and when even his own father, Lord Berwick (Norman McKinnel), doubts his innocence, Roddy leaves home.

Joining the chorus of a stage musical, he falls in love with the star, Julia (Isabel Jeans), but cannot afford her extravagant lifestyle.

Then, Roddy inherits £30,000. The sum appears very large in an intertitle:

£30,000

He buys an expensive flat, and Julia moves in with him. She is having an affair with the musical's leading man, Archie (Ian Hunter), and they squander Roddy's inheritance, living lavishly. The intertitle is now very small:

£30,000

Roddy loses both Julia and the flat.

He becomes a taxi dancer in Paris, ending up in a Marseilles flophouse, where the operators hope to collect a reward for returning him to his rich family.

Roddy finds himself on a freighter. Hallucinating, taunted by the memory of those who victimized him, he relives his downhill descent.

Awakening in an English port, he makes his way through a nightmare-like montage of familiar London scenes and arrives at his family mansion.

His father, having learned the truth of the waitress's seduction, welcomes him back, as does his alma mater.

An important scene shows Ivor Novello riding down a long escalator in the London subway. "We couldn't film in the Underground until after midnight," Hitchcock said, "so it was perfect for going to the theater. There was an opening night, and if you were in the good seats, you wore white tie and top hat.

"When the performance finished, I wore my formal attire to direct Novello going down the escalator into the Underground."

At one point in the film, Isabel Jeans leans back and looks at Ivor Novello, who has just entered her dressing room. The next shot shows what she sees, an upside-down Novello. For Hitchcock, this became a favorite moment in his films. He repeated the effect in *Notorious* with Ingrid Bergman and Cary Grant.

Another favorite moment occurs in his next film, *Easy Virtue*. Hitchcock described the scene as "actually a monologue without words."

"It lasts about one minute and is in one small set, where a hotel switchboard operator [Benita Hume] sits. She is wearing earphones, reading a romantic novel.

"She plugs into a conversation between a young woman and a young man who is proposing marriage. Neither the young woman nor the young man is shown. The audience is in suspense, along with the operator. Will the girl on the phone say yes? The switchboard operator, living vicariously, is ecstatic, showing the audience that the proposal has been accepted."

Work on *Easy Virtue* started even before *Downhill* was completed. Because Ivor Novello had not been available for his final close-ups in *Downhill*, Hitchcock arranged to shoot them while he was filming *Easy Virtue* in the south of France.

The film was adapted from a play by Noël Coward, famed for his witty dialogue, but it has few intertitles. "The only thing wrong with the silent picture was that mouths opened, and nothing came out," Hitchcock said. "The talking picture only partially solved that problem."

Larita Filton (Isabel Jeans) flees England for the French Riviera after enduring a sensational divorce trial. In the south of France, she falls in love with John Whitaker (Robin Irvine), who knows nothing about her past. He proposes, and the couple returns to England where she is introduced to his family at their mansion.

John's dominating mother (Violet Farebrother) grudgingly accepts her, but Larita seems vaguely familiar.

Fearful her past will be discovered, Larita pleads with John to take her back to the south of France, where they were happy.

John's mother recognizes Larita from a newspaper photo. While other members of the family are willing to accept Larita, Mrs. Whitaker is resolute, insisting her son divorce the infamous woman.

Larita returns to divorce court and the headlines. Touching her heart, she tells photographers on the courthouse steps, "Go ahead and shoot—there's nothing left to kill."

These last words from Larita, spoken in an intertitle, represented for Hitchcock his least favorite line written by him in any of his films. Today, the line seems more perceptive and appropriate.

The power of the media to ruin private lives, finding an individual guilty, not by conviction, but by implication, is a theme that has become even more timely. Apparently the news photographers of 1927 really were not different from the paparazzi who pursue celebrities today.

In *Easy Virtue*, Larita meets her mother-in-law in the same way Alicia Huberman, played by Ingrid Bergman, would meet hers years later in *Notorious*. A menacing figure of an older woman comes down a staircase, "descending and condescending," as Hitchcock put it, toward her new daughter-in-law.

•   •   •

TWO EVENTS THAT would have far-reaching effects on the British film industry occurred in late 1927. The first was the successful introduction of synchronized sound with *The Jazz Singer.* The second was the Cinematograph Films Act, "The Quota Act," requiring cinemas to program a certain number of British films each year.

A new film company, British International Pictures, lured Alfred Hitchcock away from Gainsborough. He was promised bigger budgets and greater artistic freedom. His first film for BIP was *The Ring.* Hitchcock wrote the screenplay for this film in a few weeks.

He had "fallen in love" with the setting of the boxing ring. Though he had never boxed, nor followed boxing, when friends took him to a boxing match, he recognized what a wonderful setting it made. "I observed those people in the best seats, close to the ring, ladies and gentlemen, and some who weren't, but who could pay the price, wearing formal clothes!" The brutality in the ring, the screaming audience in the cheap seats, and champagne being poured over the boxers to revive them, caught Hitchcock's fancy, and gave him the inspiration for *The Ring.*

> Amateur boxer Jack Sander (Carl Brisson) works in a carnival side show where he is known as "One Round Jack." His girlfriend, Mabel (Lillian Hall-Davis), sells tickets to those who hope to last more than one round with Jack, for which they will receive a prize of 2 guineas.
>
> Champion boxer Bob Corby (Ian Hunter), attracted to Mabel, enters the ring with Jack. Unrecognized, Bob knocks Jack out in the second round, but Jack impresses the champion's manager, who offers him a job as Bob's sparring partner.
>
> Though engaged to marry Jack, Mabel accepts an arm bracelet from Bob, a gift he bought for her with his prize money.
>
> With Jack's new job as Bob's sparring partner, he and Mabel can afford to get married, but Mabel is also attracted to Bob.
>
> As Jack's career advances, Mabel has an affair with Bob. Jack

and Mabel quarrel, and she leaves him. Jack publicly challenges
Bob to a fight in the ring.

The fight goes against Jack, until Mabel rushes to his corner.
Jack wins both the fight and Mabel, with Bob conceding defeat
like a gentleman. The bracelet is left on the floor of the ring.

"Before the big climax in the ring," Hitchcock said, "I instructed
the cameraman to under-crank, so that the action would seem to go
faster for the audience. I did that later in the merry-go-round
sequence in *Strangers on a Train*. Then, I told Brisson to go after
Hunter just as he would in a real match.

"After about five minutes, Hunter, who was out of shape, just sat
down on the mat. On the film, it looks as if he got knocked down. He
was complimented for a great performance by everyone."

In the background of *The Ring* is a young Tom Helmore, who,
thirty years later, would play Gavin Elster in *Vertigo*.

WHILE HITCHCOCK WAS preparing his next film, *The Farmer's
Wife,* in late 1927, the Hitchcocks were expecting their first child.

Hitchcock worked with Eliot Stannard on the adaptation of Eden
Phillpotts's play, and he also doubled as lighting cameraman, though
without credit, when Jack Cox became ill. *The Farmer's Wife* was
released in March 1928.

The wife of prosperous Devonshire farmer, Samuel Sweetland
(Jameson Thomas), dies, leaving him a widower with a teenage
daughter. His wife's last words, to their servant girl Araminta
(Lillian Hall-Davis), are, "Don't forget to air your master's pants,
Minta."

Always in good spirits, Minta takes care of Sweetland and his
daughter. Minta's drying of Sweetland's underwear, by the fire
in winter and in the sun in summer, marks the passage of time.

Sweetland's daughter (Mollie Ellis) marries. Lonely, he faces his wife's empty rocking chair.

Sweetland decides to remarry. He and Minta make a list of candidates. He imagines each one sitting in his wife's empty chair.

When all of them reject the confident Sweetland, he returns to his farm, humiliated, and Minta reassures him. As she sits in the chair vacated by his wife, Sweetland suddenly sees the truth.

He proposes to her, and she happily accepts his proposal. Some of the women who had rejected Sweetland reconsider, but they are too late.

Minta appears wearing the party dress his wife had given her, and she is beautiful. It is Minta who will sit in the empty chair.

Director Ronald Neame, at the time beginning his own film career at the Elstree Studios, said that he owed a great deal to a joke played on him while *The Farmer's Wife* was being filmed.

"I was just starting out, and I was terribly overeager. Someone sent me to fetch the 'sky hook,' which I was told was a terribly valuable piece of equipment. I looked all over until I got to *The Farmer's Wife* set. A rather plump twenty-seven-year-old director named Alfred Hitchcock was rehearsing the actors.

"For several minutes, I forgot all about the sky hook and watched the great director at work. Then I approached Hitchcock's cameraman, Jack Cox.

"This kind man said, 'You have been given a sort of initiation, because the sky hook is a leg-pull. Why don't you go back and tell them it was sold last week because it wasn't being used.'

"Because of that nonexistent sky hook, I was able to watch Hitchcock directing, and I met Jack Cox, with whom I would be working."

• • •

HITCHCOCK AND ALMA liked the area so much where they were filming *The Farmer's Wife* that they bought a Tudor cottage with surrounding land, in Shamley Green, near Guildford, about thirty miles out of London. When, in 1955, Hitchcock set up a production company for his television program, *Alfred Hitchcock Presents,* he called it Shamley Productions.

Patricia Alma Hitchcock was born on July 7, 1928. "I wanted a girl very much," Hitchcock told me, "but I never told Alma. I said I would be just as happy with a girl or a boy. I didn't like saying something to her that wasn't true, but I couldn't have her think I would be disappointed if our little Patricia had happened to be a Patrick.

"When I asked Pat's mother which she wanted, a boy or a girl, she always said she had no preference. Afterwards, she told me that she very much had wanted a girl."

THE HEAD OF PRODUCTION at British International suggested that Hitchcock make a film about champagne, because, Hitchcock told me, "He said, 'Everybody loves it.'

"I came up with a little fable about a French girl who works in a wine cellar in Rheims. She has a romantic notion about what happens to all those bottles of champagne in Paris, so one day, she decides to follow them. In Paris, instead of finding glamour, she loses her virtue and becomes a sort of fallen woman, tearful and disillusioned. She returns to her old job in Rheims, where she watches the bottles going off and wonders who will be seduced next by their false promise. They thought my story too simple. The only agreement we had on the film was that we all disagreed."

What eventually evolved was a film that bore little resemblance to Hitchcock's scenario, although it was titled *Champagne.*

Forbidden by her wealthy father (Gordon Harker) to marry The Boy (Jean Bradin), The Girl (Betty Balfour) flies one of her father's planes to the middle of the Atlantic Ocean where she crash-lands near an ocean liner carrying The Boy. Rescued, she joins him, but they quarrel, and The Girl meets The Man (Theo von Alten).

In Paris, The Girl lives lavishly, but is glad when The Boy returns. The Father arrives to tell her that they have lost their fortune. The Boy leaves. She continues to know The Man as a friend.

The Father and The Girl have to live more modestly. The Girl finds a job as a hostess in a cabaret. The Boy finds The Girl and offers to rescue both her and The Father, but she refuses, saying they still have their pride.

The Father tells The Girl that he didn't really lose his money, but was teaching her a lesson. The Man is really a family friend, keeping an eye on her for The Father. The Boy and The Girl are reunited, and the happy couple is seen through a champagne glass.

"I was quite pleased to give the head of production full credit for the story," Hitchcock said. "This was flat champagne, champagne without bubbles."

An uncredited contribution was made by the young Michael Powell. One of the legendary director's earliest jobs was as the stills photographer on *Champagne*.

The Manxman, Hitchcock's next film, released in early 1929, was based on an 1894 novel by Hall Caine, an Isle of Man writer. The film was adapted by Eliot Stannard, one of Hitchcock's favorite collaborators, primarily because Alma was not available. Just after their daughter was born, Alma was occupied in writing a screenplay, *After the Verdict,* for Henrik Galeen. It was the last time she would ever work with someone other than her husband.

For *The Manxman,* Hitchcock chose as a location the Cornwall coast rather than the Isle of Man. Danish Carl Brisson played the

Manx fisherman Pete, and Czechoslovakian Anny Ondra played Kate, the daughter of an Isle of Man innkeeper. "She was a very nice woman," Hitchcock told me. "Charming. She married the German boxer Max Schmeling."

Close friends Pete, a fisherman (Carl Brisson), and Phil, a lawyer (Malcolm Keen), are both in love with Kate (Anny Ondra). Kate loves Phil, but he aspires to be a judge, and she is only an innkeeper's daughter.

Pete is rejected by Kate's father because he is penniless, so he leaves for South Africa to make his fortune. Kate promises to wait for him. Phil promises to look after her.

Kate, hearing that Pete is dead, seduces Phil. When Pete arrives home alive, Phil convinces Kate that she must keep her promise to Pete.

Pete, now wealthy, marries Kate. Phil insists Pete must never know her child is not his. Soon after, Kate leaves Pete and her child to live with Phil, now a judge. Kate returns for her child, but Pete refuses to give her up. Kate attempts suicide.

Kate is brought before Phil as an attempted suicide. He discharges her into Pete's custody, but Kate declares she loves another man. Her father shouts out that it is the judge. Phil has to resign, and he leaves with Kate and the baby, his career ruined.

Pete is left alone.

Because British International Pictures head John Maxwell disliked *The Manxman,* distribution was delayed until after the sound premiere of *Blackmail* in 1929. *The Manxman* is sometimes listed as Hitchcock's last silent film, although a silent version of *Blackmail* exists that differs from the sound version. As a result, *Blackmail* really qualifies as both Hitchcock's last silent film and his first sound film.

Charles Bennett, author of the stage play *Blackmail,* told me, more than sixty years afterward, that he found the silent *Blackmail* "infinitely superior."

"It was Hitchcock who wanted the studio to buy it for him. After they got it, he and I talked immense hours together about what had to be done. I didn't take any credit because I had plays running at the time in London, so I didn't care." Bennett was also acting on the stage.

Bennett and Hitchcock were born in the same year and shared the experience of having grown up with the motion picture. Bennett told me, "I can not only remember when the moving pictures couldn't talk, I can remember when they couldn't move."

While Hitchcock was making *Blackmail* as a silent feature, he was planning how it could also be shot as "a talker." He was not intimidated by the introduction of sound.

"Most dialogue in a film is only a borrowing from the theater," he said, "photographs of people talking. I believed sound should liberate the cinema, not be merely a stepsister of theater.

"I foresaw sound being used in the same imaginative manner as photography had been used in film. In the early days of the cinema, they simply shot exactly what was happening on a set without any camera movement or editing, to achieve a dramatic, emotional effect."

Scotland Yard Inspector Frank Webber (John Longden) sees his girlfriend, Alice White (Anny Ondra), with another man after they have had an argument.

The man, Crewe (Cyril Ritchard), an artist, invites flirtatious Alice up to his studio. When his advances become physical, she defends herself, stabbing him with a bread knife.

She walks through London in a trancelike state, not returning to her parents' home behind their tobacco shop until dawn.

Investigating the homicide, Frank finds one of Alice's gloves, with a hole in a finger, which he recognizes. He conceals it, and later confronts Alice.

A loiterer who had been spying on Crewe, approaches them with the other glove. He is Tracy (Donald Calthrop), who has come to blackmail them.

Frank learns that the blackmailer is the prime suspect. Tracy escapes, falling to his death after a chase through the British Museum.

Not knowing Tracy is dead, Alice goes to Scotland Yard, but is stopped from confessing by Frank. Alice tells him the truth, and he accepts it. They are free to pursue their life together, though Alice looks uncertain, and there are signs that she will not forget easily what has happened.

Ronald Neame, living in California when I spoke with him, described what it was like to work on *Blackmail*.

"I was Jack Cox's assistant cameraman shooting *Blackmail*. We were shooting silent, but there were rumors that BIP was considering the addition of sound. Charles Bennett, who wrote the stage play, and Benn Levy, were brought in to write dialogue, a good hint.

"Hitch kept the sets so they could be quickly put up again. A lot of what we had already shot on *Blackmail* could be used in the sound version.

"Jack and I were installed, along with our noisy camera, in a sealed soundproof booth with a large glass window. Two men could push the booth backwards and forwards on rails to track, and they could also pivot the booth when we had to pan more than the width of our window. There was just enough room for a hotplate so we could make tea.

"Unless the microphone was practically touching the actor's head, the sound was unusable. The hum from our arc lights made so much noise we had to switch to incandescent lamps, but they weren't bright enough for the slow film stock we had in those days.

"Then, the enormous mike cast heavy shadows on the walls of the set, spoiling Jack's lighting. Jack would request they raise the mike, and they'd refuse because then it wouldn't record anything. They'd complain about the noise of our booth. Sometimes we'd retreat into our respective booths uttering words I can't tell you.

"But Hitch wasn't ever ruffled by anything. He never shouted. He wore a black suit, white shirt, and dark tie, and never seemed to perspire. The rest of us were dripping, sealed up in our booths."

The most difficult technical problem for the sound version, however, was Anny Ondra's heavy accent. Since so many of her scenes had already been filmed for the silent version, Hitchcock created his own early form of dubbing.

He engaged Joan Barry to speak for Ondra. Barry stood to the side with her separate microphone, and as she spoke the lines, Ondra mouthed them silently.

One day Hitchcock handed Neame a 16mm camera to shoot a view of the murder the audience never saw. Neame remembered it well.

"In the film, Ritchard drags Anny through some drapes into the alcove where he keeps his cot. The drapes undulate, indicating struggle. You see Alice's hand come out from behind the drapes. She reaches out for something, coming up with a knife from the table. Shortly afterwards, the artist's hand drops down from between the drapes. He's been stabbed. He's dead. Alice appears with the bloody knife in her hand.

"With that camera Hitchcock gave me, I filmed what really happened. On the other side of the drapes, a prop man ruffled them to seem like a struggle. Alice reached for the knife. Behind the drapes, a second property man smeared some 'blood' on the knife. The artist dropped his hand through the drapes to show his death. I only hope someday someone will find that film.

"Hitch liked to work late in those days, never finishing before eleven p.m., and often we were still working at midnight. At about eight o'clock, we broke for supper, and Hitch, the actors, and sometimes Jack Cox would go to a pub called the Plough, where they ate a delicious hot meal. The rest of us got a sandwich and a glass of beer.

"If we worked past the last train, we were driven home. The driver figured out how to deliver home four people who lived in opposite directions. No matter how late I arrived at my flat, I had to be back on the set the next morning by eight o'clock."

With the success of *Blackmail*, Alfred Hitchcock became firmly established as the preeminent British director.

"YEARS AGO I made a movie of Sean O'Casey's play *Juno and the Paycock*," Hitchcock told me, "and I could not for the life of me find out what to do except to photograph it in one room, with a few exteriors which aren't in the play. The film was successful, and I was ashamed to read those laudatory notices I had nothing to do with, except just to photograph the Irish players doing their job."

Sitting with Eileen O'Casey, the widow of Sean O'Casey, at London's Savoy Hotel many years after the death of her husband, I was told about his happy reaction to Hitchcock's *Juno and the Paycock*. The original play had no greater supporter than O'Casey's widow, who said the play had been a prime reason she fell in love with Sean.

"Sean was pleased about Hitchcock's making the film, and he told Hitchcock to feel free. He liked the idea of the record of the play being there for people to see in all the years to come in a great performance.

"For me, any change to the play was sacrilegious, but Sean was very cooperative and even wrote some new material for the opening scene. It was important that Hitchcock was the kind of director he was because there were some who wouldn't have gone back to Sean to make certain every word was his and to have him approve it.

"I personally preferred Sean's ending on the stage, though when I saw it some years later, I thought it was a very good film in spite of end tampering."

The ending Eileen O'Casey would have preferred was the Captain returning home so drunk that he didn't understand and couldn't comprehend the death of his son, instead of just having Juno and her daughter leave him.

"My Sean was so overjoyed, he set about writing a new play that would be right for a Hitchcock film. He wrote the screenplay. It was called *Within the Gate,* and it became a stage play. Hitchcock liked it, but it didn't happen as a movie with him. I know Sean would have liked to have done another film with Hitchcock, but he wasn't interested in doing one with any other director.

"With the film *Juno and the Paycock,* Hitchcock's name joined my Sean's, two of the great names of this century. Now I myself think how wonderful it is that it exists, *Juno and the Paycock,* an Alfred Hitchcock film, and, like Sean said, with all the great actors of that moment."

Eileen O'Casey was welcomed as a great celebrity at the Savoy, and she enjoyed it when the hotel, happy to have Mrs. Sean O'Casey as a guest, didn't present us with a check.

In Dublin during the 1920s, a Republican Army soldier has been killed after being betrayed by an informer. Angry mobs roam the streets and machine gun fire is heard.

Juno Boyle (Sarah Allgood) supports her lazy husband, "Captain" Jack Boyle (Edward Chapman) with the help of their daughter, Mary (Kathleen O'Regan). Lurking in the background is their morose son, John (John Laurie), who has lost an arm in a Republican Army skirmish.

A lawyer, Charles Bentham (John Longden), informs the Boyles that they have inherited £2,000 from a distant relative. Mary believes she and Bentham will soon be married.

The Boyles go on a spending spree, and then learn that Bentham has left for London with their inheritance. Mary is pregnant. John is losing his mind. Two men in trench coats arrive to take John away.

A neighbor tells Juno that John has just been machine-gunned as an informer. Juno and Mary make plans to leave a worthless husband and father, the Captain, who has gone to get drunk.

After Mary has left, questioning the truth of religion, Juno stands alone, still firm in her faith.

The greatest problem for early sound was post-production. There wasn't any. Everything heard in *Juno* had to be produced while it was being shot, and it couldn't be changed afterward. In one scene, Hitchcock had to direct an orchestra, a singer, a crowd, and the sound of machine gun fire, all offstage, while his camera, encased in a soundproof booth, was being dollied. "All of this at once," Hitchcock said, "and it couldn't be changed, only reshot. The amazing thing was it worked the first time."

Barry Fitzgerald, who created the part of the Captain in the first Abbey Players production of *Juno and the Paycock* in 1924, made his screen debut as the Orator. The Orator's speech at the beginning of the film was not in the play, but written specially for Hitchcock by O'Casey.

Sara Allgood, who had played Anny Ondra's mother in *Blackmail*, re-created her role from the original production and two London runs of *Juno*. Her younger sister, Maire O'Neill, reprised the role she created, and Sidney Morgan also came from the Abbey Players productions.

IN 1930, HITCHCOCK directed a short, *An Elastic Affair*, and segments of two revue films, *Elstree Calling* and *Harmony Heaven*. The revue film was an early example of sound, giving the studio the opportunity to display its stars while exploiting the novelty of synchronized sound.

The next feature Hitchcock would direct was "a talker," as the British called the new sound film, in two languages. *Murder!* and *Mary* were shot simultaneously in 1930, based on the same play, using the same sets and technical crew, but with German actors replacing the English actors for *Mary.* Herbert Marshall and Norah Baring starred in the English version, and Alfred Abel and Olga Tschechowa in the German. *Murder!* and *Mary* were based on *Enter Sir John*, a play and novel by Clemence Dane and Helen Simpson, who wrote *Under Capricorn.*

Actress Diana Baring (Norah Baring) is accused of murdering fellow actress Edna Bruce, though she claims she has no memory of the crime. She is found guilty of murder and sentenced to death.

One of the jurors, playwright-director Sir John Menier (Herbert Marshall), comes to doubt Diana's guilt. He writes a play recreating the crime, hoping that the real murderer will reveal himself when confronted with a reenactment of the murder.

Diana appears to be protecting one of the members of the troupe, someone she identifies as a "half-caste." Sir John locates the man, Handel Fane (Esme Percy). He was a member of the repertory company at the time of the murder and left to become a trapeze artist.

Reading for the part, Fane realizes he has been found out, and hangs himself dramatically in midair during one of his high-wire performances. Afterward, Sir John receives a note of confession by Fane.

Diana, released from prison, stars with Sir John in his next play, which is about the case. It's evident that she will also be starring with him in private life.

"What people most remember about *Murder!*," Hitchcock told me, "was Herbert Marshall's soliloquy in front of the shaving mirror." His lips don't move while he's looking into the mirror, but we hear him speaking his thoughts about the unfairness of the verdict in which he played a role. At the same time, a radio broadcast of the Prelude to *Tristan and Isolde* is heard.

"This was 1930, and we didn't know much about sound mixing yet. The only way to do it then was to record Marshall beforehand, and then play his voice back while we shot the scene, with a thirty-piece orchestra in the background.

"We had a chance to hear the results before we shot the German version. The orchestra had been playing too loudly, and sometimes Wagner drowned out Marshall. When we shot Abel, we had them play more softly; consequently, it's the more successful in this respect."

Hitchcock drew on his own memory for some of the comic business in *Mary*. In the opening, the wife has to dress in a hurry without taking off her nightgown because, as Hitchcock told me, "In the Victorian England I was born into, a woman would never think of exposing herself, even under dire circumstances. Because she's in such a panic to get dressed while preserving her modesty, it takes her much longer." He based this on a moment when he had glimpsed his own mother trying to get into her bloomers, putting both of her legs into the same bloomer leg.

The jury room scene comes closest to Hitchcock's early ideas of how sound film would continue the poetic tradition of the silent picture. Sir John is coerced into a guilty verdict by all of the jurors converging upon him like a Greek chorus, chanting in unison, "Guilty! Guilty!" This type of sound picture, which Hitchcock hoped to make the standard, quickly gave way to the literal, naturalistic cinema that audiences preferred.

Bryan Langley, an assistant camera operator on both *Murder!* and *Mary*, talked with me in 2003 about making those films in 1930.

"Hitchcock had been at the Babelsberg Studio in UFA, so he had a good smattering of German. On many occasions, he and the actors and everybody would be talking in German, and I was the camera assistant trying to understand what they were saying. My grip assistant, who pushed the dolly, was a Jewish man who spoke Yiddish, and he could understand German. So my instructions came from the German-speaking actors and whoever via the Yiddish-speaking grip assistant."

Langley remembered that Hitchcock said, "'Achtung!' for action, and in German, he'd say, 'Lick your lips.' This was for the girls, you see. Before the take, they had to lick their lips to make them shine."

"A great deal of the humor," Hitchcock said in discussing the two films, "is based on the difficulties of the lower class trying to adjust to the upper class and the upper class trying to adjust to the lower class. This kind of British humor doesn't travel well. In *Murder!* Sir John is an actor who becomes a gentleman, while in *Mary*, he is a gentleman who becomes an actor."

Markham's inability to speak at the opening without his false teeth is left out of *Mary*. The difficulty his modest wife has in getting into her bloomers in front of her husband without taking off her nightgown is simplified to putting on her stockings. Most of the comic exaggeration in *Murder!*, such as Markham's feet sinking ankle-deep into Sir John's rug, is not repeated in *Mary*.

At the German actor's insistence, the scene with Sir John in bed with the children and a kitten climbing all over him was modified. Only one child, a little girl, climbs onto Abel's bed and hugs him, while one little boy stands politely beside the bed holding the kitten, thus preserving Abel's dignity.

When Sir John visits Diana (Mary in the German version) in prison, the women guards are menacing. In *Murder!*, there are several ominous close-ups of them, while in *Mary*, they remain mere background figures. A scene with Diana in a cell watching the shadow of the gallows growing larger is not included in *Mary*.

At the end of *Murder!*, Sir John and Diana greet each other in a drawing room that turns out to be a stage set. This scene is omitted in *Mary*, which ends with the next-to-last scene in *Murder!*, Sir John and Mary in the back seat of his limousine, obviously in love.

The character, Sir John Menier, Hitchcock said, was lightly based on Gerald du Maurier, a famous actor-writer-producer, who was also the father of writer Daphne du Maurier and a prank-pal of Hitchcock's.

Once, Hitchcock invited Sir Gerald to a dinner party at the Café Royale in Regent Street, along with two hundred other guests. He told him that the evening was a fancy dress party, and he should wear a costume. Du Maurier arrived in an elaborate Shakespearean costume. Everyone else was in formal attire. During dessert, a naked girl entered the restaurant, crossed the room, and sat down on Sir Gerald's lap, all arranged by Hitchcock.

In *Murder!*, Hitchcock makes his cameo appearance with a woman, walking past the murder victim's house. He does not appear in *Mary*.

Alma and Hitchcock worked on both the English and German versions of the screenplay adaptation. Hitchcock's directing experience in Germany gave him enough confidence to direct the actors, but "Languages are a great deal more than words," he told me. "They're full of idiomatic expressions with subtle shades of meaning that take years of living in the language to understand and, even more important, to feel."

The Hitchcocks learned enough German to put it to use as their "secret language" at home when they didn't want their daughter, Pat, to understand what they were saying. Pat told me she wished they had used the language more often, so she could have learned it.

"THE SKIN GAME had a baronial hall," Langley told me. "There were two big Great Dane dogs who had to parade through this thing. And their feet made—their toenails, shall we say—made an awful noise on the sound recording, 'Clunk, Clunk, Clunk.' So they had to make little booties to put on their feet, and then paint their toenails on these little booties for these Great Danes to walk around in silence."

The Skin Game was based on the play of the same name by John Galsworthy, produced on the London stage in 1921. To protect their unspoiled land from outside developers, the gentry of Long Meadows resort to blackmail, but in doing so, they compromise their own integrity, and the changes are not prevented.

> Hornblower (Edmund Gwenn), a self-made industrialist who feels snubbed by the local gentry, breaks his word not to develop the rural property he bought from Hillcrist (C. V. France). He intends to develop the land the Hillcrists cherish most, the Cintry. To block him, Hillcrist persuades the owner of the Cintry to agree to an auction. In the bidding, Hornblower gets the property.
>
> Finding out something damaging about the past of Hornblower's daughter-in-law (Phyllis Konstam), Mrs. Hillcrist (Helen Haye) resorts to blackmail to save the Cintry.
>
> At the prospect of being exposed, the pregnant daughter-in-law attempts suicide. Fearing he may have lost his grandchild, Hornblower loses all interest in being socially accepted, and vows to leave.
>
> Hillcrist has beaten Hornblower in "a skin game," a swindle, but victory is not sweet. "When we began this fight, our hands were clean," he tells his wife. "Are they clean now? What's gentility worth if it can't stand fire?"

Most of the film's auction scene is shot in one camera setup, following the bidding from the auctioneer's point of view in a series of rapid pans. Then, at the climax of the bidding, it changes unexpectedly to rapid cutting as the auction takes a surprising turn.

In October of 2002, I was at the Savoy Hotel dinner celebrating the fiftieth anniversary of the British Film Institute. Seated next to me was Jack Cardiff, the acclaimed cinematographer who had worked on *Under Capricorn* for Hitchcock in 1949. Cardiff, however, had met the director much earlier, and he shared his memories with me.

"I first knew about Hitch towards the end of 1928, when I was fourteen. I was working then at Elstree, in silent films. I remember that he was on a nearby stage making *Blackmail.* I hadn't met him yet. But then, two years later, he made *The Skin Game.*

"I was then a humble numbers boy, the guy who puts the number board in, and with sound, you did the clappers. That's when you clap two pieces of wood together so the editor can synchronize the sound to the picture.

"Originally, with the first sound films, it was considered so important, the director did the clappers. After a while, Hitch got fed up with it—'Why am I doing this?'—and it was put onto the poor little numbers boy. So I had to do the numbers and also do the clappers. That was a long time ago."

"I'VE ALWAYS BEEN INTERESTED in off-center people," Hitchcock told me. "My picture *Rich and Strange* is about such people. The young couple doesn't even know they're off-center until opportunity knocks. Then, it almost knocks them over."

> Fred Hill (Henry Kendall), tired of his middle-class existence, yearns for excitement. He is granted this wish when a rich relative gives him a small fortune. Fred quits his secure but boring job, and he and wife, Emily (Joan Barry), embark on a world tour.
>
> After the shock of seminude revues in Paris, they board a luxury liner. Fred's first taste of the grand tour is seasickness. Emily, unaffected, enjoys shipboard social life. She is attracted to Commander Gordon (Percy Marmont), an older man.

Fred recovers and retaliates by fixing his attentions on an exotic woman who claims to be a princess (Betty Amann). Fred and Emily find themselves spending more time with their new interests than with each other.

In Singapore, Emily learns that the Princess is really a German actress who intends to steal Fred's money. Emily warns him, but it's too late. The Princess has left with his money. They book passage on a cargo ship.

One morning, they awaken to find the ship abandoned and sinking. A Chinese junk rescues them. On the junk, life is unbelievably hard, but enduring the ordeal reunites them.

Back home, they resume their dull, ordinary life, not seeming changed by their experience.

Only Joan Barry's voice had appeared in *Blackmail.* In *Rich and Strange,* all of her appeared.

Bryan Langley remembered that despite the low budget, a second unit was sent to Paris to shoot footage at the Folies Bergère, and background scenes were filmed in Alexandria, Egypt.

Rich and Strange may have been influenced by the Hitchcocks' own previous shipboard adventures before they married. The film, however, was based on a novel.

Hitchcock especially liked the actress who played the eccentric Miss Imrie, Elsie Randolph. It was her first screen role. He promised her that he would use her again, and Hitchcock did not forget. Forty years later, Elsie Randolph would appear in *Frenzy.*

Though *Rich and Strange* was shot before Hitchcock's next film, *Number 17,* it was released afterward, in December 1931.

FOLLOWING *THE SKIN GAME,* Hitchcock, Alma, and Pat had embarked on a world cruise. He returned to England with ideas that would be used in *Rich and Strange.* The film he wanted to do next was

John Van Druten's stage comedy *London Walls.* Instead, British International assigned him *Number 17,* a 1925 stage play by J. Jefferson Farjeon, while another director, Thomas Bentley, was assigned the Van Druten play. Hitchcock had not wanted to do *Number 17,* and Bentley had. "Typical of producers," Hitchcock said.

Number 17 is a comedy-thriller, a popular genre of the time. A group of seemingly unrelated people meet in an unoccupied house for no apparent reason. Then, as the plot progresses, it turns out they are all there for the same mysterious reason. That reason might be described as a "MacGuffin," Hitchcock's later term for something that motivates characters to take dangerous chances for something they *must* have. "MacGuffins are not totally explainable," he said, "or they wouldn't be MacGuffins."

In *The 39 Steps* it's a secret airplane engine design, in *The Lady Vanishes* and in *Foreign Correspondent* it's a secret diplomatic message, in *Notorious* it's uranium ore, and in *North by Northwest* it's rolls of microfilm. In *Number 17,* the MacGuffin is simply a diamond necklace. "It doesn't matter what it is," Hitchcock explained, "just that everyone wants it." Hitchcock explained how the MacGuffin got its name:

"Two men are traveling on a train to Scotland. One of them is carrying an odd parcel. The other man says, 'What have you there?' and he answers, 'A MacGuffin.'

"'What's a MacGuffin?'

"'It's a special device designed to trap wild lions in the Scottish Highlands.'

"'But there *aren't* any lions in the Scottish Highlands.'

"'Then, this is no MacGuffin.'

"The MacGuffin, you see, is only important if you *think* it's important, and that's my job as a director, to make you *think* it's important."

The play was a parody of melodramatic thrillers and was written for the actor who starred in it, Leon M. Lion, who also helped finance the film.

A vacant mansion is the meeting place for a gang of jewel thieves. It is also shelter for Ben (Leon M. Lion), a homeless seaman.

Gilbert Allardyce (John Stuart), a private detective, investigates. There he finds Ben, a body, and Rose, a neighbor (Ann Casson), along with members of the gang. Gang leader Sheldrake (Garry Marsh) arrives with a stolen diamond necklace.

After tying up Allardyce and Rose, the gang escapes through a basement door leading to a railway spur. Before leaving, Nora (Anne Grey), a sympathetic gang member, unties them.

The gang boards the boat train. Ben and Allardyce give chase. Ben jumps aboard a freight car. Allardyce commandeers a Green Line bus. Sheldrake and his accomplices can't control the out-of-control train.

Sheldrake is alarmed to find that he no longer has the necklace. Gang accomplice Doyle (Barry Jones) informs him that he is Inspector Barton of Scotland Yard, and they fight.

The train careens into the boat train, throwing the cars into the water. Allardyce, who arrived earlier, saves both Nora and Ben from drowning. He is the real Inspector Barton. Ben proudly reveals that *he* is wearing the missing necklace.

Hitchcock told me that he didn't care for anything about *Number 17* except the last part with the miniatures. This was his first extensive use of miniatures, a technique that would figure prominently in his later British thrillers. Bryan Langley, who shot this sequence in 1932, remembered well how it was done.

"The last ten minutes was all a model, a model train running through the countryside. Anything with the actors in it is the real train, the close-ups and so forth. But everything else was models. The scale of the models was one inch to one foot. When the train runs into the dockside, the dock was painted on what they call a Schüfftan shot. The little man you saw being run over by the train was reflected in a sheet of glass, which was put on the model track. The man, of course, was a real man, but he had to be a great distance away to be in scale to the rest of the thing. Hitchcock was there directing it, most of the time, in particular that last sequence. The man who did the models was a chap called Bill Warrington.

"The railway line was laid all around the edge of the big studio. I think it was more or less a reenactment of a real line.

"A few years back, we had a festival of Hitchcock in London, and I saw *Number 17,* and to my very great surprise, there was my name. It was put on as a credit, but nobody told me. I was a bit surprised. I'd never seen the film.

"I didn't see it because I was always working and seldom had time to go looking at films. I should have seen them, but I had my mind on the next film."

Langley paused for a moment, trying to remember something else from seventy years before.

"In *Number 17* there was a big house built in the studio, and there was a shot of a young lady at the top of the staircase listening to footsteps coming up the stairwell, and she was apprehensive as to what might happen. So, she was wringing her fingers, twisting them.

"This girl was sort of a beginner, and Hitchcock demonstrated how her hands should function. Her fingers should waggle, and he demonstrated with his big, fat fingers. It was like a string of sausages waving around. It was absolutely right, and when this slim girl did it, it was really a marvelous thing.

"From my personal point of view, Hitchcock was a marvelous man. He once said to me, 'Do you want to be a lighting cameraman?' and I said, 'Yes, very much indeed.' So he gave me two pieces of advice.

"One was to go to a museum, an art gallery, and study two or three paintings, painters like Rembrandt and so on. Get their lighting techniques in my head, the direction of light. And the other piece of advice was to take a candle and a sheet of white paper, and go into a black room, and hold the candle at varying positions to my head, and watch in the mirror the effects of front light, side light, back light, reflections, and no reflections. So, this was practical lighting, which he was kind enough to advise me to do, and it certainly worked."

Lord Camber's Ladies, Hitchcock's last film for British International Pictures, was only produced by him, and was directed by Benn Levy. The author of the original play, H. A. Vachell, had written the stage adaptation of *The Lodger* that Hitchcock saw in 1915. The cast of this film included Gertrude Lawrence and Gerald du Maurier, as well as Nigel Bruce in the title role. Hitchcock considered this and his next film the low points of his career.

WHEN I MENTIONED to Hitchcock that I'd never seen *Waltzes from Vienna,* he said, "That's a good girl. Don't."

I hadn't, because there was no opportunity. Finally I was able to see the film in 2003 when a British Film Institute print was shown at Anthology Film Archives in New York City. As I left the theater, I wished I could tell Alfred Hitchcock that I had enjoyed it.

After some commercial disappointments at British International Pictures, *The Skin Game, Rich and Strange,* and *Number 17,* Hitchcock signed a short-term contract with Alexander Korda. Nothing came of this, so when Ivor Novello's producing colleague, Tom Arnold, approached him about doing a musical, Hitchcock was initially receptive. Based on a 1933 German film, Ludwig Berger's *Waltzerkrieg* ("The Battle of the Waltzes") had recently been adapted by Guy Bolton for the London stage as *Waltzes from Vienna.* When the stage musical was adapted for the screen, however, nearly all of the dance numbers were taken out, prompting Hitchcock to refer to it as "a musical without music."

For the hero, Johann Strauss, Jr., called "Schani," Esmond Knight came from the stage production, where he had created the role in English. For the heroine, Rasi Ebenezar, Jessie Matthews, one of Britain's most popular musical comedy stars, was selected. She had starred in *The Good Companions* and soon would appear in her most famous film, *Evergreen*. Other members of the cast included two Hitchcock favorites from the London stage: Edmund Gwenn as Strauss, Sr. and Fay Compton as Countess Helga von Stahl, the "other woman" in Schani's life. As well as having just appeared in *The Skin Game,* Gwenn would play in two more Hitchcock films, *Foreign Correspondent* and *The Trouble with Harry.* Compton had played the title role in *Mary Rose,* the James Barrie stage play that had impressed the young Hitchcock so much that it would haunt him for the rest of his life.

Jessie Matthews (1907–1981) was offered the opportunity to dance in Hollywood musicals with Fred Astaire, but she chose to remain in England with her husband, dancing partner, and director, Sonny Hale. Matthews's career declined as she gained weight, and by the 1960s, she was a radio voice.

Esmond Knight (1906–1987) was blinded in World War II during the naval battle with the Bismarck. Recovering partial sight, he was eventually able to resume his career. Among other parts, he played a British captain in the film, *Sink the Bismarck.*

Countess Helga von Stahl (Fay Compton) commissions "Schani" Strauss (Esmond Knight) to set her lyrics to music, hoping his famous father will play it.

Inspired by young Rasi (Jessie Matthews), and the rhythms of her father's confectioner's kitchen, Schani composes "The Blue

Danube Waltz" and dedicates it to her. Then, the Countess asks him to dedicate it to *her.* Rasi tries unsuccessfully to interest Strauss, Sr. in the waltz, but is angry when she sees the double dedication.

The Countess shows "The Blue Danube" to a music publisher who exclaims, "It has to live." They arrange to have it played.

As Strauss, Sr. arrives at the concert, he hears a new waltz, which receives an enthusiastic reception. It is his son's.

Searching for Rasi, Schani rushes to his apartment, hoping she will be there, but the Countess is there instead. The Prince (Frank Vosper), suspecting his wife of infidelity, goes to challenge Schani to a duel. Realizing she loves Schani, Rasi arrives first so she can change places with the Countess. The couple is reunited.

Afterward, the elder Strauss is asked for his autograph. He signs his name, adding "Sr." and smiling wistfully. Now, there will be two composers named Johann Strauss.

Waltzes from Vienna shows the influence of Ernst Lubitsch, whom Hitchcock greatly admired. In the scene of the Prince and the Countess taking their morning baths, they communicate through messages given for delivery to the butler and the maid who are attending them. We see only the servants, as they rush back and forth, at the same time carrying on their own little affair. Soon, their kissing and the conversation become so intense, they forget and start to go to the wrong bathrooms.

The film also follows the vogue of historical musicals, which began at UFA in 1929 in answer to sound. The original approach had been pictures with only a minimum of dialogue, such as Fritz Lang's *M.* A reaction against this trend was the series of historical musicals, including *Waltzerkrieg,* on which *Waltzes from Vienna* was based, and culminating in *Viktor und Viktoria* and *Amphitryon,* both written and directed by Reinhold Schünzel, who later, as an actor in Hollywood, became one of Claude Raines's co-conspirators in *Notorious.*

Waltzes from Vienna did respectable business in 1934, even during the depth of the Depression. Hitchcock was still the best known British director, but he needed another success like *The Lodger* and *Blackmail* to reestablish himself as the great British hope. His next film would do that and more.

BRITISH STAR

❦

The Man Who Knew Too Much to *Jamaica Inn*

I LIKE TO SKI," Hitchcock told me, "in my mind."

Hitchcock was actually agile and graceful until illness limited his physical activities, although he never enjoyed doing anything he couldn't do well.

"I knew very early I was not a skier, but some of my happiest hours were spent watching people ski. *Watching* is the key word. I enjoyed their passion for play and their lack of fear of consequences. I, myself, have lived a life in which fear of consequences has always played a part. I was not an impulsive sort. I could not imagine myself at the top of a slope rushing down on skis. I'm not really built for it."

His daughter, Pat, remembered him getting into his ski pants at St. Moritz to sit on their balcony and drink hot chocolate while he watched the skiers and skaters, or read. "He liked reading at St. Moritz. Both my father and my mother liked to read. At home, they would read together while they listened to classical music."

Writer Charles Bennett and his wife sometimes went to St. Moritz with Hitchcock and Alma and Pat. Bennett recalled Hitchcock working every day in his suite, looking at the view while the others skied.

Bennett played a role in the development of the quintessential Hitchcock romantic thriller, having worked with him on *The Man Who Knew Too Much, The 39 Steps, Secret Agent, Sabotage, Young and Innocent,* and *Foreign Correspondent,* as well as informally on *Blackmail.* All of these films except *Young and Innocent* share the still quite relevant themes of political terrorism and international espionage.

I talked with Charles Bennett in 1993, not long before his death at ninety-six. At the time, Bennett reminded me, more than once, he was interrupting work on a script to speak with me. With great hope and with great enthusiasm, he was working on a new screenplay of his stage play *Blackmail.* He said he was "bringing it up to date."

Bennett sat at the bar of his just-out-of-Beverly Hills house. "Less expensive," he said, "because of being in the unfashionable postal zone." It was late morning, but none too early for Bennett to have a drink. He placed a bottle and one glass in front of him. I had gone to his home with his friend, film archivist Dan Price. We were offered drinks, but declined, which didn't inhibit Bennett.

As he spoke, he rocked back and forth on a high bar stool. He began by rocking only slightly, but as his words became more animated, he would rock back farther and farther, making it difficult for us to concentrate on what he was saying. Bennett, who appeared much younger than ninety-five, was agile, fit, and filled with energy, both verbal and physical.

We were uneasy, but our warnings about the possibility of his falling went unheeded as he became more engrossed in talking about Hitchcock. Then, just as we weren't expecting it, he rocked back too far. Price and I rushed forward, trying to cushion his fall. It was probably for the best that we failed, because we might have caused him to injure himself.

He fell straight back, continuing his comments about Hitchcock from the floor, never missing a beat. Then he righted himself and boarded his stool again, all the while never interrupting his reminiscences.

Finally he paused, but only to pour himself a drink, making no mention of his fall. That he had fallen in that way and not been injured seemed miraculous, yet I had a vague feeling that it wasn't the first time he had suffered that mishap, and perhaps it might not be the last.

Bennett talked with us about *The Man Who Knew Too Much.*

"I had been asked to write a picture about Bulldog Drummond by British International Pictures, which owned the rights. I came up with this little idea of Bulldog Drummond's baby, and to keep his tongue quiet, they snatched his child so an assassination could take place.

"Hitch had had some flops, and they didn't quite go ahead with the picture, so he went straight to Michael Balcon at Gaumont-British and said there's a picture I want to make about Bulldog Drummond.

"British International Pictures wouldn't sell their Bulldog Drummond rights, but let the story go, which was my story, *The Man Who Knew Too Much.* It was the recipe for the blending of melodrama, comedy, and romance. It was my first Hitchcock film and the first real Hitchcock picture."

In a Swiss ski lodge, French skier Bernard (Pierre Fresnay) is shot while dancing with Jill Lawrence (Edna Best). As he dies, he warns her about an assassination attempt in London, and gives her the key to his room. Jill's husband, Bob (Leslie Banks), searches the room and finds a cryptic note. Before he can contact British Intelligence, he is informed that their young daughter, Betty (Nova Pilbeam), has been kidnapped to ensure his silence.

In London, the Lawrences avoid the police, while Bob and an Uncle Clive (Hugh Wakefield) investigate. They find the taberna-

cle hideout of a gang of professional assassins led by Abbott
(Peter Lorre). Bob is captured and held prisoner along with
Betty. Clive escapes after learning about a planned assassination
that evening at Albert Hall. He warns Jill, who rushes to the hall.

There, she recognizes Ramon, a sharpshooter from Switzerland. In the auditorium at the climax of the music, Jill sees him
taking aim and screams, saving the intended victim. Police follow Ramon to the tabernacle.

During a shoot-out, Ramon attempts to escape over the
rooftops while holding Betty as a shield. When a police marksman won't risk a shot, Jill, a competitive marksman herself,
shoots Ramon, saving her daughter.

Inside the tabernacle, Abbott is killed, and Bob is released.

"Bennett and I worked backwards at our task," Hitchcock said. "I
thought first of 'where.'

"St. Moritz was chosen because Alma and I had spent our honeymoon there, and we've always loved it. Thus, I have a certain personal feeling for the first *Man Who Knew Too Much* because it exists
for me not only as a film, but as that time in my life when I was
young.

"It was also in perfect contrast to the bleak streets of East End London, where most of the action was to take place. Then, we got even
more contrast with a church and finally a gala concert at the Royal
Albert Hall. This is more or less how we worked: choose a colorful
location and then people it with believable characters.

"The other rule we stumbled upon was that the comedy-thriller-
melodramas would be more effective if they had something to do
with important events taking place in the world. At the time, it was
obvious that another war was on the horizon. That meant that espionage, assassinations, and all of the intrigues which accompany such
times would be good dramatic material for films. My melodramas are

relevant to the times, which I mention in defense of the criticism that they are only escapist."

For the villain, Hitchcock chose Peter Lorre, an outstanding German actor, who didn't yet speak English.

"Sometimes he was speaking his lines without knowing what he was saying," Hitchcock said. "But he was one of those actors who, with a hint of an expression or a slight gesture, could enhance his character in a way that was beneficial to the plot. He had left Germany as a Jewish refugee, fleeing for his life after having made *M* in which he played a child murderer. It wasn't necessary to direct him because he knew what *not* to do. Understatement is priceless, especially in melodrama.

"In person, Lorre was a charming man, very funny. I saw this and cast him in his first comic villain part." During the shoot, Lorre got married, not having enough time to remove his makeup for the ceremony.

For the child who is kidnapped, Hitchcock chose twelve-year-old Nova Pilbeam, who had just starred in a film called *Little Friend*. "The part I was offering her was smaller," Hitchcock said, "and she was fully aware of it. She had a lot of ideas of her own for building her part, which she passed on to me gratuitously, not all of them suitable.

"Sometimes I had to 'persuade' her to do something she didn't believe in, like at the end when she's reunited with her parents. At that age, even a short separation seems a long time, so I wanted her to greet them almost as strangers. It turned out to be one of the most interesting moments."

The tight budget precluded shooting the Albert Hall sequence with a house full of extras, so the Schüfftan process was used as it had been for the British Museum scenes in *Blackmail*. Some realism was injected by having one or two heads moving in the audience as Edna Best searches for the assassin.

The most controversial part of *The Man Who Knew Too Much* was the final shoot-out, which was based on an actual event. In 1911, a foreign gang of criminals thought to be anarchists were cornered in a building on Sidney Street, where police used rifles to subdue them. The "Sidney Street siege" became a cause célèbre, not just because British police are forbidden to carry guns, but also because Winston Churchill as home secretary had sanctioned it. A policeman's rifle becomes important when Edna Best saves her daughter with her sharpshooting skills. The script was altered to the censor's satisfaction by having the policemen's rifles requisitioned from a local gunsmith's shop.

Distribution of the film was delayed when Michael Balcon left for a business trip to America and C. M. Woolf was placed in charge of Gaumont-British. Woolf didn't like *The Man Who Knew Too Much* and limited the film's distribution. "The name of Woolf wasn't a favorite in our home," Pat Hitchcock remembered.

Hitchcock considered *The Man Who Knew Too Much* the turning point in his career. "It was made a second time with Jimmy Stewart and Doris Day, and it wasn't good," Bennett told me. "I don't understand why Hitch remade the picture at all, especially when he not only didn't do better, he did worse."

"EVER SINCE I READ John Buchan's *The 39 Steps,*" Hitchcock told me, "I thought it would make a great movie. But I didn't do anything about it until years later when I reread it.

"Then, I was surprised to find that, despite being full of action, it wasn't a natural screenplay. Many things didn't carry over to the screen.

"In the novel, the hero is running from a gang of assassins. We changed that to the police chasing him while he's chasing the spies to prove his innocence. I also added comedy. There isn't a great deal of humor in Buchan, and there is no romantic interest. That wouldn't do for the screen since it's so often the women who decide which movie the men are going to see. They weren't going to choose one without a heroine, but Buchan wrote his 'shockers' for men."

Buchan said, in fact, that he wrote *The 39 Steps* for himself when he found himself with no "shocker" to read. The novel's hero, Richard Hannay, resembles Buchan.

"Hitch and I both admired Buchan," Charles Bennett told me, "with this sudden eruption of terror in the life of an ordinary man. But I didn't like the novel. I thought it was horrible, but with possibilities. Hitch and I liked the double chase.

"Alma's credit on *39 Steps*'s continuity was a way Hitchcock got more money. What *is* continuity? Alma was an adorable person, but I don't remember her making much of a writing contribution to that film. But one advantage of working with Hitchcock was the wonderful food when Alma cooked."

Again, C. W. Woolf tried to stop *The 39 Steps* from being made, instead assigning Hitchcock and co-producer Ivor Montagu to a biography of Leslie Stuart, the composer of *Floradora,* a turn-of-the-century musical. They placated Woolf until Balcon came back from America and rescued *The 39 Steps.*

> Shots are fired, and a music hall audience panics. An attractive foreign woman (Lucie Mannheim) asks Richard Hannay (Robert Donat) if she can stay the night at his flat.
>
> Early the next morning, she is stabbed. Before she dies, she tells Hannay he must stop "the 39 Steps" from smuggling a state secret out of England. Clutched in her hand is a map of Scotland, with a town marked. Hannay, now a fugitive, leaves for Scotland to prove his innocence.
>
> On the train, he seeks help from a beautiful young blonde, Pamela (Madeleine Carroll), but she informs the police. He escapes and makes his way to Scotland.

He locates Professor Jordan (Godfrey Tearle), the 39 Steps leader, but Hannay is arrested. He escapes, and then is again arrested by two plainclothesmen, after being identified by Pamela.

The men, not really policemen, handcuff Hannay and Pamela together, but in handcuffs they escape and register at an inn. Finally, Pamela believes Hannay's story and agrees to help him. They go back to London.

Returning to the music hall, Hannay sees an act he remembers from his previous visit, Mr. Memory (Wylie Watson), who can answer any question of fact. Hannay asks, "What are the 39 Steps?" As Memory compulsively recites the answer, Jordan shoots him, and the police shoot Jordan.

Dying, Memory tells Hannay and Pamela his proudest achievement—memorizing the complex secret formula that was to be smuggled out of England.

"Mr. Memory is one of my favorite characters," Hitchcock told me. "I have many favorites among those who people my films, but none of whom I'm fonder than Mr. Memory. The character is based on a real person named Datas, who had an act in London when I was young. I found Memory's compulsion to answer quite fascinating.

"He was neither a magician nor a genius, you see. Memory had this one special talent. Otherwise, he would have been ordinary, but his pride in it made him a victim. He couldn't help showing it off, even at the cost of his life."

Madeleine Carroll had not been Hitchcock's first choice to be Pamela, but Alma had persuaded her husband to cast her. For Carroll, the part was expanded.

"She would have played the smaller role if I'd asked her," Hitchcock said. "But she understood what a good part it was for her, and I wanted to get more of her real personality on the screen.

"She was extremely likable. Before *The 39 Steps,* she'd played rather cold, humorless types, but she was a good comedy actress. She was a wonderful sport about Robert Donat dragging her over the Scottish moors during a rainstorm. The weather was our regular problem.

"I am often accused of perpetrating inconsiderate practical jokes, but I never purposely left Robert Donat and Madeleine Carroll handcuffed together for a whole day, as rumor had it. The key being misplaced was accidental, and certainly not for long. We did, after all, have other scenes to shoot with them. I would never risk time or money, placing my film in jeopardy.

"It is true, however, that I played a bit of a joke on Robert Donat. When he complained that his suit had been ruined in the waterfall scene, I went out and bought him another one from a nearby thrift shop—a child's sailor suit. Then, I told him I'd had a fine tailor make it especially for him."

When the picture came out, Hitchcock took Pat to see it. "She was only seven and frightened when the woman was stabbed, so I told her, 'It's only a movie.'"

Pat said, "It was just a very normal life at our house. My father was a wonderful father, so dear and funny. He liked it when I was mischievous. He was. Sometimes when I was very young, I would wake up and look in the mirror, and he had drawn a clown's face on me. This happened a lot. He never woke me, and I never knew who I would be."

"THERE IS A NO-MAN'S-LAND between good and evil. It is this gray area which interests me," Hitchcock told me. That was the theme of *Secret Agent*.

The film was drawn from two Somerset Maugham short stories, "The Traitor" and "The Hairless Mexican," which were included in the *Ashenden* collection. Balcon had become interested in the subject when he saw a play by Campbell Dixon based on "The Hairless Mexican." The project was given to Hitchcock and Montagu. A key difference between Dixon's play and the Maugham story was the addition of a female spy who provides the love interest, an essential of the Hitchcock touch. Hitchcock also chose glamorous settings, such as the Alps, grand hotels, and international trains, his own preferences.

Maugham had based his Ashenden spy stories on his own experiences as a British spy during World War I. Driving an ambulance in France, Maugham volunteered for espionage duty and was posted to Switzerland. The character of Robert Ashenden became Maugham's alter ego in a series of short stories based on his real career as a spy.

> Novelist Edgar Brodie assumes a new identity as a secret agent. As Richard Ashenden (John Gielgud), he is assigned to kill a German agent going to a meeting with Arab leaders sympathetic to Germany.
>
> In Switzerland, Ashenden is joined by a professional assassin, the General (Peter Lorre), and, as cover, a beautiful wife, Elsa (Madeleine Carroll). Courting Elsa is an American playboy, Robert Marvin (Robert Young).
>
> They mistakenly kill the wrong man (Percy Marmont), a sympathetic Englishman traveling with his devoted German wife and their beloved long-haired dachshund. When the elderly Englishman is killed and his wife left alone, the General finds the mistake funny and laughs, but Ashenden and Elsa decide to resign.
>
> Ashenden and the General discover that the German spy is Marvin. Not knowing this, Elsa departs for Greece with Marvin. At the station, Ashenden and the General find Elsa waiting for him. Seeing Marvin board the Constantinople train without her, they follow.
>
> On the train, Marvin finds Elsa alone and confronts her.

Ashenden and the General arrive as planes bomb the train. Mar-
vin, dying in the wreckage, shoots the General.

After a montage of successful Allied advances in Turkey, a
postcard to London announces: "Home safely, never again, Mr.
and Mrs. Ashenden."

John Gielgud was selected for the film because Hitchcock saw a
resemblance between Ashenden and Hamlet, and he was fond of
using stage actors because "they weren't afraid of speaking." He
found Gielgud "arrogant," however, and the actor felt that he
received no help from his director. Gielgud was well into his eighties
when I spoke with him in New York City.

"My performance was taken for granted, and I was unaccustomed
to being taken for granted. Hitchcock was, I learned later from others
who worked with him, rather stingy with praise. In the theater I was
used to the nourishment, after a performance, of audience applause.
In film work, one looks primarily to the director, or possibly a co-star.
Not only was little forthcoming from Hitchcock, but I didn't establish a warm relationship with Madeleine Carroll. She was very good,
but when our scenes ended, she seemed to be inhabiting another
world. I might say the same for Peter Lorre, except that he really *was*
in another world, drugs, you know.

"He was also an accomplished film actor who knew how to steal a
scene by inserting business into the take that he hadn't used in
rehearsal. At the time, I was annoyed. I think now it was my own
inexperience with the film medium which was responsible for my
insecurity and subsequent stiffness. Then, too, I didn't feel I was
good-looking enough to be a screen leading man, especially with
someone as beautiful as Madeleine Carroll. But when I saw the film
rather recently, I was struck by how well we all played together.

"I have always been a passionate film fan, being an early member
of the London Film Society, along with Hitchcock, whom I would

see there. But in those days, it was considered beneath one's dignity, as a stage actor, to accept employment in films. So, when I did take a few parts in the silents, I didn't tell anyone and hoped my friends wouldn't notice.

"I avoided making films. It was terribly exhausting to have to get up early in the morning after you'd been working in the theater the night before. And then, you'd always be thinking about the performance that evening. I must admit that I really did *Secret Agent* for the money.

"Your faults are hidden on the stage, and you seem grander than you are. In the films, every defect is magnified. And it's forever.

"For many years, I stopped making films entirely, and I blamed Hitchcock for this, but it wasn't his fault. Looking back, I realize I didn't have much confidence in my talent as a film actor and, when I first saw the film, I thought my performance was rather poor. When I saw it decades later, I was stunned—by how young I looked.

"Actually, I rather enjoyed working with Hitchcock. He was a great joker. Now, I love the film and treasure my appearance in it."

Making her English-language film debut in *Secret Agent* was Lilli Palmer, who plays Peter Lorre's girlfriend, Lilli. Tom Helmore is the colonel in the steam bath. Michael Redgrave makes a brief appearance as an army officer. The coachman is the legendary French actor Michel Saint-Denis, who was a friend of Gielgud's. Robert Young, already an established star in Hollywood, assumed the role of the villain, a part that was tempered with comedy.

The murder of the sympathetic British man mistaken for a German spy changed the tone of the film from spy thriller to tragedy. He is an outstanding example of another Hitchcock wrong man, although Hitchcock preferred to think of that character as "a man on the spot."

"'DESMOND TESTICLE. Where are you Desmond Testicle?'

"My most vivid memory of *Sabotage* was Alfred Hitchcock calling out to Desmond Tester," Sylvia Sidney told me. "Desmond was the boy who played my little brother. Tester was his last name, and I could never forget it, because whenever Hitchcock would call upon him, he would call out in that incredible voice of his, every syllable clearly enunciated, 'Is Des-mond Tes-ti-cle here?'"

It was in 1998 at New York City's legendary Players Club that Sidney talked with me about her memories of 1936, more than sixty years earlier, when she was the star of Alfred Hitchcock's *Sabotage*.

"The boy was terribly embarrassed, but Hitchcock seemed to get a great deal of pleasure out of that. I didn't think the joke was funny in the first place. I certainly didn't think it was funny in the second place. And it didn't get funnier with repetition for anyone except Hitchcock, who seemed to enjoy it so much. I personally thought it was a cruel thing to do to a child who couldn't do anything about it except be red-faced. Fortunately, it never seemed to affect the boy's performance, which was very good. I often wondered what became of him.

"Then, some years later, I met someone who had been working on the *Sabotage* set, and he said he happened to run into Desmond, somewhere like Australia, I think. The person told me that they were reminiscing about the picture, and he expressed his sympathy to Desmond about how Hitchcock had made fun of him. And you know what? Desmond said *he* thought it was very funny!"

Sidney and I were standing in front of a painting of the celebrated nineteenth-century actor Edwin Booth. Indicating Booth, she said, "His fame as a great actor was eclipsed by his brother, John Wilkes Booth, who killed Abraham Lincoln. The negative always gets more attention than the positive.

"If I'd known how famous Alfred Hitchcock was going to be, I would have paid more attention to what he was doing. And if I'd known how long people were always going to be asking me how it was to work with Hitchcock and Fritz Lang, I would have taken notes.

"I guess I preferred Hitchcock to Fritz, who could be cruel. Hitchcock wasn't unpleasant, but he was strange. He seemed to be more interested in things than in people. He treated props like actors. When we did the murder scene at the end, where I kill Oscar Homolka, Hitchcock was more interested in the knife than in either of us. He would just tell us, 'Look to the right. Not so much. Less. Look away.' He never said, 'You're doing it right.' When he stopped giving you any directions, you knew you were doing it right."

Charles Bennett remembered Sylvia Sidney as being extremely unhappy during the shooting of *Sabotage*. "She just hated Hitchcock! He called her and courted her for the picture, and then paid no attention to her. I thought she was very good. Hitch was a very tubby, brilliant man. He was tough to love and easy to hate."

Sabotage is loosely based on the Joseph Conrad novel *The Secret Agent*.

Disguised as a greengrocer's assistant, police sergeant Ted Spencer (John Loder) investigates a suspected saboteur, Mr. Verloc (Oscar Homolka), a cinema owner. He makes friends with Verloc's young wife (Sylvia Sidney) and her younger brother, Stevie (Desmond Tester).

Desperate for money, Verloc agrees to blow up the Piccadilly tube station during a parade. Before the parade, he receives a bomb set to go off at 1:45 p.m. Hiding it in a film can, he gives the can to Stevie to deliver to the Piccadilly underground station, admonishing him to do so before 1:30. As Stevie passes Spencer and Mrs. Verloc, they notice the film can.

Stevie, distracted along the way, is late. The bomb goes off on a London bus, killing him and the other passengers, including a small, friendly dog.

Spencer, finding pieces of the film can in the wreckage, understands what has happened. Mrs. Verloc confronts her husband, who admits his guilt, but blames her "Scotland Yard

friend" for Stevie's death. As he moves toward her threaten-
ingly, she kills him with a carving knife.

The bomb maker returns to remove any evidence of his complicity, and accidentally blows up the theater along with Verloc's
body.

Mrs. Verloc and Spencer are free to find what happiness they
can.

Robert Donat was originally scheduled to play the part of Verloc,
but he suffered from very bad asthma and was incapacitated by it just
before shooting started. Sylvia Sidney remembered Oscar Homolka
as "very old school, very old-fashioned in his approach to acting. I
wasn't used to this."

Sidney had looked forward to working with Hitchcock, the most
famous British director of that moment. She was enjoying a fine Hollywood career, which included playing the lead in Fritz Lang's *Fury*.
During a visit to England, she had been signed by Michael Balcon for
Sabotage. She was, in fact, the reason the picture could be made.

The actress had expected to learn something from Hitchcock, but
when he wanted to shoot the end of a scene before the beginning,
even before they had rehearsed it, she began to wonder. His methods
were so unorthodox she decided that "maybe he was going to have
the rehearsal after the wrap, but he seemed to know what he was
doing." When she saw the film and her performance in it, she
decided that while he was a bit aloof, he was a great director.

Sidney loved dogs, so she was particularly offended by what she
considered "the unnecessary death of the darling dog." She told
Hitchcock so and was unsatisfied then and through the years by his
reply: "It's only a movie, Sylvia."

"I think Hitchcock made a terrible mistake when he had the people in the bus, my young brother, and that adorable little dog blown
up," Sidney continued.

When Sidney died, she left her white bulldog to New York City's Players Club, a favorite place of hers, where he became their mascot.

Hitchcock, however, was well aware that he had broken a prime rule of his own by killing Stevie. "Once you have established the heroes and heroines, you must rescue them at the last second," he told me. "That's because you have transferred the feelings of danger facing your characters to the audience. The only way they can enjoy the sensation of the hero and heroine facing death is knowing they will be saved. If you don't do this, you have betrayed this unspoken agreement with your audience."

Sabotage was not shot on location. An entire city block was built for it on a field near Harrow in order to avoid the pitfalls and inconveniences imposed by shooting on the streets of London. "But there was one I couldn't avoid, the English weather. We were held up for the same reason we would have been held up in the West End. Rain."

WHEN *YOUNG AND INNOCENT* was released in early 1938, it was widely anticipated not only as a new Hitchcock thriller, but also as Nova Pilbeam's first adult role. She was fourteen when she played the girl who is kidnapped in *The Man Who Knew Too Much,* and eighteen for *Young and Innocent.*

"I felt she had great appeal for women," Hitchcock said. "I believed she had a brilliant future, and I was planning to use her for the part Margaret Lockwood eventually played in *The Lady Vanishes.*

"She was fresh and natural-looking. Hollywood makeup people would have put a mask on her, but she didn't care a bit about Hollywood. I didn't, at the time, know why. The reason was love."

In 1939, she married Penrose Tennyson, whom she had known since 1934 when he was an assistant director on *The Man Who Knew Too Much.* Tennyson became a director for Michael Balcon after *Young and Innocent* and made three films for Ealing before he joined the navy at the outbreak of World War II. He was killed in a plane crash in 1941, at the age of twenty-nine.

Pilbeam returned to films after his death, acting in twelve pictures until she retired from the screen in 1948.

Young and Innocent is best remembered for the wide overhead traveling shot in the hotel ballroom which finishes on a close-up of the twitching eye of the blackfaced drummer. Hitchcock used this shot memorably in *Notorious,* and again in *Marnie,* each time to point up something small in a large setting that is really the most important element of the scene.

To accomplish this in one take, Hitchcock asked the studio's camera workshop to design and construct a variable focal-length, zoom-type lens that, when used with a specially built elevator dolly, would allow the camera to move from a high overhead view of the ballroom to a close-up of the drummer's twitching eye.

Bryan Langley recalled Hitchcock's expert knowledge of camera lenses: "He could draw a setup with background, larger or smaller, according to the focal length of the lens, which no one else I've ever seen was able to do or even understood that it's necessary."

Young and Innocent was based on a novel by Josephine Tey, with the screenplay by Charles Bennett, Edwin Greenwood, Anthony Armstrong and Alma Reville, who was uncredited.

After a violent argument with her husband, a famous star is discovered by her ex-lover, Robert Tisdall (Derrick De Marney), drowned on a beach. Police arrive and arrest Tisdall on the testimony of witnesses who saw him with the body. He is accused of the murder.

As he is about to go on trial for murder, he escapes from the courthouse with the help of Erica Burgoyne (Nova Pilbeam), the resourceful daughter of the police constable (Percy Marmont) . At first, Erica doesn't really believe Tisdall is innocent, but she's so attracted to the young man, she continues to help him elude capture while searching for the real killer, risking her life and her father's reputation.

Their only lead is provided by Old Will (Edward Rigby), a china mender, who can identify the murderer, a man with a noticeably twitching eye. They track him to a grand hotel, where the murderer is revealed to be the blackfaced drummer in the ballroom's dance band. Robert's innocence is established.

Although Erica's father is not thrilled with Tisdall as a future son-in-law, her expression in the final close-up indicates she will have her way.

Hitchcock appears onscreen in a scene outside the courthouse, wearing a cap and holding a small camera, annoyed because people are blocking his view, and he can't get his picture. "My cameo appearances," Hitchcock told me, "were a deliberate move away from realism, reminding the audience, 'It's only a movie.'"

IN AUGUST OF 1937, the Hitchcocks made a trip to America on the *Queen Mary.* Hitchcock and Alma had talked about a possible move to Hollywood, and they were anxious to explore the possibilities firsthand.

Very privately, he had employed an American publicist to be certain the press knew of his arrival. He already was represented by the brother of David O. Selznick, agent Myron Selznick, who lived and worked in England.

The trip did not produce anything in the way of offers, but a personal relationship was established with David Selznick's representative in New York. The Hitchcocks returned to England in September 1938, where he completed the editing of *Young and Innocent.* They had made no American commitment, nor did they have in mind their next British film. *The Wheel Spins,* a 1936 novel by Ethel Lina White, who specialized in mysteries about young women on journeys, was considered. It developed into *The Lady Vanishes*.

A screenplay had been prepared at Gainsborough for the Hollywood director Roy William Neill, later known for his Universal Sherlock Holmes films. Neill, however, dropped out of the project, so it was given to Hitchcock. He was struck by the resemblance of the story to one he had wanted to do, one that had inspired a German film of 1938 (Veit Harlan's *Verwehte Spuren*) and later *So Long at the Fair*, a 1950 British film with Jean Simmons and Dirk Bogarde directed by Terence Fisher and Anthony Darnborough. It is based on the true story of a woman who disappears without a trace at the Paris Exposition of 1890 because she has contracted the plague.

"Our vanishing lady disappears because of a different plague coming on the scene—World War II," Hitchcock said. "The heroine is supposed to be imagining things because of a bit of a bump on the head she has had."

I met Sir Michael Redgrave at his last birthday party, in New York. We had the opportunity to speak about what it was like working with Hitchcock during the director's late British period.

Redgrave remembered it as "life-changing, my first film," though he had appeared briefly in *Secret Agent*. At the time, he thought of himself as "of the theater, one of the theater folk" who scoffed at acting in films.

"I was appearing on the stage," Redgrave said, "but I didn't have a next part coming up that I really liked, so I decided to try a film. My fellow actors were discouraging, but that only made me feel more determined to do it." John Gielgud advised him to give it a try for the experience, but Peggy Ashcroft, who had worked in *The 39 Steps*, advised him to "stick to the stage."

"I loved to go to the cinema, but I approached it with trepidation as an actor." Redgrave took the screen test and was offered the lead in *The Lady Vanishes*.

"I was more or less the right type for the part. I was sufficiently trained to be able to memorize and rattle off my lines, and though I was more of a Redgrave than a Redford, I was not especially self-conscious in front of a camera.

"I wasn't vain because I really didn't have anything to be vain about. I didn't think about camera angles or which was my best side. I didn't think I *had* a best profile, or if I did, I couldn't find it.

"The first thing I did after signing was to regret it. It was like so many decisions we all make, where one immediately has second thoughts. But I was curious to see what picture making was all about, and I assumed I'd learn something."

The first words of wisdom he heard from the most famous of British film directors were: "Learn your lines, hit your marks, and don't worry too much."

"I don't think Hitchcock thought much of me as an actor. But he didn't seem worried because I believe he thought he would get a performance from me in the cutting room through his skill. I thought I'd been chosen because I photographed well.

"I can say definitely that Hitchcock said, quote, 'Actors are cattle,' unquote, because he said it in my presence. I never knew if it was aimed specifically at me or if he had already had the thought."

Hitchcock told me, "You don't have time to massage actors' egos. If you do, it has been my experience that the appetite grows with the eating. It can be a full-time job for an octopus, holding all those hands."

In the theater, Redgrave had never enjoyed "hitting chalk marks."

"I was a stage actor accustomed to being expansive. I believed that there must be a great deal of improvisation in acting, and that the part should be developing continuously."

Redgrave had some ideas he thought quite clever business, and he thought Hitchcock would be pleased by what he had brought to the character. Quite the contrary. He was allowed to finish his small addition. Then, an extremely serious Hitchcock said, "You can't do that. It won't match the other shots."

Redgrave felt mortified by the rebuke in front of the cast and crew. "I did not like Hitchcock. I particularly didn't like his sense of humor.

"I was bored. I'd never been bored in the theater. Not for one minute. I was certain I would never agree to make another film, even if anyone wanted me to, which I was certain they never would after this. I expected to writhe in shame when the picture was released.

"Being in the theater at night and getting up early for the film, I was always tired. I had a terrible time waking up in the morning and I was sleepwalking all day. We had a lot of time to talk since most screen acting is waiting around.

"One day, that fine actor, Paul Lukas, who was in the film, told me he had seen me the night before in *The Three Sisters.* 'You're a *real* actor,' he said. 'But here, you hardly seem to be trying at all.'

"I agreed with him. I not only found it boring, but I was really exhausted, putting all my energy into my nightly performances in the theater.

"'But, my dear boy,' he told me, 'it's all going into the can, forever. After the director has called, 'Print!' it's too late for you to do it better next time. There *is* no next time. It's all there in the can.'

"There is a scene in *The Lady Vanishes* in which a foreign agent mentions that his perfect command of English is due to his having been educated at Oxford. My character picks up a chair and hits the agent over the head.

"'Why did you do that?' I'm asked.

"I say, 'I was at Cambridge.' I found this an utterly terrible line to say. Embarrassing. I considered asking Hitchcock to cut it, but to do so might have been disruptive to our relationship.

"When the film opened and as long as it played, everywhere my line, the one I would have wished to have taken out, got the biggest laugh of the film.

"Well, here we are, so long afterwards. The audiences that watched me as a young man are as old as I am and some of them are gone, taking their memories with them. The film screen has a much longer memory. I understand now that when I am gone, I shall probably be remembered best for *The Lady Vanishes,* about which I was at the time flippant and nonchalant. I had occasion to see the film not long ago, and I felt gratitude to Paul Lukas for helping me gain perspective. I felt gratitude to Mr. Hitchcock for casting me. I came to admire Mr. Hitchcock very much, but never his sense of humor.

"At the time I made the film, I had so little confidence in the way my face would look blown up big on a screen. Seeing the film just a little while ago, I noticed how young I look, and that is forever."

A group of British tourists, snowbound in an Alpine lodge, finally catch a train out of a Balkan country. One passenger, Iris Henderson (Margaret Lockwood), is unenthusiastically returning to London to get married. She meets an older lady, Miss Froy (Dame May Whitty), who disappears after a bandaged patient is brought aboard. When Iris calls attention to Miss Froy's disappearance, no one will admit that a Miss Froy ever existed, with the exception of an eccentric young musician, Gilbert Redman (Michael Redgrave). They tell their story to Dr. Hartz (Paul Lukas), who is really a member of the conspiracy to kidnap Miss Froy and take her off the train as the bandaged patient.

Iris and Gilbert find Miss Froy and free her. She is an English spy on her way to London with an important message encoded in a melody. Before escaping, she teaches Gilbert the melody, in case she doesn't make it.

The train is diverted and the passengers are attacked by troops, until they manage to commandeer the engine and drive out of the country.

In London, Iris chooses Gilbert instead of her fiancé. They go together to the War Office where Gilbert finds he cannot remember the tune. Then they hear Miss Froy playing it in the next room, and they are reunited.

"I'll tell you the kind of image I'm proud of," Hitchcock said. "In *The Lady Vanishes,* there is a lady disguised as a nun. The audience believes she is a nun, and then I cut to the hem of her robe. When you see her high-heeled shoes, that picture tells the story. No nun, this one.

"This kind of image may come out of my early days in silent films, or it may be just the way my mind works."

Hitchcock was reunited with cinematographer Jack Cox on this film; it was their twelfth picture together. Director Roy Ward Baker, who was an assistant director on the film, told me, "Cox was very tall, a man of very few words, with a complete lack of pretense, and a sardonic wit. He didn't chatter, you know. He just got on with his lighting.

"If we had to put the camera up on a rostrum, what you call a parallel lift, Hitch wouldn't climb up, because he always was fat, even in those days. What he did was to make a sort of thumbnail sketch of what he wanted and give it to Jack Cox. And that was it.

"He always claimed that he could see the film in his mind's eye, complete, as it would be when it was finished. It was a kind of boast, 'Only a leg-pull, really,' as he would say.

"At the same time, that was his principle, that you don't build a great set and call a lot of actors and a crew and everything, and then sit down and wonder what you're going to do next. The most vital ingredient for the success of any film is that the people who are making it know what they want and know what they're doing."

Baker described Hitchcock as "not particularly friendly, but he wasn't unfriendly. He was professional, you know. He didn't waste time on pleasantries. He got on with the work, and so did I.

"I think everyone enjoyed working with Hitchcock. He was an eye-opener, a plucky chap. There was no larking about, wasting time, and stupidities. He was quite a disciplinarian, but he didn't emphasize it at all; he just *was* it. The whole crew's behavior will derive from the behavior of the director, in any case.

"Hitch called on the art director to build one of the sets for *The Lady Vanishes* in false perspective. It was the platform of a small country railway station, which was made to look much longer than it was by foreshortening each end of the platform to a false vanishing point. Hitchcock had the idea to have some small children dressed as grown-ups and to have them at the rapidly diminishing ends of the platform where there would be normal-sized adult people and buildings in the foreground.

"If it had been anyone but Hitchcock, I would have been dubious about the effect, but he could imagine everything and work it out that way in advance, and when you did it, his technical conception was infallible. And it was always that the technical was only there to carry the story forward in the best possible way, and frequently in the most money-saving way. Hitchcock was able to work within limitations, and when he did, they were no longer limitations.

"I was Hitchcock's second assistant director, that's all. But it was a privilege to have worked with him, and it taught me a great deal about the inside, the nuts and bolts, of how you make a film.

"I saw him later when I came to Hollywood to make pictures myself. I visited him at Universal, and he was very genial and amusing, you know, as he always was, at least to me. He gave me tea.

"He was quite a connoisseur of good food, and he fancied the food hampers of Fortnum & Mason. I always remember the image of Hitchcock with his little daughter, of whom he was so proud, having lunch in the train's make-believe wagon restaurant. We were shooting that day in the dining car. There, in the make-believe restaurant, they had a little make-believe champagne, which had the bubbles, but no alcohol. With a few working lights, the two of them were dining.

"*The Lady Vanishes* showed the varying moods of people towards what everybody knew was an oncoming war. It was shown in late 1938 in London, and of course it was a tremendous success because he got it bang to rights."

On the subject of Hitchcock's legendary love of practical jokes, Baker said, "People warned me to beware of his practical joke side, which apparently amused him, jokes which he found hilarious and no one else did, especially the victim. I must say that during the course of the film, I, personally, never saw any instance of any practical jokery on the part of Hitchcock, only serious determination and focus on planning. The methodical planning of everything in advance was what I learned from him, and, I repeat, on a Hitchcock set there was no larking about.

"The nearest I ever got to a firsthand account of a joke was from a production manager who worked for Hitchcock. His name was Dicky Bevill.

"Hitch invited Bevill to drive down to his country house at Shamley Green in Surrey for a Sunday lunch. 'But, Hitch, my car is being repaired.'

"'No trouble,' Hitch said. 'Come by Green Line bus. It passes by your door.' Hitch was a student of public transportation and could tell you how to get anywhere by bus or train.

"Still, Bevill was skeptical. 'Are you sure? I've never seen a bus running on Elgin Avenue.'

"'Take the 11:10 a.m. bus and you'll be there in good time.'

"'But, Hitch . . .'

"'Don't argue. Just do as I say.'

"So, on Sunday morning, just as Hitch had said, a Green Line bus appeared at 11:10 going to Shamley Green. Of course, Hitch had hired the bus, complete with driver and conductor."

Bryan Langley offered an explanation for Hitchcock's often criticized fondness for practical jokes. "He was a great joke maker, but he wasn't the only one. In those days, soon after the First World War, people were full of practical jokes. This was the fashion at the time in the studios, and I do believe really it was a reaction from the events of the First World War. Many of these people were either in the war or had grown up as children with it."

Practical jokes in England came into their own even earlier, at the end of the Victorian period, and were especially popular during the Edwardian era, which lasted from 1901 until 1910. In its heyday, people would spend fortunes and great effort and ingenuity to devise elaborate pranks. Hitchcock's reputation for practical jokes was exaggerated, but he did grow up during this period and admitted he had a liking for them.

As *The Lady Vanishes* was being completed, Myron Selznick negotiated a seven-year contract with his brother, David, for his client, Alfred Hitchcock. Though other studios had shown interest, the Selznick offer was the only firm one. Seven years seemed a rather long commitment to Hitchcock, but at the same time, it held the promise of security for his family and justified the move to California. Though the Hitchcocks had high hopes for their future in Hollywood, they kept their home in Shamley Green, and paid an exploratory visit to America.

Hitchcock had agreed to do one more film in England, a film he really didn't want to make, *Jamaica Inn.* After it was completed, he liked it even less, and said, "I would have preferred to have vanished after *The Lady Vanishes.*"

In 1938, before going to America, he had been persuaded by Charles Laughton to direct a costume epic. Laughton had formed a production company with Erich Pommer and Mayflower Pictures, and this was to be their third film. Hitchcock was persuaded by the prospect of doing a Daphne du Maurier novel. Although tentatively scheduled to make a picture about the Titanic with David Selznick, Hitchcock knew that Selznick had recently purchased film rights to du Maurier's *Rebecca,* and he hoped to direct it.

After he agreed to do *Jamaica Inn,* Hitchcock saw the first script and had second thoughts. He entrusted the revision to his personal assistant, Joan Harrison, and left for a trip to America. On his return to London, he encountered more than script problems.

Laughton had gone from being the hero to being the villain. "It

would be like casting Laughton as the butler in a whodunit," Hitchcock said. "I would have had to change it into a 'howdunit.' In the
novel the villain is a clergyman, which made the film difficult to distribute in America, so he was changed into a village squire and the
local magistrate."

Maureen O'Hara told me that she did *Jamaica Inn* because she was
under contract to Charles Laughton, who had discovered her, and the
enthusiasm for the film was all his. She felt that Hitchcock had little
interest in the film, and that he didn't make much of an impression on
her, "perhaps because I was so young."

In 1820, Mary Yellin (Maureen O'Hara) leaves Ireland and comes
to Cornwall to live with her Aunt Patience (Marie Ney). Patience's
husband, Joss Merlyn (Leslie Banks), operates the Jamaica Inn,
whose tenants are wreckers. Led by Joss, they cause ships to be
grounded, then plunder them. Their real leader is the local magistrate, Sir Humphrey Pengallan (Charles Laughton), who deals
only with Joss. Pengallan admires Mary's beauty.

One of the gang, Jem Trehearne (Robert Newton), suspected
of stealing from them, is hanged, but Mary saves him by cutting
him down after they have left him for dead. She then has to
leave with him when Joss discovers her complicity and duplicity.

They go to Pengallan's mansion where Jem reveals he is an
undercover police officer. Pengallan accompanies them back to
the Jamaica Inn and pretends to arrest Joss. Jem is recaptured
by the gang, and he and Mary are tied up. Patience releases
them and they escape.

Mary is recaptured after she foils the gang's attempt to
wreck an approaching ship, and Joss is shot for defending her.
After shooting Patience, Pengallan forces Mary to come with
him. Jem intercepts them with the militia at the port, where
Pengallan climbs a ship's rigging and leaps to his death.

Trehearne comforts Mary, and they leave together.

Emlyn Williams, who appeared in the film as a character named Harry, told me that he took the part as a favor to Charles Laughton, and because he was curious about what he might learn from "the great Alfred Hitchcock. What I learned from Hitchcock was that it was a good time to go to Hollywood."

After *Jamaica Inn,* Hitchcock, Alma, and Pat returned to America on the *Queen Mary,* taking Hitchcock's assistant and family friend, Joan Harrison, with them. This time they were going to stay. "It was what I wanted," Hitchcock said, "though I didn't think I was going for my whole life. Alma was less certain about the move than I was and then she was more certain about staying. She loved the southern California weather.

"Our daughter, Patricia, adjusted to wherever her parents were. We brought a cook and a maid, who left us. Our dogs—Edward, an English cocker spaniel, and Jenkins, a Sealyham terrier—seemed to have no opinion on the subject. Grass is grass."

Sitting with Pat Hitchcock in her suite at New York City's Plaza Hotel, late in 2003, I asked her about her feelings, all those years ago. Did she mind leaving her home, her school friends, England?

"No. I didn't think about it. We were together. I was an only child, and we were very close. We could weather anything."

When their cook left, Alma bought some cookbooks. "We both enjoy French food," Hitchcock said, "and she learned to cook everything just as I like it. Happily, she likes it the same way.

"When we got off the ship in New York, reporters immediately asked me a question which really seemed to me had no special pertinence, but they were wedded to it. 'What is your favorite food?' I said, 'Steak à la mode.'

"No one laughed. No one even smiled. Then, I found myself reading that quote, over and over again. Steak à la mode. Disgusting.

"Alma was over the moon when she saw California," Hitchcock said. "She loved the flower-scented air, the orange blossoms. It was love at first smell."

Alma told me she liked what she saw as the absence in America of the class system that prevailed in England.

When Hitchcock left for Hollywood, he was England's most famous director, both respected and popular. Bryan Langley, cameraman for five of Hitchcock's earliest English sound films, seventy years later, said to me with great feeling:

"He was a very good bloke."

III.

HOLLYWOOD

THE SELZNICK YEARS

❦

Rebecca to The Paradine Case

I CAN'T BELIEVE I was ever that thin."

This was Joan Fontaine's comment on just having seen herself in *Rebecca,* fifty years after she had starred with Laurence Olivier in the Hitchcock film.

We were having dinner at New York City's Le Cirque restaurant with ICM's Milton Goldman, her agent and friend.

"What's your most striking memory of *Rebecca*?" Goldman asked.

"That's it," she said, "I can't believe I was ever so naive. And so skinny.

"Do you remember when Olivier takes me to the grand hotel? I ate scrambled eggs." She made a face.

Just at that moment, owner Sirio Maccioni appeared with the menu and a few special suggestions. Fontaine did not order scrambled eggs. She continued talking about *Rebecca* in her life.

"You never know when a chance meeting or a dinner you almost didn't accept is what changes your career and life forever. I was invited to a dinner party at Charlie Chaplin's where I was seated next to a heavy man wearing glasses. He was very pleasant, and we began chatting about books. I happened to mention a book I'd just read and enjoyed, Daphne du Maurier's *Rebecca*. He said, 'I just bought the book today!' I assumed he meant he bought a book, as did I. He went on.

"'My name is David O. Selznick. I bought the film rights to *Rebecca*.'

"He asked me if I would like to test for the part of 'I.'

"I tested several times. I was encouraged when it was Alfred Hitchcock who directed my test. Then, I heard about all of the others who were testing for the part of the young girl who has no name until she becomes 'the second Mrs. de Winter.' It was simply *everyone*. Loretta Young, Susan Hayward, Anne Baxter, Vivien Leigh. I didn't dare hope.

"I was marrying Brian Aherne, and a week before my wedding, Mr. Selznick called and asked if I'd mind postponing my wedding to test again. I thought, yes, I do mind, but I didn't say it.

"I'd really wanted my career, but on my honeymoon, I was no longer certain.

"I had the part and Mr. Selznick wanted me to sign a long-term contract. The long-term contract, seven years, was a condition I had to agree to if I wanted the part.

"I found Hitchcock rather distant, but only at first, not after you got to know him. I was shy. He would say disparaging things about people on the set when they couldn't hear him, so I assumed he did the same about me. Laurence Olivier didn't want me. He had wanted Vivien Leigh with whom he was having a notorious affair.

"Just after we began filming, Hitchcock confided that Olivier didn't think I was very good. You can imagine how that made me feel. I was as friendly and cooperative as I could be. But after what I'd been told, if I convinced Olivier of my good feeling towards him, then I *really* deserved an Oscar. I never knew if Hitchcock said it without thinking, or if he had thought it out in order to divide and conquer.

"Later, I wondered if knowing this hurt me or helped me in my part. At the time, I was certain it hurt me, but later I wondered if Hitchcock might have known me better than I knew myself.

"Practically the whole cast was British, and very cliquish. Gladys Cooper told me, 'You don't belong here.' I couldn't let that pass, not only was I British, too, but I told her that my grandmother was the honorable Mrs. de Havilland of Guernsey, the first lady of Guernsey. That's like being the first lady of Catalina.

"Alma, Hitch's wife, was so petite it was possible, if you looked quickly, to overlook her. She was quiet as a mouse. I suppose mice *are* quiet. I never saw her say anything to Hitch on the set, but I bet she saved it all for when they were home alone. Pillow-to-pillow, pretty powerful stuff. They seemed very close.

"He had a great visual sense, and he knew acting. I've heard that he wasn't an actor's director, but I learned a lot from him.

"I'll never forget this wonderful drawing he made. It wasn't of me, it was of 'I,' the character I played. He would show me the drawings to help me understand how he wanted me to be. It was a wonderful way."

The drawing she best remembered was her character shrinking into an oversized chair. Hitchcock showed the light on her face in such a way that the fear in her eyes was highlighted. The rest of the drawing was in darkness. From it she said she was able to grasp her character.

She said she wished she had that drawing, but it wouldn't have occurred to her to ask for it because she was too much the timid young girl she was playing.

Olivier told me about his first meeting with Hitchcock. He said to the director, "Call me, Larry."

Hitchcock responded, surprising Olivier, "Call me Hitch, without a cock."

"I'd certainly heard the word before," Olivier said, "but I wasn't expecting it from the seemingly decorous Hitchcock."

Olivier said that Hitchcock didn't say to him the much quoted

"Actors are cattle," but rather he said, "Actors are chess figures."

During a stay at New York's Wyndham Hotel, Olivier talked with me about *Rebecca*.

"At that time, I wasn't so interested in films. I preferred the stage. Hitchcock saw the part of the young heroine as the important one, and it turned out that way. I saw film as a director's medium and the stage, an actor's.

"When they called to say someone named Joan Fontaine had been given the role playing opposite me, I can't say I was thrilled. I'd certainly never heard of her. Then I met her and what I noticed was how young and skinny she was. I didn't really understand what my character, Maxim de Winter, could see in her. As I understood Max better, I decided that she was just what he wanted—someone exactly the opposite of Rebecca. He'd had enough of Rebecca, and he was looking for docile, even wilted.

"I admit I was prejudiced from the start. I'd exerted my influence to persuade Selznick that the best possible choice for the part was Vivien. Vivien had her heart set on playing opposite me, and she loved the part, which she had tested for. She was a very good actress, and it was rather mortifying for me not to have been more influential. It affected our personal lives for a while.

"Joan Fontaine gave an amazing performance. I don't think anyone could have done it better, even though I didn't realize it while it was happening, which surprises me because I consider myself rather a good judge of performances.

"As for Hitchcock, I rather enjoyed the experience. I don't remember him giving me a lot of direction. Just simple things, like 'Don't mumble.' He was quite right about that.

"Mr. Hitchcock—I never thought of him as Hitch—he didn't make me feel that he was overly thrilled with what I was doing. Perhaps because he wasn't. I thought of myself as a stage actor who was acting in a film. When I saw the finished film, I was not ashamed. I respected Mr. Hitchcock, but I don't remember liking him much during filming. I came to like him very much afterwards. If he had asked me to do another film with him, I would have said yes. But he never did. I did regret that I hadn't given the young Miss Fontaine my helping hand. As it turned out, she didn't need it.

"I felt she didn't like me. Here, we were supposed to be having a flirtation, a courtship, a love marriage. When the camera wasn't on, she never said anything hostile to me, but she scarcely spoke to me at all. I wondered if she was aware that I had spoken to Hitchcock on behalf of Vivien.

"I didn't like having to plead Vivien's case. But I couldn't say no to her. Hitch was very decent about it. But the worst part of it was I really didn't want to have her get the part. There was already so much strain in our personal life, our divorces, leaving a wife and child, and a husband and child in England, the European situation, the war. It was perhaps better for us to have a little vacation from constant togetherness.

"Vivien thought I didn't try hard enough for her with Hitchcock for the part in *Rebecca*. Well, I didn't. I hadn't felt she was right for that part, if the truth be told.

"Vivien was exactly the opposite of Scarlett O'Hara, who said something like, 'I'll worry about it tomorrow.' She worried about everything—yesterday, today, and tomorrow. But she was *so* beautiful.

"All through the filming, my respect for Joan only grew. Then, when I saw the film, it was over the top."

DAME JUDITH ANDERSON preferred the stage, too. She did not enjoy being in *Rebecca* because she believed she wasn't allowed to bring anything to her part. "There was only one way to play Mrs. Danvers—Hitchcock's way," Anderson observed. She was nominated for an Oscar for best supporting actress in *Rebecca* in 1940.

She could never forget Joan Fontaine coming up to her on the set, and saying, "Slap me."

"I just looked at her," Anderson told me.

"So she went up to Hitch and said something. Then, he just hauled back and slapped her. She reeled and staggered out in front of the camera, looking fragile, hurt, as though her eyes were just about to well up with tears, in the mood for the next scene she had to play. Hitch and she had their way of working together."

Widower Maxim de Winter (Laurence Olivier) marries a timid young woman (Joan Fontaine), a lady's companion he has met in Monte Carlo.

At Manderley, Max's estate, the young woman is over-whelmed by Mrs. Danvers, the haughty housekeeper (Judith Anderson), who humiliates her whenever possible, comparing her to Max's first wife, Rebecca, who had drowned in a boating accident.

Finally realizing that Mrs. Danvers is doing this deliberately, the young woman confronts her. Mrs. Danvers suggests to the sad young woman that taking her own life might be the answer.

Then, a sunken boat is found in the harbor. It is the de Winter boat, with Rebecca's body on board. Max becomes a murder suspect.

Jack Favell (George Sanders), Rebecca's "favorite" cousin, offers to suppress evidence that might convict Max, for a price. His contention that Rebecca was pregnant is proven to be false by a visit to her doctor (Leo G. Carroll). Rebecca was dying of cancer, raising the possibility of suicide. Max is cleared.

Mrs. Danvers, insane, sets fire to Manderley. She dies in the flames, along with the spirit of Rebecca, whom Max has revealed he hated. The couple is set free, though certainly haunted by memories.

"It's important that the house was dying," Hitchcock told me.

He wanted to show how cold the house was, so he placed an electric fan there to blow Joan Fontaine's perfect hair and show that she feels a chill. "Whenever possible, you *show* what is happening, not *say* it."

Hitchcock and Selznick often disagreed. Selznick was passionate about being faithful to the novel, while Hitchcock believed the novel should be changed for the screen. Hitchcock particularly disliked one idea of Selznick's more than any other. "He wanted the smoke from the burning Manderley to spell out a huge R. Can you imagine! How the audience would have laughed!"

While Selznick was preoccupied by *Gone With the Wind,* Hitchcock was able to replace the smoky R with the burning of a monogrammed lingerie case. He also edited the picture in the camera, a method of filmmaking that didn't allow Selznick to reedit the picture. Otherwise, Hitchcock considered *Rebecca* more Selznick than Hitchcock.

"Our personalities did not mesh," Hitchcock said. "For him, I was an obstreperous employee. He did not like to hear the words 'Yes, but.' He wanted to be totally involved in a way I have never experienced with any other producer. He wanted to be the director and the writer as well as producer. I was introduced to those letters called memos which he insisted on sending me every day."

Daniel Selznick, the son of David Selznick, didn't remember his father talking about Hitchcock, or being involved socially with the Hitchcocks. The only time he met Hitchcock was after his father and mother, Irene Mayer Selznick, had separated, and it was his mother who took him to the Hitchcock home.

Joan Fontaine believed it was Selznick's idea for her to wear light makeup for *Rebecca,* so it appeared that she wasn't wearing any at all. He had the same idea for Ingrid Bergman, when she came to Hollywood to remake *Intermezzo* for him.

The changes in Joan Fontaine's hair as the story develops were even more important. Her hairstyles became sleeker and more sophisticated, making it clear that circumstances were forcing her to grow up, even though her husband had told her that she should never be thirty-six.

"Hitchcock could be devastating," Fontaine said, summing up her *Rebecca* experience. "He could be sarcastic. He kept us actors in line. He didn't say let's try this or let's try that. Never. He knew exactly what he wanted,

"I think Mr. Hitchcock felt comfortable with me. I don't think he felt so comfortable with any of the other actors. I felt alone, and I think he did, too. I wanted his help, and he wanted to help me, but he didn't give me what I needed most, confidence. I was terrified, but I think *he* thought it helped my performance."

While gathering location footage for *Rebecca* on the Monterey coast, Hitch and Alma decided that they would like to have their American country home there. Joan Fontaine had grown up in this area, and her parents, who lived nearby, suggested Scotts Valley. In 1940, the Hitchcocks bought a ranch and a vineyard in the Vine Hill area near Scotts Valley. They had some furnishings sent from their London flat and their English country house, which gave the house a slight British air.

During the shooting of *Rebecca,* World War II began, and Alma went back to London. She returned with her mother and sister. Hitchcock tried to persuade his mother to come to California, but leaving the world she knew was unimaginable for her.

Rebecca won the Oscar for best film, which went to Selznick, but Hitchcock, who had been nominated as best director, did not win.

NEEDING MONEY to finance *Gone With the Wind,* Selznick loaned out some of his contract stars to other producers and studios at a profit. After *Rebecca,* Hitchcock became one of Selznick's most valuable properties and was loaned out to Walter Wanger to direct *Foreign Correspondent.*

Initially, Hitchcock wanted Gary Cooper for the role of the unsophisticated but intelligent hero. Cooper turned it down. "He thought that being a thriller, it had to be bad," Hitchcock told me. "That was the perception Hollywood had of the kind of picture I did. In England, there was a different sensibility. The best actors—Donat, Gielgud, Redgrave, Laughton—all worked with me. Afterwards, Gary Cooper admitted to me he'd made a mistake. It probably was his agent who made the decision."

Foreign Correspondent was based on *Personal History,* a book by newspaperman Vincent Sheean. The screenplay was by Charles Bennett and Joan Harrison.

In 1939, Johnny Jones (Joel McCrea), an insubordinate city desk reporter, is sent to London as a totally unqualified foreign correspondent. There he interviews Van Meer (Albert Bassermann), leader of a peace movement endorsed by Universal Peace Party head Stephen Fisher (Herbert Marshall). Johnny finds Fisher's pretty young daughter, Carol (Laraine Day), more interesting.

In Amsterdam, Van Meer apparently is assassinated. Johnny and journalist Scott ffolliett (George Sanders) follow the assassin into the countryside. Johnny investigates a windmill and finds the real Van Meer, a drugged prisoner. His captors escape with their prisoner, and Johnny's story is not believed.

After attempts on Johnny's life, Carol believes him. Now in love, they return to London, where Johnny realizes that her father is actually the leader of the conspirators.

Johnny tries to protect Carol, who is totally innocent, but she misinterprets his motives, and they quarrel. He and Scott try without success to convince Scotland Yard of Fisher's conspiracy to stall peace efforts. Then, war is declared.

On board a Clipper plane, Fisher explains to his daughter that he was only being loyal to his native country. Johnny, also on the plane, tries to make up with Carol.

After the plane is shot down, Fisher dies saving the other passengers. Rescued, Johnny and Carol are reunited when he defends her father in his news report.

Hitchcock in particular liked the character of Stebbins, the veteran correspondent who had never filed a report with his paper, only expense vouchers. Hitchcock considered him unbelievable, however, unless the contributing writer who created him, Robert Benchley, played the part. Benchley accepted the offer. Hitchcock had admired Benchley's series of comedy short subjects, and said later that they had influenced his personal appearances on his own television series.

For his performance in the film, Albert Bassermann was nominated for a supporting actor Oscar. He was one of the foremost German stage actors of his generation, holder of the highest acting award that country offered, the Lessing Medal. Fritz Lang told me how Bassermann managed to smuggle his prized medal out of Nazi Germany.

When Bassermann was forced to leave Germany, he knew the Nazis would never allow him to take the medal with him, so he had another one struck and wore the copy when he left, hiding the genuine medal in his luggage. The counterfeit Lessing Medal was confiscated, as Bassermann had anticipated, and he kept the real one, which he wore to the Oscar ceremonies in 1940.

Joan Brodel, the actress named in the credits as Joel McCrea's sister, afterward changed her name to Joan Leslie and became famous for roles in *Sergeant York* and *Yankee Doodle Dandy*. Leslie told me that she was not directed in her exceedingly small part by Hitchcock, but by an assistant. Then her bit in *Foreign Correspondent* was cut out, so she described it as "a nonpart." She can be seen, however, for a few seconds in the background of the ship's stateroom scene when Johnny Jones's family says goodbye to him.

For the film, several blocks of Amsterdam were rebuilt on a Hollywood soundstage, complete with running streetcars and a sewage system to drain the artificial rainfall.

When the Clipper plane crashes, it is seen from the viewpoint of the pilot's cabin, with water pouring in on impact. This effect was achieved with a rear screen transparency made of paper, behind which a water tank was positioned, tearing the screen open when the water was released.

"The set with the plane in the ocean," Hitchcock said, "was a huge rubber tank they had built at Goldwyn with back projection screens all around and pieces of the plane's fuselage mounted on tracks under the water so we could move them around without any cuts."

Foreign Correspondent went over-budget and took longer to produce than expected, but it was well received by critics and the public alike. Selznick considered it a return to Hitchcock's little British comedy-thrillers, but the director's reputation grew, and he became more in demand on loan-outs. He had become one of Hollywood's best-known directors, but because of his contract with Selznick, he was earning a fraction of what other famous Hollywood directors received. Hitchcock didn't feel any debt of gratitude to Selznick for launching his Hollywood career. "I had paid and repaid him," he said.

Among the studios bidding for his services was RKO, headed by George J. Schaefer, who had given Orson Welles carte blanche in the making of *Citizen Kane.* They offered Hitchcock two films, *Before the Fact* and *No for an Answer,* both of which would become Hitchcock films under different titles: *Suspicion* and *Mr. and Mrs. Smith.*

Before the Hitchcocks found their own home in California, they rented Carole Lombard's house, and became good friends with her and with her husband, Clark Gable. Lombard had moved in with Gable at his ranch.

"I liked her very much," Hitchcock said. "She had a bawdy sense of humor and used the language men use with each other. I'd never heard a woman speak that way. She was a forceful personality, stronger, I felt, than Gable.

"Carole wanted me to do *Mr. and Mrs. Smith,* so I made the picture because it wasn't easy to say no to her."

Hitchcock said that *Mr. and Mrs. Smith* was one of two times in his life that he made a film on the urging of a beautiful woman. "As a favor to another actress, I made the same mistake again. Ingrid Bergman suggested *Under Capricorn.* Who could say no to Ingrid?"

Hitchcock allowed Lombard to direct his cameo in the picture, the only time he permitted such a stunt. He said he really didn't plan to use her take, but it turned out to be good. "She might have become a director one day. She had the personality for it.

"When she was killed in a plane crash while working for the war effort, Gable was heartbroken. After her death, he mourned deeply and aged terribly. I don't think he was ever the same."

The original story and screenplay for *Mr. and Mrs. Smith* were by Norman Krasna, who also wrote Fritz Lang's *Fury* and René Clair's *The Flame of New Orleans.*

One day, Ann and David Smith (Carole Lombard and Robert Montgomery) find out that because of a technicality, they aren't really married. They have an argument about whether they would marry each other again, and David goes to his men's club for the night, assuming everything will be all right the next day.

Ann, however, has other ideas. She changes her name and gets a job as a sales clerk. She seeks advice from David's law partner, Jeff Custer (Gene Raymond), who has always liked her.

A friend of David's arranges a blind date for him. Ann becomes jealous and takes Jeff home, where his gentlemanly behavior leads her to believe his intentions toward her must be serious.

During a misadventure at Lake Placid, Jeff realizes Ann and David were meant for each other. David pleads that he really

does love Ann, but he is not believed, and they have another argument.

Ann asks Jeff to marry her. When he accepts, she has second
thoughts. She is worried about David.

Ann and David have another argument, but this time they
quickly make up, glad to be together again.

Hitchcock wanted Cary Grant to play Mr. Smith, but accepted
Robert Montgomery, who was paid more money than the director.

Betty Compson, who plays a small role in the film, was, in 1923,
one of Hollywood's biggest stars. Victor Saville, looking for a Hollywood name for Gainsborough, had been able sign her for a two-
picture deal, the first of which would be *Woman to Woman,* directed by
Graham Cutts, with Hitchcock as the assistant director and art director. Hitchcock remembered her as someone who was considerate and
encouraging to him before he became famous. Years later, he recipro-
cated when he was casting *Mr. and Mrs. Smith,* and she was no longer
remembered.

JOAN FONTAINE LIKED the character of Lina in *Suspicion* so much,
she sent Hitchcock a note after she read the novel, on which the
screenplay was based, offering to play the part for free, if necessary.
Cary Grant was equally enthusiastic.

"Cary had been thrilled to be cast as Johnnie," Fontaine told me,
"because he liked to do serious parts and didn't want to be typecast
for comedy just because he did it so well.

"I thought *I* was interested in my career, but it was nothing com-
pared to the way Cary felt. He had focus and took his career very seriously. I was easily distracted by my personal life. His professional and
personal life were one. He knew his best camera angles and exactly
how the lighting should be to show him at his best. Actually, I don't

think he had any bad angles, and there wasn't any way you could light him that he wasn't at his best.

"As for my own best profile or how I should be lit, I hadn't the faintest. He watched his rushes with great interest. He encouraged me to watch mine, but when I did, I became too self-conscious after I saw myself. I thought about what I should do in the scene to make what I did come out right on the screen. It confused me, and Cary said I didn't need to watch rushes anymore."

Suspicion was based on a 1932 novel, *Before the Fact,* by Anthony Berkely Cox, writing under the pseudonym Francis Iles.

Against her parents' wishes, wealthy Lina MacLaidlaw (Joan Fontaine) elopes with handsome Johnnie Aysgarth (Cary Grant), and then finds out he is penniless and in debt. He can't seem to hold a job, and he sells their wedding gift chairs from her father to cover his gambling debts. She is persuaded not to leave by Johnnie.

Johnnie's friend Beaky (Nigel Bruce) dies under mysterious circumstances, and Lina fears that Johnnie is responsible. He denies this, but cautions her not to tell the police about his financial dealings with Beaky.

Lina finds a book on poisons among Johnnie's things. Then she learns that Johnnie has been unsuccessfully trying to borrow on her life insurance policy. He can collect only on her death.

Lina discovers that Johnnie has been making inquiries about an undetectable poison. When he brings her a glass of milk, she doesn't drink it. In the morning, she leaves for her parents' family home. Johnnie insists on driving her.

On a winding road, Lina fears Johnnie will kill her. When the car stops, she tries to run away, but he stops her.

She asks about the poison, and he says he was going to take

it himself. He assures her he had nothing to do with Beaky's
death.

They return home together.

The glowing glass of milk that Cary Grant carries up the stairs was illuminated by a small flashlight inside.

"The ending of *Suspicion*," Hitchcock said, "was a complete mistake because of making that story with Cary Grant. Unless you have a cynical ending, it makes the story too simple. *Suspicion* deals with a man whose wife suspects he's a murderer. When he brings her up that glass of milk at the end of the picture, she knows he's going to murder her, but in our film, we have to make it a harmless glass of milk. In truth, the ending of the picture should be Joan Fontaine accepting that she is going to be murdered. I had an idea for an ending in which she knows.

"She writes a letter. 'Dear Mother, I'm in such terrible straits. I know he's going to kill me, but I love him so much I don't want to live anymore, and I do think society should be protected.' Then, she seals the letter and leaves it by the bed. Johnnie brings up the milk, and she says, 'Could you mail this for me?' She drinks the fatal glass of milk, really committing suicide, and you fade out on her death. Next you have a cheerful, whistling Cary Grant popping the letter into the mailbox. That's how I wanted to end the picture. Black humor, you know.

"The problem of having the leading man, Cary Grant in this case, be guilty was the same problem we had faced in *The Lodger*. In those days, the audience wouldn't have put up with Ivor Novello being guilty, especially women, and a lot of the audience would be women anytime he was in a film.

"For the sake of their own careers, important stars won't be villains. The idols that we put up there must do no wrong. If they do, audiences don't approve of that sort of thing.

"In Mrs. Belloc Lownde's book, the Ripper got away with it. Having Cary Grant as the hero meant I had to compromise. The best you could have was a bit of doubt, and not much of that. Once the decision was made to have Grant, it was like Novello, he *had* to be innocent.

"There was a new head of RKO who came up to me one day smiling, and said, 'I've solved all the problems of *Suspicion*. I've cut it down to fifty-five minutes.' What he had done, you see, was to take out every mention, every hint that Cary Grant was a murderer. Well, what do you have left?"

Grant told me, "I'm sure I didn't do it. My character wasn't that sort of chap at all. He couldn't possibly have murdered her. My character was a rogue, not a rat."

HITCHCOCK'S DAUGHTER, Pat, decided shortly after *Suspicion* that she wanted to be an actress, and she told me how that career began.

"John Van Druten, a good friend of Auriol Lee, who was in *Suspicion,* was looking for a thirteen-year-old to do a Broadway play of his called *Solitaire.* He asked my parents if they would let me read for it. They said only if she doesn't know what she's reading for, because they didn't want me to get all excited about it and be hurt if I didn't get it. I read, and he decided he wanted me to do it. Unfortunately, it opened right after Pearl Harbor, and that was the end of that, but not the end of my wanting to be an actress."

Alma was anxious to move into a home of their own in California. She felt it was important for their daughter not to live in a temporary house, so Alma and Pat looked at many houses. Finally they found one they both immediately loved.

Hitchcock at first feigned lack of enthusiasm, and they were disappointed. Then he bought the house himself, surprising them. From then on, he and Alma never lived anywhere else except their northern California weekend house, and Pat lived with them until she married.

"He'd learned to drive," Pat told me, "but he didn't drive very much. He had a license, but he didn't like it. My mother loved it and she did all the driving."

"WHEN HITCHCOCK BEGAN a picture, he glowed," Robert Boyle told me.

"In those days, if Alma didn't drive Hitch to the studio or wherever they were working, he would arrive in a taxi. At the end of the day, she usually drove by for him. Alma was so small, you could barely see her head over the steering wheel. But he would see her, and his eyes would light up. Whenever there was a discussion of some importance to ponder, Hitchcock would say, 'I'll discuss this with the Madame.'

"I became an art director in 1941 on *Saboteur.* He was really retelling *39 Steps,* as he did later with *North by Northwest.*

"We would sit on either side of the desk, and he'd make these funny little drawings, and I'd draw, and then we'd compare. After we had made all these roughs, they would be transferred into better sketches. But they never were better, because his originals, these little stick figures and things, always gave you the proper image size. Then, every shot was prepared and outlined, and everything worked out. When all this was finished, he said, 'Now I will be bored making the picture.' Actually that wasn't quite true. He just liked to say it because it was a funny thing for him to say. I think he enjoyed making the picture.

"No one taught me more than Hitchcock about film language. He thought that each shot should relate to all the other shots, with no such thing as a throwaway shot.

"No other director could ask for solutions to such difficult problems, because no other director knew what questions to ask. He knew enough about getting difficult shots and the sort of effect he wanted to create, so that you could somehow get it for him, though it might cause you some sleepless nights trying to figure it out.

"Hitchcock would push the technical aspect of any shot to any length *if* it would satisfy what he felt is that gut feeling of whatever he was trying to do. And sometimes he'd push it so far that it didn't quite make it. The shot became a little too strange, a little too far beyond the capabilities of the medium. But he never really was worried about that.

"He bent reality to his purpose to get the real truth."

Of Boyle, Hitchcock said, "I would say to him what I wanted to do, knowing it was not impossible, only close to impossible, and he would do it."

After *Suspicion,* Selznick loaned-out Hitchcock to Universal to do *Saboteur.* For *Saboteur,* Hitchcock originally had hoped to get Gary Cooper and Barbara Stanwyck for the leads, and veteran western actor Harry Carey, Sr., as villain. John Houseman was assigned by Selznick to supervise the writing of the script, which began a lifelong friendship between Houseman and Hitchcock. The film was shot in fifteen weeks and came in almost within budget.

Los Angeles aircraft worker Barry Kane (Robert Cummings) evades arrest after he is unjustly accused of sabotage. Following leads, he travels across the country to New York trying to clear his name by exposing a gang of saboteurs led by apparently respectable Charles Tobin (Otto Kruger). Along the way, he involves Pat Martin (Priscilla Lane), eventually preventing a major act of sabotage. They finally catch up with Frank Fry (Norman Lloyd), the man who actually committed the act of sabotage at the aircraft factory. Pursuing him to Bedloe's Island, Barry is unable to save Fry from falling to his death from the Statue of Liberty.

One of the most memorable images in any of Hitchcock's films is that of Norman Lloyd dangling from the top of the Statue of Liberty. Lloyd explained to me how that was done.

"Hitch had the hand, torch, and balcony built to scale at Universal. The inside of the crown was also built to scale. When in panic I went over the railing, there was a mattress and a grip below to catch me. For the long shot, stuntmen took over for me and Bob.

"For the next shots, which were close-ups, Hitch had the torch dismantled. The thumb and the forefinger piece of the torch, and the crotch of the thumb and forefinger were arranged on the stage floor. The camera was angled at me lying on my stomach on the set piece, and I did all my close-up reactions in that position. Bob Cummings came down the forefinger, but he could only reach the sleeve of my jacket. Then there were intercuts between my close-up, Bob Cummings's close-up, and the seam where the sleeve was stitched to the jacket, which began to tear.

"When I fell, it had to be in one continuous shot, of Fry in close-up to Fry falling all the way to the base of the statue. People have wondered to this day how this was done.

"The thumb and forefinger section was taken to another studio and attached to a platform six feet high. This platform was on counterweights and rigged to the top of the stage. A hole was cut in the platform, and a camera was placed so it could shoot down through the hole, towards the set piece fixed beneath it. Underneath the whole thing was a saddlelike thing on which I sat, on a pipe about four and a half feet high, based on a black cloth. On a cue, the camera, on the counterweight system, started from a close-up of me, went up in the air to the grid, together with the set piece of the thumb and forefinger, and left me behind, giving the illusion of my falling.

"This was shot at different speeds, in which I did movements of falling rather slowly, like a ballet dancer. By the time the camera got to the top of its move, it had gone from an extreme close-up of me to a very long shot of my apparently falling figure. The small saddle was not visible; the pipe and black cloth, which still could be seen, were painted out later in a traveling matte. As the camera pulled away from me, I gave my best Shakespearean scream."

"There is one device I have employed many times in assorted variations—the dangling," Hitchcock told me. "The so called danglee is sometimes held by the so-called danglor, and may or may not fall."

Hitchcock was later uncertain about whether having the villain dangling from the Statue of Liberty instead of the hero was a good idea. "It would probably have been more effective if the hero were in danger," he said. "On the other hand, the hero thinks he has to save the villain in order to clear his name. He's also a decent fellow who would try to save the life of anyone who was in trouble. *Res est sacra miser,* a person in distress is a sacred thing.

"Well, it was probably best the way it was. No one could have dangled better than Norman."

"He left an indelible mark on me of what it means to be a director and how to conduct oneself on the set," Lloyd said. "Hitch always dressed in a dark suit, white shirt, and dark tie. He looked more like a banker than a film director.

"He projected a very special world. He had about him an international aura of the Orient Express, St. Moritz, the best foods, cigars, and vintage wines—all of the fantasies one saw on the screen."

For Lloyd, the essence of the Hitchcock touch was the blending of humor with real danger, as in the Radio City Music Hall sequence, where real shots are being fired, and the audience is laughing. "It was typical of the balance he could achieve in everything he did. Nobody else could achieve this balance, and then, finally, neither could Hitch."

Norman Lloyd told me about a lady tourist from Virginia who somehow got mixed up among the extras during location filming. It didn't bother her that she had to keep getting on and off the boat, before she was allowed to go up in the Statue of Liberty. She had the time of her life, thinking that the coffee and doughnuts and box lunches served to the extras were how everyone was treated in New

York. It was discovered too late that she wasn't an extra, and she couldn't be located to sign a release, so none of the shots with her could be used.

The scene of Fry looking out at the capsized *Normandie* was inspired by newsreel footage Hitchcock had seen, and incorporated after the script was written. The navy was concerned because there were plans to press the passenger liner into service as a troop carrier, and sabotage was suspected.

Hitchcock fans have long wondered who played Barry Kane's friend, Ken Mason, in *Saboteur.* He sets the plot in motion by bumping into Fry, and then his death in the sabotage fire puts Barry in the position of being the man on the spot who quickly becomes the man on the run. He is not listed in the credits.

In 2004, Norman Lloyd told me why the actor had been so difficult to identify. "Hitchcock was looking for someone to play Ken, a small but crucial part. Then, one day on the set, he found him.

"'That's the one' he said, indicating a tall, well-built young man, good-looking and sympathetic. He wasn't an actor at all, but a grip. He eventually became the head grip at Universal. His name was Virgil Summers and that was his only screen appearance."

UNIVERSAL NEGOTIATED WITH Selznick to employ Hitchcock again, and at a considerably higher fee, $150,000 for eighteen weeks. Of this, Hitchcock would receive $50,000, Selznick the rest. Hitchcock was also to get above-the-credits billing for the first time in his career.

For his next subject, Hitchcock chose a short story by Gordon McDonell, "Uncle Charlie," which was based on a real-life serial killer who murdered twenty-two wealthy widows for their money. To help develop the screenplay, he turned to Thornton Wilder, whose stage play *Our Town* he greatly admired. Since Wilder was about to join the army's psychological warfare unit, he was only able to supply a treatment and limited material for the story, and to help Hitchcock select locations. They chose Newark, New Jersey, and Santa Rosa, California, as sharply contrasting locales for *Shadow of a Doubt*. Alma finished the script, working with Sally Benson, who wrote *Meet Me in St. Louis*.

The film opens with turn-of-the-century couples dancing to the "Merry Widow Waltz."

Serial killer Charles Oakley (Joseph Cotten) finds a safe hiding place with his sister's family in Santa Rosa. They believe he is a successful businessman. Uncle Charlie has brought his name-sake niece, Charlie Newton (Teresa Wright), a ring, which has an inscription, but not to her.

Uncle Charlie won't let his picture be taken for the local newspaper, and he avoids two men who want to interview him. One of the interviewers, Jack Graham (Macdonald Carey), confides to young Charlie that they are really detectives. Uncle Charlie is a murder suspect.

Young Charlie reads about the "Merry Widow murderer," who kills wealthy widows for their money. Her ring has the last victim's initials on it.

Uncle Charlie pleads with her not to say anything. He will be leaving soon. Afterward, she suspects Uncle Charlie of trying to kill her.

Another suspect is captured, and Uncle Charlie, feeling safe, decides to stay. Charlie demands that he leave in exchange for her silence.

As the train pulls out of the station, he tries to push her into the path of another train. Instead, he is killed.

As Santa Rosa mourns the death of Charles Oakley, Charlie is consoled by Jack Graham, who is in love with her.

William Hitchcock and his son, Alfred Joseph, in front of the family store, about 1906. A mosaic version of this picture appears in the Leytonstone tube station in London. *(British Film Institute)*

Hitchcock directing *The Mountain Eagle* at the Emelka Studios in Munich, 1926. Alma stands behind him, and the cameraman is Baron Gaetano di Ventimiglia, who was the cinematographer for Hitchcock's first three films. *(British Film Institute)*

In the 1920s, Hitchcock first drew this caricature of himself, and he continued to draw it throughout his life. He drew this one for the author. *(Collection of Charlotte Chandler)*

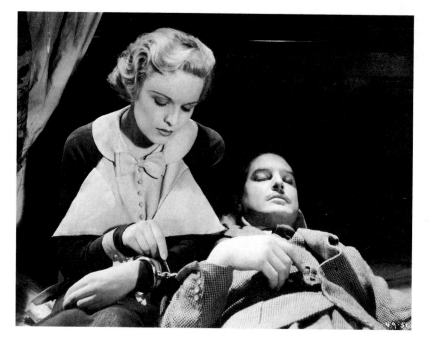

Madeleine Carroll and Robert Donat in *The 39 Steps*. Hitchcock denied the rumor that he lost the key and the couple had to stay handcuffed for a whole day. *(British Film Institute)*

Peter Lorre, Madeleine Carroll, and John Gielgud in *Secret Agent* (1936). Gielgud was later sorry he had made so few films after this one. *(British Film Institute)*

Michael Redgrave and Margaret Leighton are consoled by Paul Lukas, who is really the villain. In 1938, *The Lady Vanishes* anticipated the coming European war. *(Museum of Modern Art Collection)*

Laurence Olivier and Joan Fontaine in *Rebecca*. Fontaine thought Olivier wanted his wife, Vivien Leigh, to play her part, but she later found out she was wrong. *(British Film Institute)*

MacDonald Carey, Wallace Ford, Teresa Wright, and Joseph Cotten
during an early crucial moment of Hitchcock's own favorite Hitchcock
film, *Shadow of a Doubt*. *(Museum of Modern Art Collection)*

Walter Slezak adjusts the clasp of Tallulah Bankhead's diamond bracelet
in *Lifeboat*. The Cartier bracelet symbolizes all of Constance Porter's
hopes and dreams. *(The Sunset Boulevard Collection)*

Hitchcock with his daughter, Pat (left), and wife, Alma, in Bel Air
during 1945. Hitchcock had just lost weight on an orange diet,
and he is demonstrating how not to eat one.
(Collection of Robert Haller)

The famous kissing scene between Cary Grant and Ingrid Bergman
in *Notorious* that found its way around the three-second limit
for film kisses. *(British Film Institute)*

Hitch makes himself useful for Ingrid on the *Under Capricorn* set between shots. *(British Film Institute)*

Hitchcock and Marlene Dietrich discuss a serious matter during the
shooting of *Stage Fright* in London. Dietrich was more likely
concerned about her appearance than about her character.
(Museum of Modern Art Collection)

The four stars of *Rear Window*: James Stewart, Grace Kelly, Alfred Hitchcock,
and the celebrated courtyard set of Joseph MacMillan Johnson.
(Museum of Modern Art Collection)

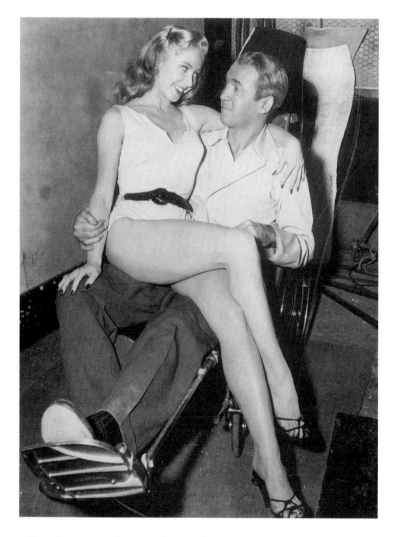

Georgine Darcy, who played Miss Torso, with James Stewart between scenes of *Rear Window*. The pink shorts she saved provided the key to the color restoration of the film. The cast Stewart wore is standing behind them. *(Collection of Georgine Darcy)*

Edith Head's original sketch for Kim Novak's unforgettable white coat in *Vertigo*. *(Collection of Charlotte Chandler)*

James Stewart making arrangements to follow Kim Novak more closely than her husband had asked him to. *(Potsdam Museum)*

Cary Grant, Eva Marie Saint, Alfred Hitchcock, and James Mason
during a promotional appearance for *North by Northwest*.
(Collection of Eva Marie Saint)

Hitchcock, Grace Kelly, and Alma enjoy a joke during the filming of
To Catch a Thief. *(Museum of Modern Art Collection)*

Hitchcock regards the "bad" aspect of Janet Leigh's character in *Psycho*, symbolized by her black bra and half-slip. In the opening scene, before she steals the money, she wears white lingerie. *(Collection of Robert Haller)*

Rod Taylor and Jessica Tandy assist an injured Tippi Hedren after she has endured a nightmarish attack by *The Birds*. The birds themselves seem unperturbed. *(Collection of Robert Haller)*

Pat Hitchcock, right, during her stay in New York at the Plaza Hotel, just after Christmas, 2003, with the author. The photograph was taken by Trisha, the great-granddaughter of Alfred Hitchcock.
(Collection of Charlotte Chandler)

"It has been said," Hitchcock told me, "that I based the character of the mother in *Shadow of a Doubt* on my own mother. I can tell you that I did not deliberately do so, nor did I deliberately avoid doing so. My characters have their own identities, and for a time, at least, I share my life with them, more perhaps than I do with any except the closest members of my family.

"In this particular case, however, I have to admit that it was a time when I was thinking about my mother, who was in London. There was the constant danger from the war, as well as her own failing health. She *was* in my thoughts at the time. I suppose that if we think about a character who is a mother, it is natural to start with one's own. The character of the mother in *Shadow of a Doubt,* you might say, is a figment of my memory."

Hitchcock was terribly troubled by the bombing of London and what it meant to his mother, to members of his family, to friends of his and Alma's. While Alma had gone back to London to fetch her mother and sister, he had been unable to persuade his own mother to come to California. Instead, he had convinced her that she should leave her London home for his Shamley Green country house. Still, he worried, Pat Hitchcock recalled.

Alma Hitchcock remembered their family having a wonderful time filming *Shadow of a Doubt.* Their daughter, Pat, was there helping in the coaching of the young sister of Charlie, and it was a happy set.

"Everyone knows about how my father said he saw the whole picture in his head before he made the film," Pat Hitchcock told me. "Well, at home he said that he was happy if he got 75 percent of what he'd seen in his head. Sometimes he got more, and then he was very, very happy."

"When I met him to talk about being in the film," Teresa Wright told me, "he described it as if he were seeing it in his mind. The way I think of him is that he had a little projection booth up there in his head.

"On the set, he never raised his voice. I never felt any tension. He would tell you what he wanted without too much instruction, and you would know exactly what to do. You couldn't make a mistake. If you did, you knew he would be there for you. At the same time, you felt a sense of freedom.

"I remember the actress who played my little sister was from Santa Rosa, and her father owned a grocery store. Hitchcock asked to see it, and he said it reminded him of his own childhood and his father's greengrocery.

"*Shadow of a Doubt* is the picture I have taken with me all my life. I wasn't Charlie. I was an actress. But I think maybe in some ways after that, Charlie journeyed with me all my life. More people ask me about that film than about all the others put together."

Joseph Cotten told me that Hitchcock was not only a great director, but "really wonderfully easy to work with, one of the best directors I've worked with, including Orson [Welles], when we did *Citizen Kane,* and one of the easiest to get on with."

Hitchcock said, "*Shadow of a Doubt* was the rare occasion when suspense and melodrama combined well with character. You know, the family can be so frightening. I do not give my first priority to character, but when good characters come through, it makes me very happy. No ice box chatter there." This was how he described discussions in the kitchen after the film, when the audience arrives home and "starts taking apart plot discrepancies and character deficiencies."

"Some of it was shot in the original town," Hitchcock said, "and at that time, they were shooting an awful lot on the back lot, so it had a freshness.

"The selection of the right house for the family was essential. I had it shopped for very carefully. I wanted to know what it would cost to buy or rent the house. It was very important that the family didn't live beyond its means. They weren't that sort. It was also important that they didn't live *below* their means. This was a family that knew its place. They didn't talk about money, or feel the need to think about it.

"We located the perfect place, and the people who owned it were very happy to have their house play in a movie. In fact, they were so happy, they painted it and fixed it up, so it wasn't right anymore. Fortunately, we were able to undo it all."

In May 1964, Alfred Hitchcock was invited to speak at the university in Belgrade. It was a great occasion for those fortunate film students who were to have the opportunity to hear Hitchcock speak, to see one of his films, which he was bringing with him, and even to ask questions of the great filmmaker. The film Hitchcock had chosen was *Shadow of a Doubt.*

Everyone looked forward especially to the question-and-answer part of the program, and began to think of his or her question. At that time, film studies were taken more seriously in Eastern Europe than in the West, and cinema was regarded as something more than art or entertainment.

During the years after World War II, American films were rarely shown in Yugoslavia. Most of the pictures seen there came from Russia, with an occasional politically correct Italian or French film, not intended purely for entertainment and usually with a message. In spite of this, film students in Belgrade were familiar with the name and reputation of Alfred Hitchcock, though few had ever seen one of his films. There was great excitement about his upcoming visit.

Vlada Petric, who was to become a world-acclaimed film professor and the director of the Harvard Film Archive, was at the time a film student in Belgrade and one of those invited to the Hitchcock event. He remembered that everyone liked *Shadow of a Doubt,* "which he told us was his own personal favorite."

Petric had given serious thought to what question he might ask, a worthy question that would produce an interesting answer.

When the moment came, he asked Hitchcock his question: "You are fascinated by mystery and suspense, you treat fear. How did you become so interested in these themes?"

Hitchcock said, "That's a very interesting question. I've never told this to anyone before, but I do know exactly. It happened when I was in my cradle.

"I was lying there, too small to move, and over me was the huge face of one of my father's sisters. My aunt was bent over the cradle, and her big face was moving closer and closer, getting bigger and bigger as it came towards me. Suddenly, this huge face was making horrible sounds, 'B-bibble, b-bibble, b-bibble,' as she ran her fingers over her lips."

Petric always remembered Hitchcock's answer. Through the years, he noted that while Hitchcock didn't use the close-up often, he did use it to great effect to create a feeling of horror. Some of the most memorable images in Hitchcock films are in close-up to create intense emotion. Whenever Petric saw one of the horror close-ups, he remembered that evening in Belgrade and thought of the image of that huge face peering into baby Alfred's cradle.

"THERE WERE ACTUALLY three lifeboats," Hitchcock told me discussing his next film. "It was like Citizen Kane's sled, Rosebud. We needed to have a stand-in for the lifeboat and then a stand-in for the stand-in. The difference between the lifeboats and the sleds was when the film wrapped, everyone wanted to take home Rosebud, and no one wanted our lifeboat."

Starring in *Lifeboat* was Tallulah Bankhead, a celebrated nonconformist. Among her eccentricities was a disdain for undergarments. George Cukor told me about "Tallulah's panties" or lack of them. He'd had his own somewhat embarrassing experiences with Tallulah after she asked if she could swim in his pool. "Of course, my dear," he said. He hadn't realized she meant without a bathing suit.

Not that it bothered him, but his gardener and cook and guests were sometimes surprised, sometimes shocked. "George, there's a naked woman in your swimming pool," British actor John Mills mentioned to him. "Do you know her?"

Cukor did. "You knew her well, or you didn't know her at all." Then he told me the "Tallulah's panties" story from the days of Hitchcock's *Lifeboat.*

"The dear girl never wore any panties. In fact, she was way ahead of her time, ahead of Marilyn in not liking to wear any underwear. She was especially against panties.

"Well, she told me that she spent the entire film in the lifeboat. Having the part involved a great deal of climbing in and out of the lifeboat. Every time she got into it, those already sitting there got a pretty good view of her at that rather unusual angle, and it was quickly no secret that she didn't consider panties part of her costume.

"Someone complained, and the word got back to Hitch, who was told by the powers-that-be that he was supposed to say something about it to her, or delegate that responsibility to someone.

"No one ever said a word to her, and for the entire filming, she never had to don panties.

"I imagine that Hitch saw for himself and thought it funny. He would have been much too staid to say anything to her, but not too staid to have a look.

"Hitch, you know, was full of beans."

Elizabeth Japp Fowler believed she was the model for the Tallulah Bankhead character. An American living in Ghana, she persuaded the captain of a freighter to allow her to travel on his ship in 1942. The ship was torpedoed on its way to New York, and she spent ten days in a lifeboat with thirty-four men, surviving thirst, hunger, cold, freezing rain, and circling sharks. The press reported that she mourned the Burberry coat she had lost, as the journalist in *Lifeboat* misses *her* fur coat, camera, typewriter, and her Cartier bracelet.

Hume Cronyn, who played the sunken ship's radio operator in

the film, talked with me about Hitchcock in general and *Lifeboat* in particular.

"The notion that Hitch was not concerned with his actors is utterly fallacious. I never knew how actors and people could say that. For *Lifeboat,* we began by sitting around a table for days in long read-throughs, as we would do in the theater. The lifeboat was actually very like a stage.

"Hitch would listen carefully and every once in a while, he would interrupt us with some suggestion like, 'Speak more slowly,' or 'Emphasize that word'—you know, that sort of thing. He very much didn't try to show us how to play our parts any more than he would have told a mike boom operator how to stay out of the frame. He expected us to know our jobs. That was why he had hired us. I don't consider that being unconcerned with your actors.

"He had faith in you, and that made you feel good and gave you confidence. There are directors who are backseat actors. They don't give you a chance to do what you can do.

"I could sense that as we read, Hitch was seeing our words more than he was hearing them. He had such a visual mind, and I feel he was watching the movie unfold in his mind's eye as all of us spoke the words of the characters. He was working backwards, you might say, from what he saw to what he heard. Other directors work from the dialogue and action to the visual elements of the film. Hitch, I think, had a total concept of the finished movie before we sat down to read, and he was just guiding us all toward what he saw on that screen in his mind."

Walter Slezak, who played the German U-boat commander, also disagreed with the notion that Hitchcock was unconcerned with his actors. "Far from it," he told me, "and he knew more about how to help an actor than any director I've ever worked with. I remember a young actress who was having trouble with an emotional scene. He told her to lower her voice three tones, take a deep breath, and not breathe again until she'd finished her speech. It worked beautifully."

John Steinbeck wrote the novella on which *Lifeboat* was based. Darryl F. Zanuck, who had done Steinbeck's *Grapes of Wrath,* was the producer. Jo Swerling and Ben Hecht wrote the screenplay.

In a lifeboat, columnist Constance Porter (Tallulah Bankhead), wearing a fur coat, high heels, and a Cartier diamond bracelet, photographs her own personal tragedy as if it were any other news story. Fellow survivors from the ship torpedoed by a U-boat join her: ship's engineer Kovac (John Hodiak), radio operator Stanley Garrett (Hume Cronyn), nurse Alice MacKenzie (Mary Anderson), seaman Gus Smith (William Bendix), steward Joe (Canada Lee), and Mrs. Higgins (Heather Angel), a hysterical Englishwoman holding her dead baby. After the baby is buried at sea, the mother drowns herself. Though the inhabitants of the lifeboat come from vastly different backgrounds, they quickly set aside the social and economic differences that divide them in a united effort to survive.

A German seaman, Willi (Walter Slezak), is picked up. Constance interprets. Willi suggests in German the direction toward Bermuda. During a crisis, he shouts at them in English. He was the U-boat commander.

Gus's leg must be amputated, and Willi, a surgeon in civilian life, performs the operation. Feverish, Gus becomes a burden, and Willi encourages him to slip overboard. When the group realizes Willi is actually steering them toward a rendezvous with a German supply ship, they push him overboard.

An approaching German ship is sunk, and a young German sailor (William Yetter, Jr.) is pulled from the sea brandishing a pistol. He is quickly disarmed, and they are soon rescued.

When I asked Hitchcock if he thought the characters would keep in touch, he answered, "No, it was a wrap." When making a film, people become friends, fall in love, vow at the wrap party to always keep in touch, and then return to their lives, forgetting it all.

Hitchcock makes his cameo appearance in a before-and-after reducing ad on the back of a newspaper salvaged from the debris. Conveniently, Hitchcock had just lost more than 100 pounds on a recent diet.

Pat Hitchcock told me that after *Lifeboat,* her father received many letters from people who had seen the film and, not realizing Reduco was a fictitious product, wanted to know where they could buy it.

"I had wanted to get into the lifeboat," Hitchcock said, "but Tallulah wouldn't let me. She was afraid I would sink it. And I would never do anything so undignified as float by, as someone else suggested. What really hurt was they said I would be just as recognizable floating face-down as face-up. I immediately went on an extreme diet, and that was when I thought of using before-and-after photographs of myself on a page in a newspaper."

NOT LONG AFTER HITCHCOCK moved to Hollywood, Michael Balcon wrote an article about British film people who were deserting England in time of war for Hollywood, singling out a certain "plump" director, whom he didn't name.

Making light of it, Hitchcock said that what he minded most was being called "plump." There were attempts at restoring the old relationship between the two men, though it never truly happened. "The words had hurt too much," Hitchcock said.

Hitchcock, who felt physically cut off from England and World War II, wanted to make a contribution to the war effort. His friend, Sidney Bernstein, director of the British Ministry of Information, offered him the opportunity.

In December 1943, before beginning *Spellbound,* Hitchcock flew to London. He spent a month there, early in 1944, filming two propaganda shorts to be shown in unoccupied France.

Hitchcock was given a token salary of £10 a week and a suite at London's Claridge's Hotel. He had never stayed there before. Thereafter, Hitchcock frequently stayed at Claridge's when he visited London.

Writing the scripts with Hitchcock was Angus MacPhail, who was at the time also working on *Spellbound*. The actors were drawn from members of the Molière Players, a French refugee group performing in London. They would remain anonymous to avoid the possibility of reprisals against their families in occupied France. The cinematographer was Günther Krampf, who, before he left Germany in 1932, had photographed *Nosferatu, The Student of Prague,* and *Pandora's Box.* One British actor appeared, John Blythe.

Hitchcock was concerned that occupied France be shown authentically. "We had to be careful not to leave any crusts of bread on the tables, and certainly not any cigarette butts."

In *Bon Voyage,* Sergeant John Dougal (John Blythe), a young Scottish airman, has just escaped from a German prisoner-of-war camp. In London, a colonel of the Free French Army listens as John describes his "miraculous" escape from occupied France with the help of a fellow escapee, a Polish prisoner of war.

They were taken by members of the resistance to a farm where they stayed with the farmer and his young daughter, Jeanne. John is rescued by a British plane with room for only one passenger. The Polish escapee will leave later.

The French officer tells the Scottish airman that he has been duped, part of a plot to expose the resistance, and that the other man is really a Gestapo agent. This leads to the death of members of the resistance, among them the appealing Jeanne. Members of the resistance take their revenge.

"*Bon Voyage* shows that the enemy is clever and ruthless, and one must be extra-vigilant," Hitchcock said.

In *Aventure malgache,* the Molière Players are rehearsing a play in London during World War II. It is based on the experiences of Paul Clarousse, a Madagascar lawyer, who is playing himself. One of the actors is having trouble understanding his character, who is shown in flashback as Jean Michel, a police chief who was publicly accused of corruption by Clarousse. When the Vichy government takes over Madagascar, Michel joins them, while Clarousse secretly sides with the Allies.

Michel is able to have Clarousse jailed as a traitor when he is caught helping people flee Madagascar to join the Free French. His death sentence is commuted because of his World War I record. Clarousse is offered better prison conditions by Michel if he will reveal the location of a secret Free French radio transmitter, but he refuses. When the British arrive Clarousse is freed, and Michel changes sides again and professes loyalty to the Allies.

When Clarousse tells the actor playing Michel that he greatly resembles his old enemy, the actor gets angry, and explains he is only rehearsing his part.

The point of *Aventure malgache* is to show "how the same spirit animated even the furthest colonies," Bernstein said.

In *Bon Voyage,* the scene between the French girl and the escaped impostor is cinematically worthy of the best Hitchcock films. With the camera on Jeanne, a shot is fired, and she collapses. Without a cut, a man's hand comes up into frame holding her address book, and then her delicate lady's wristwatch. The scene anticipates the murder of Juanita in *Topaz.*

The two shorts have a visual style similar to that of Hitchcock's later television series. They are examples of what Hitchcock could achieve at the peak of his creative powers with almost no money, and with unknown actors speaking French.

Bon Voyage and *Aventure malgache* did not play any part in the British war effort. They were not widely circulated in France. Fifty years afterward, the British Film Institute, which had surviving prints, made them available.

WHEN THE EXTERMINATION CAMPS were liberated by the British, Russian, and American armies in 1945, the full horrors of what they found became known, and Sidney Bernstein went there personally for the British Ministry of Information. He believed it imperative that army photographers document the scene as they found it in each camp; the dead, the dying, and the few survivors, as well as those who ran the camps. The only person Bernstein wanted to have supervise the editing of a film of the horrors was his friend, "the greatest film genius, Alfred Hitchcock."

Hitchcock agreed immediately. He knew that he was going to be working with unimaginable horrors, if only on film, without his personally having visited the camps. The films proved to be more horrible than Hitchcock anticipated. He told me that even though the tragic images remained in his mind, he never regretted doing it.

Ultimately, the British government decided not to show the film to the Germans, feeling it would work against the morale and rapport of the German citizenry, which was needed to rebuild the country. The relatively unseen film, therefore, remained officially F3080, and unofficially, *Memory of the Camps.*

Hitchcock had three ideas he considered important in making the film. The first was to film the dead in the extermination camps in wide, slow panning shots, the longest possible with no editing, so that there could be no accusation of trickery.

He wanted to have as many prominent Germans as possible who lived in the vicinity of the camps appear in the film, documenting their presence as the horrors were revealed by the liberating troops. They would then be witnesses who could never deny what they had seen.

He suggested a montage of the possessions of the victims, who, having been told they were going to new homes to be resettled, took with them what they could of their most treasured belongings. These were mostly wedding rings, brooches, handbags, children's toys, and eyeglasses.

Hitchcock had the idea, which proved very effective, of showing the life of the German countryside in the pastoral areas surrounding the camps, with carefully tended farms. Most startling were the local inhabitants, seemingly not disturbed by their proximity to such unspeakable horror. They ought to be shown, Hitchcock felt, going about their daily lives, involved with their own concerns, even those as close as one mile away, where the overpowering stench made it impossible to ignore what was happening.

The anonymous corpses were stripped of their identities, and from what remained, it often wasn't possible to tell men from women. The German civilians who lived in the area and who were forced to witness the atrocities appear well dressed and well fed, many of them, indeed, *too* well fed. Even living as they did, within sight and smell of the camps, they nonetheless claimed they were unaware of what was happening there. Viewing the camps from the inside with a close look at the piles of corpses that had been people and the few pitiful survivors, some of the women wept.

The guards, having become prisoners themselves, remained arrogant, claiming they were only obeying orders. They handled the corpses like store mannequins.

The film wasn't shown until the late 1980s, on British television, under the title *A Painful Reminder,* to an audience that tuned in never expecting to see such a disturbing program. Many turned away, unable to bear it.

Hitchcock, like Bernstein, was frustrated because the film he created from work by British, Russian, and American cameramen was not shown. His name on the project did not guarantee its showing, but it did help to preserve it.

. . .

WHEN *SPELLBOUND* BEGAN SHOOTING, David Selznick's own psychiatrist, Dr. May Romm, was brought in as technical advisor. Norman Lloyd, who played Garmes in the film, recalled that Hitchcock's melodramatic approach to psychiatry didn't always coincide with Romm's conventional approach.

"I was there on the set one day," Lloyd told me, "when the technical advisor, Dr. Romm, was objecting to something Hitch did in a scene which was a violation of psychoanalytic theory. Hitch said, 'It's only a movie, May, and in a movie, we don't have to stay absolutely faithful to facts.'"

Selznick, who had great faith in psychiatrists, had wanted to do a film with Hitchcock about psychiatry. Hitchcock chose as his subject a book by Francis Beeding called *The House of Dr. Edwardes,* set in a Swiss asylum. (Edwardes was changed to Edwards for the film.) While he was in London making the French shorts for the British Ministry of Information, he and Angus MacPhail began working on a screen adaptation.

Selznick wasn't satisfied with MacPhail and replaced him with Ben Hecht, who was more familiar with psychotherapy. Hecht and Hitchcock produced a screenplay quickly after Hecht did some research at mental hospitals around New York City.

Selznick felt no compulsion to follow the novel faithfully, as he had with *Rebecca.* The original story deals with a madman who takes over an insane asylum. Selznick was most interested in the love story that Hitchcock and Hecht would have to add to the screenplay. "Though David would not have characterized himself that way, he was an extreme romantic," his first wife, Irene Mayer Selznick, told me. "He was Don Quixote, with a dash of Cyrano and some Parsifal. And he was Faust, who sold his soul."

Hitchcock saw psychiatry as an interesting element in a suspense film, but he could not imagine telling his own innermost thoughts, feelings, fears, and desires to a stranger, "not even to a friend, to Alma, not even to myself," he told me. He was, however, fascinated by one aspect of it, the study of the criminal mind.

> Dr. Anthony Edwards (Gregory Peck), sent to replace Dr. Murchison (Leo G. Carroll) as head of Green Manors mental hospital, is an impostor. When Murchison calls the police, Edwards leaves, followed by Dr. Constance Peterson (Ingrid Bergman), who has fallen in love with him and wants to treat his amnesia. She believes he is a medical doctor whose name is John.
>
> As snow falls outside, John is upset by the parallel lines of sled tracks, and recalls skiing at St. Gabriel Valley with Edwards. Constance accompanies him to the ski resort.
>
> Skiing down a long slope, accompanied by Constance, John relives the memory of his brother being impaled on an iron fence with parallel bars, an accident for which he feels responsible.
>
> He remembers that he is Dr. John Ballantine. After a traumatic military plane accident, he went to Dr. Edwards for treatment. They went skiing together, and Edwards went over the precipice.
>
> Police find the body, but there is a bullet wound. John is accused of murder.
>
> Constance returns to Green Manors, where she confronts Dr. Murchison, accusing him of the murder. When he aims a revolver at her, she calmly rises and leaves. He turns the gun on himself and fires.
>
> It was Dr. Murchison who killed Edwards at the ski slope, and John was a witness. John is cleared, and he and Constance are reunited.

On the original prints of the film, the firing of the gun aimed at the camera, from Dr. Murchison's point of view, is in color. "Audiences weren't expecting it," Hitchcock said, "and I was rather disappointed when people didn't seem to notice it. I hope they noticed subliminally. That would be best of all." The red color has been restored on new prints.

Before the gun is fired, Ingrid Bergman is seen in the background from Murchison's point of view. Hitchcock asked camera director George Barnes to temporarily abandon his low diffuse lighting on female stars in order to increase the camera's depth of field. He wanted both the gun and Bergman to be in focus, so the lighting had to be increased. "Ingrid didn't need any help from the lighting," Hitchcock said.

For the musical score, Miklos Rozsa won an Oscar. His music featured an electronic instrument known as the theremin. Selznick was furious when he learned that Rozsa had also used it in Billy Wilder's *Lost Weekend*. That score was also nominated.

"I knew Hitch liked working with me," Ingrid Bergman told me. "I could feel it, and I felt that way about him. He was a wonderful director, so sensitive. There were actors who said he wasn't a good actor's director, but something was wrong with them. He was so sympathetic. He never seemed bored by my concerns, professional or private. He always listened. Hitch was someone I could tell just about anything.

"He had a delicious sense of humor, and he could be a little shocking. It wasn't so much *what* he said, but *when* he said it, always at some inappropriate moment when one wasn't expecting it. Hitch could talk me out of being nervous and uncertain, which I always was, and he could make me giggle."

Gregory Peck found a different side of Hitchcock.

"Hitch didn't seem to like to be personally involved," Peck told me, "and I got the impression that what he was saying was that he wanted *me* not to be involved. That was the message I got. Now, maybe it wasn't the right one, but it was what I understood and what I acted on. I asked him how he wanted me to play a certain scene where I would be in close-up. 'Blankly,' he said. I wondered if he was making fun of me. I didn't know how to do blank."

While in school, Peck had thought of becoming a doctor, but then he discovered acting. *Spellbound* gave him an opportunity to live out his early dream. He said it was one of the great advantages of being an actor. "You can live all different sorts of lives. And then, best of all, you can leave them behind on the set and go home to your own life.

"Ingrid was warm and wonderful. She was very young, and she had a fresh quality, but she had more confidence than I did. No wonder. She was beautiful, more beautiful in person than on the screen.

"She was always very encouraging to me, if I felt neglected. Hitch gave Ingrid much more attention than he did anyone else, including me. Especially me. Well, I don't blame him. The most important thing she understood right away, I didn't understand. She told me, 'Hitch will tell you if you aren't doing it right. It's a great compliment if he *doesn't* speak to you.' I wanted to believe her. Now, I know it was true. I wish I could say, 'Thank you, Hitch,' but I don't have the number up there.

"He was a very reserved man on the outside. Perhaps on the inside, too. I wouldn't know about that. Personally, I always felt he was having a very good time working, and that he had great warmth.

"The Hitchcock movies seem so new. It's hard to believe he isn't making them now."

At Hitchcock's suggestion, surrealist painter Salvador Dali was brought in to help design the dream sequence, which was to be directed by the legendary production designer, William Cameron Menzies. Very little of what Hitchcock and Dali planned was used in the film, and Menzies declined credit for his work on the sequence. Peck remembered parts of the dream sequence that were cut.

"Selznick agreed to make my nightmare an unforgettable visual, as Hitchcock wanted. He went to Dali with the commission. As I would be lying there, the audience would share my nightmare.

"There were four hundred human eyes which looked down at me from the heavy black drapes. Meanwhile a giant pair of pliers, many times my size, would appear and then I was supposed to chase him or it, the pliers, up the side of a pyramid where I would find a plaster cast of Ingrid. Her plaster head would crack and streams of ants would pour out of her face. Ugh. Well, the ants ended up on the cutting room floor.

"I asked Hitch about why I was having a greatly curtailed nightmare. He said, 'The ants' contract was canceled. We couldn't get enough trained ants, and Central Casting said all of their fleas were already gainfully employed. Aside from that,' he added, 'David [Selznick] decided it would make audiences laugh.'"

I WAS SITTING BETWEEN Kim Hunter and Elia Kazan at the Players Club in New York during the memorial tribute for playwright Sidney Kingsley, as Hunter told us about her experience with Hitchcock.

"I was under contract to Selznick at the time and not working, so I was put to work as a stand-in for Ingrid while Hitchcock auditioned a group of actors trying out for the part John Emery finally got [Dr. Fleurot]. He's the psychiatrist who's trying to seduce Ingrid.

"Anyway, Hitch gave an expansive, articulate description of the character, who he was, what he wanted, and then the story of the whole film in wonderful detail. I didn't need to see it anymore.

"After he'd done this, he turned to me and quietly said, 'Have I left anything out, Miss Hunter?' I blushed and stammered something inane, but I knew what he was trying to do. He was trying to put the other actors at ease at my expense. I was kind of embarrassed, like suddenly being called on in school when you aren't prepared. But what he did didn't work. They were all even more nervous. They thought he would do it to them."

Spellbound was nominated by the Motion Picture Academy for best picture, best director, best supporting actor, best cinematography, best special effects, and best musical score. Only music won. The picture was an enormous critical and popular success.

AFTER *SPELLBOUND*, Selznick once again became enthusiastic about making movies with Hitchcock. Hitchcock had in mind a story somewhat like *Vertigo*. A woman is coached to participate in a confidence scheme in which she might marry the victim. From Selznick's story department came a 1921 magazine short story called "The Song of the Dragon," and *Notorious* was begun.

Writer Ben Hecht and Hitchcock took so long developing the story and writing drafts, Selznick grew impatient. He was especially unhappy with the MacGuffin they finally decided on, uranium ore, which he considered implausible, so he sold the property to RKO— a few months before the first atomic bomb was dropped on Hiroshima.

> FBI agent T. R. Devlin (Cary Grant) recruits Alicia Huberman (Ingrid Bergman). Because her father was a German spy, it is believed she will make a convincing undercover agent. She is trying to repay her father's debt as if it were a bankruptcy. It is a moral debt to America, the country she loves and feels her father has betrayed. Alicia and Devlin have an affair.
>
> Her assignment in Rio de Janeiro involves resuming an acquaintance with a wealthy German businessman, Alexander Sebastian (Claude Rains), who had been attracted to her. She is to infiltrate his circle of German scientists.
>
> Against the wishes of his mother (Leopoldine Konstantin), Sebastian asks Alicia to marry him. She accepts, and they marry, though she is disappointed when Devlin raises no objections.

Alicia explores the mansion, but finds the wine cellar is locked.

Devlin tells Alicia to invite him to a party at Sebastian's mansion. She is to take the key to the wine cellar from Sebastian's key ring without his knowing it.

At the party, Devlin and Alicia investigate the wine cellar, where they find some bottles of sand. When Sebastian finds them together in the wine cellar, they convince him they are having a tryst.

Noticing that the key was missing and then replaced, Sebastian suspects Alicia of being a U.S. spy. His mother plots to poison her slowly, with arsenic, because she has become a woman who knows too much.

Devlin visits Alicia at the mansion, finds her in bed, desperately ill, and realizes what is happening. He helps her down the stairs and out of the house. Sebastian and his mother, fearing exposure, are forced to aid him as the Nazi guests watch.

Sebastian begs Devlin to take him with them, but he is left to his fate, certain death.

The sand proves to be uranium ore.

Bergman's dresses were designed by Edith Head. *Notorious* was the first of many Edith Head credits on Hitchcock films.

Pat Hitchcock told me that *Notorious* was her favorite of her father's films. "What a perfect film! The more I see *Notorious*, the more I like it. It has a wonderful cast, too. My mother's favorite was *Shadow of a Doubt*, and *Notorious*, too. My second favorite is *Rebecca*."

A celebrated scene in *Notorious* is the long kiss between Cary Grant and Ingrid Bergman. Hitchcock defeated the Production Code limitation on the time a kiss could last—only a few seconds—by breaking up their long kiss into many short ones, as they discuss dinner. "My father rather enjoyed getting away with something," Pat Hitchcock told me.

The actor who played the genial Dr. Anderson, Reinhold Schünzel, was the writer-director of *Viktor und Viktoria*, one of the most popular German films ever made, which has been remade several times, the most famous version being with Julie Andrews playing Victor and Victoria. Schünzel is said to have been Hitler's favorite director until it was discovered he was one-quarter Jewish. Afterward, he went to Hollywood, where he was chiefly an actor.

Although Leopoldine Konstantin entered films in 1913, she made only this one Hollywood film. She was primarily a star of the German stage, appearing in Max Reinhardt's Deutsches Theater from 1908 until 1937. Her husband was Constantine Shayne, who played Pop Leibel, the loquacious bookstore owner in *Vertigo*. She was recommended for the part of Mrs. Sebastian by Schünzel after Ethel Barrymore turned it down. Madame Konstantin, as she is listed in the credits, played a part similar to that of the disapproving mother in *Easy Virtue* who also descends an imposing staircase to meet her son's choice of a wife. Another memorable shot from Hitchcock's silent era recurs in *Notorious* when, from her position in bed, Ingrid Bergman sees Cary Grant upside-down .

HITCHCOCK HAD one year left on his Selznick contract, and one more film, but he was already making plans for the pictures he would be filming with Sidney Bernstein at Transatlantic Pictures, the new production company they were starting. Ingrid Bergman and Cary Grant had told Hitchcock they would love to make a film for him at Transatlantic. There was even some talk of a Cary Grant *Hamlet* in modern dress.

Hitchcock told me that if he hadn't been a director, the career he would have liked was that of a criminal lawyer. "I have always been interested in the law as well as in food, you might say, torts and tortes." With a hint of mirth, he added, "I would like to have been a hangin' judge."

The Paradine Case was the last picture Hitchcock made on his seven-year Selznick contract, though Selznick did not want him to leave. Selznick had already offered him a new seven-year, nonexclusive contract, with more generous financial terms. Hitchcock would receive $100,000 for one picture each year of the contract with a percentage of the gross receipts, and he would be free to make films with other producers. Hitchcock's heart, however, was in his project with his friend Sidney Bernstein, Transatlantic Pictures, so he turned Selznick down and started work on the final film of his contract.

The Paradine Case was adapted from a 1932 novel by Robert Hichens, based on a real court case that Selznick had long wanted to make into a film.

> Anthony Keane (Gregory Peck), a famous lawyer, is engaged to defend Maddalena Paradine (Alida Valli), a European woman who has been charged with poisoning her wealthy, blind British husband, Colonel Paradine. Although Keane is happily married, he becomes obsessed with his client, and he is convinced of her innocence.
>
> He becomes so involved with the case that his wife, Gay (Ann Todd), understands she is losing him to Maddalena. She feels that if he wins the case, she will lose him to a living woman, and if he loses, she will lose him to an ideal woman he can never possess. She prefers competing with a real woman, and wants her husband to win his case.
>
> The trial turns against Keane and his client. He tries to incriminate the valet, André Latour (Louis Jourdan), who admits to having had an affair with Maddalena. When Latour commits suicide, a distraught Maddalena, who until that time had appeared coolly unemotional, turns against her lawyer. On the witness stand, she admits to killing her husband because she doesn't care about living now that the man she loves, Latour, is dead.
>
> Keane returns to his loving wife.

A memorable image in *The Paradine Case* occurs when Maddalena is taken from her life of luxury and confined to a bare jail cell. The slamming of the iron door behind her as she enters the cell recalls one of Hitchcock's own memories, that of the six-year-old Alfred being locked up in the Leytonstone jail.

Ben Hecht and James Bridie wrote a screenplay based on Alma's adaptation of the story, but Selznick wasn't pleased. He rewrote their script and took credit as a screenplay writer, along with Alma. He also edited the trial sequence after Hitchcock had been prevailed upon to shoot the long and difficult scene with four cameras running simultaneously.

The ninety-two-day shoot was Hitchcock's longest and the picture his most costly up to that time. Opening on the last day of 1947 in order to qualify for the Oscars, *The Paradine Case* was a critical disaster and box office loser.

Hitchcock said, "Many times, people have told me how much they enjoyed *Witness for the Prosecution.* They thought it was my film instead of Billy Wilder's. And Wilder told me people asked him about *The Paradine Case,* thinking he had done it. Well, I would be happy to make an exchange."

After Claude Rains turned down the part of the judge, Hitchcock went against his customary preference for "negative acting," in other words, low-key, and chose Charles Laughton, never low-key.

"I have been asked what I mean by 'negative acting,'" Hitchcock said, "a term I have used many times with actors. It seems obvious. Clearly it doesn't mean *not* acting or *non*-acting, or I wouldn't need professional actors.

"I used Leo G. Carroll so many times because he was the perfect screen actor. He brought nothing to his part except himself, exactly what I wanted. Negative acting is actually a layer below what I call 'obvious' acting, and it requires great subtlety.

"After *Jamaica Inn,* I swore I would never again use Laughton, who was the most 'obvious' of actors. This, however, was the perfect vehicle for him."

Peck thought he looked too young for the part, but no matter what he did, he couldn't age himself as much as he wanted. He also worried about his speech, not certain about how far he should go toward British diction. His model was Anthony Eden, although he didn't feel he sounded much like Eden in the finished film.

Selznick saw in Alida Valli the possibility for creating another Ingrid Bergman. Valli told me that she had the impression that Hitchcock particularly wanted her for *The Paradine Case,* but after she began making the film, she had the feeling that "he wanted my look and not me. I had the feeling he was disappointed, but perhaps not in me, but in the film. Now, with Gregory Peck, it was all different. He was always helpful, and *so* attractive."

It was Hitchcock who selected Ann Todd. Selznick found her "too British," but he accepted her because for him everything depended on the key role played by Valli.

"David was a remarkable man," Irene Mayer Selznick told me, "but he wanted to be even more remarkable. Nothing was ever enough. *Gone With the Wind* wasn't enough. From then on, he had to surpass it. Like for Orson [Welles], Rosebud was elusive. David was a man of passion, a romantic, intense, desperate. When I was his wife, he wanted me to be the best-dressed woman in Hollywood, not something I aspired to be. He was the husband who wanted me to buy more clothes, and more expensive clothes.

"His real death was the death of his confidence."

"When our contract was finished, I knew I wouldn't miss those memos," Hitchcock told me. "Those memos were the essence of the man. Selznick wore his mind on his sleeve."

TRANSATLANTIC INTERLUDE

Rope to Stage Fright

"R OPE WASN'T MY FAVORITE PICTURE," James Stewart told me. "I think I was miscast, though not terribly so. So many people could have played that part, probably better. But it was a very important part for me because it started my relationship going with Hitch, and it led to *Rear Window, The Man Who Knew Too Much,* and *Vertigo.*"

"When I adapted *Rope* to the screen," Arthur Laurents told me, "homosexuality was an unmentionable word in Hollywood, referred to as 'it.' Now, here was a play about three homosexuals in which 'it' had to be self-evident to everybody except the Hays Office or the Legion of Decency. Without 'it,' nothing makes sense. There isn't a scene between Brandon and Phillip, the two murderers, that doesn't imply 'it.'

"Casting was of the utmost importance. Hitchcock and I wanted Cary Grant to be Rupert, the college professor, and Montgomery Clift to be Brandon, the dominant one in the relationship between him and Phillip. This would have been dream casting. Instead, we got James Stewart and John Dall.

"I think the casting of Jimmy Stewart was absolutely destructive. He's not sexual as an actor, and the implication in the British play was that Rupert and Brandon had been some kind of lovers. Cary Grant was not a homosexual, but he was the finest screen actor of his time, and he was always sexual."

Pat Hitchcock articulated her father's feeling for Stewart. "He believed an American audience would identify more with James Stewart than any other actor," she told me. "I think Jimmy personified Everyman for my father."

Clift told Hitchcock that he couldn't do the part of Brandon because he didn't want to do a role that would "raise eyebrows." John Dall who had been nominated for an Oscar in 1946 for his work in *The Corn Is Green,* replaced him.

"The problems started with the adaptation from English to American English," Laurents continued. "What was accepted as ordinary everyday speech in London was perceived as 'homosexual dialogue' in Hollywood. I drew from some silver and china queens.

"But when I started to Americanize the dialogue, Sidney Bernstein, Hitch's associate producer, kept returning English expressions to the original play because what I was writing didn't sound 'literary' enough to him. He especially liked the phrase, 'My dear boy,' commonly used in England with no homosexual connotations. When he put it back, it never failed to elicit a blue-penciled HOMOSEXUAL DIALOGUE condemnation from the Hays Office. Since Sidney began or ended every sentence he spoke with 'My dear boy,' this really mystified him.

"Hitchcock never referred to the homosexual relationships in *Rope,* though he understood it very well. 'It' was just implied and taken for granted. And the play's relationship to the Loeb-Leopold murder case, that was never discussed either.

"I thought the showing of the murder itself was a big mistake. That wasn't done in the original stage play. The suspense was, *was* there or was there *not* something in the chest? Well, the suspense is over at the beginning. But that's what he wanted, and Hitchcock did what he wanted. On that film, at any rate. You have to remember that he had formed a special company. The whole purpose was to do what he wanted, and Sidney Bernstein, who was his partner, just adored him and thought everything he did was wonderful. He thought he was a great artist. He was. But Hitch didn't listen to people. Not that I know of, except for Alma. She kept him on track. She was his core. He had a very good marriage."

For those who have seen the film's trailer, the murder takes on an added dimension. Instead of the usual short excerpts from the film being previewed, *Rope*'s trailer shows David Kentley (Dick Hogan) meeting his fiancée, Janet (Joan Chandler), on a park bench. They discuss their future together, and then David gets up and leaves her—forever. This trailer could have been the opening for the film, though it wasn't in Laurents's script. Hitchcock said, "It was just an idea that wouldn't have worked, because if the public had established sympathy for the young couple, it would have been impossible to watch the murderers."

UNDER CAPRICORN WAS TO BE the first Transatlantic Pictures production, but its star, Ingrid Bergman, was unavailable. While Hitchcock and Bernstein waited, they chose to make what seemed to be a simple one-set picture. Patrick Hamilton's 1929 one-set play, *Rope's End,* seemed an ideal vehicle to test Hitchcock's experimental ideas. Instead of shooting in conventional camera setups, he would shoot the entire play straight through, interrupted only by the need to change the nine-and-a-half-minute film reels. He envisioned a continuous filmed drama that is shown exactly as it happens in eighty minutes.

To achieve this feat, a special set had to be built, with everything, including the walls, silently mobile so that the six-thousand-pound motorized dolly with its massive motorized Technicolor camera could move anywhere at any time.

"Our roving Technicolor camera had to poke its lens into every nook and cranny of the collapsible Sutton Place apartment of the killers," Hitchcock told me. "Prop men were crouching everywhere, set to pounce on furniture and pull it out of the way of the camera, and then replace it after it had passed. Everyone was signaling everyone else to move something that had to be moved. Even the actors were moving chairs, or catching people who had to fall out of the way of the camera. Then, if someone fluffed a line, even in the last few seconds of the nine-minute take, we had to shoot it again, from three to six times. This was especially trying for Mr. [Dick] Hogan, whose performance after being garroted consisted of lying in the dark of an antique chest for almost ten minutes, listening to the mayhem."

This "mayhem," the rolling of walls on Vaseline-lubricated rollers, the scraping of furniture being shuffled back and forth, the rustling of actors trying to avoid getting in the picture or being run over by the camera, the breathing of prop men, all of this was caught along with the dialogue by the four microphones placed above the set at various locations. It became evident that some post-synchronization of sound would be necessary.

Since the action of the play takes place during the early hours of an evening, the view of New York City from the Sutton Place apartment must change, from daylight, to twilight, to night. To achieve this effect, a complicated cyclorama was built, showing a thirty-five-mile panorama of the city. Model buildings were built to scale in front of the cyclorama to give the effect of depth. This was lit by thousands of incandescent bulbs of various sizes, and numerous neon signs controlled by a complex lighting console.

This was Hitchcock's first color film, and he had definite ideas about what colors he wanted. "The set and the costumes had been carefully muted down," Laurents recalled, "and the first prints that came out, it was like fiesta time in Mexico. Hitchcock was furious, and it took a long time before it suited him."

All of the action takes place in the living room of the fashionable apartment.

> Two college friends (John Dall and Farley Granger) strangle a
> third friend for the intellectual thrill of committing the perfect
> crime, and then serve hors d'oeuvres and drinks to the victim's
> relatives and friends on the antique chest containing his body.
> After the party, their crime is discovered by the professor (James
> Stewart) whose teachings were misinterpreted as justification
> for the murder.

Farley Granger described some of his *Rope* experiences: "The studio had been yelling for me to get back from New York. It was to do *Rope*. Of course, as soon as I knew it was a Hitchcock film, I could have flown back without a plane.

"Those tricky long takes caused so many problems. The camera, for instance, was an enormous monster. As the camera moved, they would break away the walls and there'd be people moving the lights at the same time to keep you in the light. Then, for instance, you have to sit down just out of camera range, and there was always a stagehand there with a seat to slip under you at just the last minute. I saved Constance Collier once because I saw she was ready to sit down and there was no chair.

"She and Sir Cedric Hardwicke were the jolliest of the group. All the young people were taking it very seriously, and they were having a ball.

"Hitch would say, 'What next?' And he'd go over and look at the book. Then, he'd say, 'Oh, yes, okay.'

"Hitch was very definite in what he wanted, you know, because it had all been planned and done with the drawings, so he had to be sure that everything was right. In this film, he had to be more certain of everything because of the way he was shooting it.

"The crews were crazy about him. They respected his knowledge of everything. He really understood lenses, and he was jolly with them."

Hume Cronyn told me, "When Hitch asked me if I would like to work on Patrick Hamilton's play *Rope* for the screen, well, I was very complimented, to say the least. But why would he choose a relatively inexperienced writer like me when he could get anyone he wanted?

"He had two reasons. First of all, we got along smashingly. He may have felt more at ease with Canadians than with Americans. I think Hitch liked people intuitively, the way a child does. When he liked you, he *really* liked you.

"Second, since he planned to do *Rope* exactly as it appeared on the stage, with no editing and in reel-long takes, he wanted someone who had a lot of stage experience as well as film knowledge. Then, he brought in Arthur Laurents, but Hitch and I got along well enough for him to ask me to do the same for his next film, *Under Capricorn.*"

Arthur Laurents wondered about the Cronyn connection. "When I saw Hume Cronyn's name next to mine for the writing credit, I was, to put it mildly, astonished. I had never been given one word of his 'adaptation,' nor did I even know he was writing one. I was always under the impression that we were doing the play pretty much as it was onstage, and that I was supposed to 'Americanize' and bring it up to date."

Gary Stevens, the publicist for *Rope,* described his first meeting with Hitchcock. Hitchcock played a practical joke I recognized from my own experiences with him.

"It was in a sixteenth-floor suite at the St. Regis Hotel in New York," Stevens said. "We got into the elevator, and on the fifteenth floor, two elderly ladies got on. As the elevator went down, he said to me, out of nowhere, 'Gary, did you clean the blood off the knife?' I looked at him, but I didn't say anything. The two women stared at us, and when the elevator stopped at the eleventh floor, they were so frightened, they rushed out, not waiting to go down to the lobby. That was how my first meeting with him went.

"I took him to a very popular morning program. They started to talk about his picture, and he went into his own monologue. It was breakfast time, and Hitchcock went into a tirade about eggs. He said, 'Oh, what a horrible dirty thing an egg is. You open it up and it's slimy and runs out.' People all over the city must have had their breakfasts ruined, and it was a hell of a time before they got him out of it. By that time, he knew I was on to him, and he gave me a sly wink."

"When I worked on *Rope,*" Arthur Laurents told me, "I was included as a member of Hitchcock's extended family, and it was a laughing and loving family. I was invited frequently to have a family dinner at their home in upper-strata Bel Air or at the country house in northern California. I was a regular at Alfred Hitchcock's table at Romanoff's. Romanoff's was *the* Hollywood restaurant. He always ordered steak with some potatoes, wine, and some black coffee. I understood that eating there with Hitchcock at his table was special, and that eating there without him would never quite be the same. I was soon to find out.

"After the completion of *Rope,* I was invited to one of those family dinners at the Hitchcocks, and Sidney Bernstein was there. After dinner, I was given a novel to take home and read, *Under Capricorn.* I knew what it meant. I was quite flattered. It meant he really liked what I did. And I was prepared to like *Under Capricorn—better* than like it.

"I was lightly admonished, as if I needed to be, not to waste any time in getting it read, and then, as if I needed any extra incentive, I was told, 'Ingrid will be doing it.'

"As soon as I got home, I began reading. I thought I would try to get through it that night. I didn't make it. The next day, I was still limping along.

"What Hitchcock and Ingrid saw in *Under Capricorn* was a mystery to me. I felt it was wrong for *all* of us.

"Hitch and I were friends, but I was hesitant about saying, 'Why did you buy this?' Instead I simply said I would very much like to work for him again, but I was the wrong writer for *Under Capricorn*. It just wasn't my cup of tea.

"He changed the subject. I realized I had been excommunicated.

"Later, Sidney [Bernstein] tried to get me to recant. I had hurt Hitch with my 'disloyalty,' loyalty for him being an unquestioning 'yes,' disloyalty, a 'no.' But if I said 'yes,' it would make me *really* disloyal. I never again sat at his table at Romanoff's."

HITCHCOCK HAD RECEIVED an unpublished treatment of Helen Simpson's 1937 novel from Selznick's office in 1944. He saw enough promise in the story to buy the screen rights for a token price, and then he put it aside for later consideration. He and Sidney Bernstein were already making plans for their Transatlantic Pictures venture, and they would need properties to develop. It appealed to Ingrid Bergman, who agreed to make the picture for Transatlantic, and who encouraged Hitchcock to make the film. Before James Bridie was brought in to write the screenplay, Hume Cronyn worked on a treatment, to which Alma made contributions.

"I did *Under Capricorn* because Ingrid liked it," Hitchcock told me. "From that, I learned that it was better to look at Ingrid than to listen to her."

Charles Adare (Michael Wilding) arrives in Australia in 1831 with his uncle, the new governor (Cecil Parker). Unsuccessful in Ireland, Charles hopes to make his fortune in Sydney.

He is befriended by Samson Flusky (Joseph Cotten), a prosperous ex-convict. Sam's wife, Lady Henrietta, "Hattie" (Ingrid Bergman), was a friend of Charles's sister in Ireland. Sam hopes that the young man will be able to cheer up his wife, who is a mentally unstable alcoholic. Meanwhile the attractive housekeeper, Milly (Margaret Leighton), secretly loves Sam, and encourages Hattie's drinking.

Sam had been sent to an Australian prison after he confessed to a killing that Hattie actually committed. She had followed him and waited for his release.

Charles's efforts to rehabilitate Hattie conflict with Milly's intentions. Eventually, Sam becomes jealous, and in a rage, accidentally shoots Charles. This time, Hattie accepts the blame for the shooting.

Milly, seeing her chances to win Sam slipping away, attempts to poison Hattie, who is saved in time. When Charles recovers, he tells the authorities that the shooting was accidental.

Hattie stays with Sam, whom she really loves, and Charles leaves for Ireland because he sees no future for himself in Australia.

Jack Cardiff, the film's cinematographer, described for me what he called "the daunting challenge" of shooting *Under Capricorn*.

"They built a huge composite set of the entire mansion. It filled the largest stage at Elstree's M-G-M Studios. I wondered how on earth I could possibly light so many sets at once! Since the camera was going to have to track on a crane noiselessly all over the place, I worked more closely with the director than usual.

"Each long take had to be covered in one shot with one camera. For example: Michael Wilding enters through the front door of the mansion, into a large circular hall with a winding stairway. He turns to his right and walks along a narrow corridor into the servants' quarters. After saying something, he returns to the hall, along another passage into a large drawing room. More dialogue and more camera movement, and then the camera follows him back to the hall. Now he goes up the stairs and walks down a hallway to a door. He opens the door and enters a bedroom, approaching a large bed where Ingrid

Bergman is sleeping. As he and the camera near her, the bed itself tilts towards the camera to avoid the camera having to crane up for an overhead shot.

"We rehearsed the whole day and shot the next day. I had to light all of the sets we'd be using in one go. The noise was indescribable. As the electric crane rolled through the sets, whole walls opened up, furniture was whisked out of the way by frantic prop men, and then just as frantically put back as the crane made a return trip.

"The most incredible take was when the camera ends up in a dining room with eight people sitting at a long Georgian table. Hitch wanted a shot of the guests, looking down the table, then to track in to a close-up of Ingrid Bergman at the far end.

"The Technicolor camera, inside its enormous blimp, was more than four feet high. To crane above the table, over the candlesticks, the wine, and the food, it would have been necessary for the camera to be very high up, looking down on the heads of the actors. The problem was solved by cutting the table into sections, and then fastening everything down very firmly—food, plates, silverware, glasses, napkins, salt shakers, everything.

"Each actor had a section of the table. The camera is now positioned at table level instead of six feet above it. At the beginning of the scene, the guests are all sitting in their places enjoying a leisurely banquet. The camera moves forward, bearing down on each guest, but at the last moment, each of them falls back on a mattress while holding on to his section of the table with all the props stuck to it.

"I don't know how Ingrid kept a straight face while watching her fellow actors fall back like dominoes. It was hilarious, but it worked. I think a film of *Capricorn* being made would have been far more successful than *Capricorn* itself."

Cardiff recalled that Joseph Cotten hated the new technique especially the electric crane-dolly. "He was a complete professional and never complained. But he told me that he could always feel the monster sneaking up behind him and was terrified it would run him over.

"Practically all of Hitchcock's energies were spent on pre-production. Everything was worked out in detail, every page timed. If a page was just a few seconds off, everything would have been off. No wonder Hitch sometimes found the actual shooting of the film something of a bore.

"During a ten-minute take, he would have his back to the set, aimlessly looking down at the floor. Then, at the end, after he had said 'Cut,' he would ask my camera operator, 'How was that for you, Paul?' If Paul nodded yes, he would accept the whole reel. He hardly ever watched the rushes of the day's work. From the moment he had drawn pictures of the camera setups, he had the picture all firmly in his mind.

"On his other films, using normal techniques, he used his camera in a way no one else ever had, cutting from shot to shot to obtain rhythmic emphasis. I think that's where *Under Capricorn* failed. Despite Hitch's brilliant ideas on how to keep the camera moving, he couldn't overcome the inevitable loss of tempo. Having to shoot the whole reel without any cuts, the camera had to move cumbersomely all over the place in order to obtain the same angles the editor would have used in cutting."

Sound director Peter Handford told me that there was absolutely no post-synchronization at all. It was all done at the time on the set.

"We had a very, very good editor. Without him, it would have been difficult. Most editors would have said, 'Oh, this is ridiculous. Post-sync is just as good.' But Hitchcock wanted it done properly on the set.

"He was a wonderful man, Hitchcock. Years later when he did *Frenzy,* he sent for me. After all that time!

"He had the largest studio in M-G-M, and the whole floor of the stage, covered in carpet. All that carpet came from Sidney Bernstein's cinemas. Carpeting was rationed, you see, because of the war.

"He would do a scene, and then, as soon as he'd done the take where there was a problem, he would ask me to tell him what the problem was. He would then clear the stage as soon as he had the take he considered to be best, and he'd get the actors to do the whole scene over again with all the movement, but without the camera.

"And it worked, because they were good actors, and problems of synchronization, of course, had to be put together by the editor. There was no problem then, because their timing was exactly the same as it was when they had the camera. They had the timing from the rehearsals. He was very strict about timing in the rehearsals. This does work with real actors who knew exactly what was wanted.

"It's true. We didn't do any post-sync at all. I want to repeat that, because it was so amazing. It was all done with the actors as if it was a proper take of the camera. That's why it worked. If you had a man a long way from the table and another close, the sound perspective was exactly right.

"Some big scenes were rehearsed for two or three days, mainly because of the complicated camera movement. Even with the rehearsal, things could go wrong, and sometimes did. Ingrid Bergman said it was not exactly fun, but interesting.

"I worked with her again much later, on *Murder on the Orient Express*. I didn't realize at the time she did *Under Capricorn* what a terrible stress she was under, because she was leaving her husband. You would never know she was under such a strain as that.

"Hitchcock had a wonderful sense of humor, and he loved playing jokes on people. For instance, if we were doing a take, he would suddenly come up to me, and he'd lift my headphones and tell me some awful joke and try to get me to laugh.

"He was very fond of steam trains, railway trains. And he found out it was one of my major loves, steam railways, and we would talk about that for a long time. On steam trains, the wagon behind the engine was called the tender, the one full of coal. Hitchcock came up to me once and said, 'Do you know why the locomotive was so unhappy?' and I said, 'No, not at all.'

"And he said, 'Because it had a tender behind.'"

• • •

HITCHCOCK WAS UNHAPPY, disappointed, when Ingrid Bergman left Hollywood to be with Italian director Roberto Rossellini.
Divorcing her husband, Peter Lindstrom, she starred in several
films of Rossellini, whom she married and with whom she had
three children. It was quite a while before she was welcomed back
in Hollywood, "forgiven" for the "scandal," and bankable again.
Bergman told me that Hitchcock had never said anything to her
about "Roberto," though she knew he wanted her to be in *his*
movies, not Italian films.

"Finally, after several years," she said, "when I was visiting Los
Angeles, Hitchcock said to me, 'It's a shame. He ruined your career.'

"I laughed. 'Oh, no, dear Hitch, Roberto didn't ruin *my* career. I
ruined *his.*' I didn't belong in those pictures of his."

She didn't remember why she had chosen *Under Capricorn.* She
told me, "You would have to ask the person I was."

Under Capricorn was Hitchcock's second and last Transatlantic
picture. Though their company had not been successful, Hitchcock's friendship with Sidney Bernstein continued. Hitchcock
always regretted that he hadn't produced a big success for Bernstein, who never ceased to describe his friend as "a unique genius."
Bernstein told me that he felt honored to have known and worked
with him. "No regrets. I'd like to have had a success because I
would have liked to be able to go on. It's a friendship of a lifetime
that I treasure."

"With Transatlantic," Hitchcock told me, "I had complete freedom, but that of itself is in a way a handicap, because one enters into
the field of financial ethics. No doubt one can do whatever one
wants, but you become restrained by a kind of responsibility. I did not
understand at the time that I was being self-indulgent. I called it artistic freedom. My next picture, *Stage Fright,* was my attempt to return
to more responsible filmmaking, but I was too late for Transatlantic."

Hitchcock didn't see Jack Cardiff again until 1960, when Cardiff was in Hollywood after having directed *Sons and Lovers.*

"Hitch was pleased to see me, of course, but he had this strange look on his face when we shook hands. He seemed kind of stunned, a bit puzzled.

"'I saw *Sons and Lovers,*' he said. Then he added softly, 'It was bloody good.' It was obvious he couldn't believe that a mere cameraman could have directed such a good movie. Of all the critical praise I received for *Sons and Lovers,* Hitchcock's 'It was bloody good' were the words I treasured most."

"THEY WERE LIKE a couple of kids. They really were just like a couple of kids talking about their movie and their plans, and the script, and what everything meant."

That was how Richard Todd characterized his first meeting with the Hitchcocks to discuss his role in *Stage Fright,* a lunch filled with energy and enthusiasm. More than half a century later, Todd recalled for me that day and his subsequent *Stage Fright* experience.

"I remember it well. First of all, meeting Hitchcock. It was the third or fourth picture I ever made, so I was still pretty green, and I was very flattered that this world-famous director wanted *me* to play the lead in his film.

"He asked me to come and meet him at the Savoy Hotel where he and his wife were staying and have lunch. That was flattering, too. And what struck me about him, he was *so* enthusiastic. He spent a couple of hours telling me all about the story. 'You see, we do this, and then we do that, and this happens, and then that happens,' and she [Alma] kept piping up as well.

"His wife had written the script. She was chattering away as much as he was. She was totally involved. So I came away just about as enthusiastic as they were.

"I got on with him very well, right from the very first day I met him. Then he arranged for me to have lunch at the Savoy with Marlene Dietrich, who was to be my girlfriend. It seemed a bit strange then, and still does, in the movie. I got along with her very well. I got on with Jane [Wyman], too.

"Then when we started actually working in the studio, it was a very different kettle of fish. He worked like no other director I know of. He was very impersonal with his actors. I can now believe that he actually did say 'Actors are cattle,' because he didn't take an awful lot of interest in what they were doing. I was lucky. I was the one he sort of cottoned on to more than most. At one point, he said I had very expressive eyes. So he kept on doing close-ups of my eyes. This was the first time I was aware of speaking with the eyes.

"It helped me particularly, this thing about expressive eyes. Hitchcock wanted to light them and come in close on them all the time. Well, that made me feel that I certainly was getting something out of it. Hitchcock didn't give the kind of hints directors give at all, but I didn't mind.

"I wasn't too sure of myself, because as I said, I hadn't made all that number of movies. I just hoped I was doing the right thing. But he'd let it go, and so I thought, 'Well, it must be all right then.'

"He was more interested during the filming in his setups, in his camera positions and so on than he was in his actors, how they played their roles. Most of the time, what he did was as soon as we'd finished a setup, and it was in the can, he would give the first assistant director a note of how he wanted people to move, where they were to stand and be. Then he would go off to his office; and he didn't come back onto the floor, the set, until we were ready to shoot. All the arrangements had been made by the first assistant director. I'd never come across *that* before. After that, I never came across it again.

"I was newly married at the time, less than a year, and my little wife and I had a very nice address in Park Street, Mayfair. The only trouble was, it was a converted house, and our flat was at the top of four stories, and we didn't have a lift. We had asked Hitch and

Jane Wyman to supper one night, and they came. Alma wasn't there.

"Hitch simply waltzed up the stairs. No problem at all. Jane Wyman was huffing and puffing. He was remarkably fit."

The year before, Richard Todd had received an Oscar nomination for his performance in *The Hasty Heart.* Though his success seemed to come quickly, Todd's acting career had been delayed by his six years of military service during World War II.

"Funny thing was that I had just finished making *The Hasty Heart* with Ronald Reagan, and he was a bit down in the dumps because his marriage with Jane Wyman had broken down. He was terribly sorry about it all.

"And then, less than a year later, I was working with Jane. So, I heard *her* side of the story. I think she had a lot of regrets, too. I continued to see Ronald Reagan for years. We became great friends."

Stage Fright was based on *Man Running,* a novel by Selwyn Jepson, the first of several in which Eve Gill is an amateur sleuth. It was inspired by a sensational murder of the 1920s involving an actress, a case that had long intrigued Hitchcock.

During early 1949, he and Alma worked on the treatment and script. Later, playwright Whitfield Cook contributed dialogue. Cook had written the play *Violet,* in which Patricia Hitchcock starred on Broadway.

When it came time for her to choose a college, wanting to become an actress, Hitchcock's daughter made the decision to study at the Royal Academy of Dramatic Art in London. Her father, knowing that she wanted to study drama, had suggested RADA, and she enthusiastically agreed.

She made her feature film debut in *Stage Fright.* Jane Wyman, who was the star, played a RADA student. Their daughter being there inspired the Hitchcocks to place their heroine at RADA as an acting student and to use it as an important setting. Though it was only a small part for Pat, Hitchcock was pleased, and it led her to a more important role in *Strangers on a Train.* This was the ultimate sign of approval from her father. In *Stage Fright,* she brings more to her role than might have been expected from her relatively few lines.

Pat was the recipient of some technical advice from Marlene Dietrich.

"I was able to give his young daughter some valuable tips based on what I had learned about camera lighting," Dietrich told me in Paris many years later. "The wrong lighting, the wrong lens, being photographed from the wrong angle, this ages you. The wrong lighting could have taken away her freshness.

"She listened with great attention, but I think she was not very vain, about makeup or wardrobe, either. She was more deeply involved with her acting. For me, acting is only part of it."

Pat Hitchcock told me that she really loved best being onstage, and would have chosen to be a stage actress. "It's a career that lasts longer. I'm glad I had the opportunity to be in films and television. As it turned out, being in the films of my father was the most lasting part of my career. But the most fulfilling part of my life has been being a daughter, a wife, a mother, and a grandmother.

"People think it's much easier to be an actress if you have a relative in the business. Well, it has the obvious advantage, but it's also much harder because there are people who think it's the *only* reason you got the part.

"Some people took such a hard look at what I did. They thought I was getting jobs because of my father, but my father would never have cast me if I hadn't been right for the parts. He was very particular about casting. I wish I'd fit more parts. I'd like to have done more."

A common occurrence in Hitchcock's films is a wrong man being on the run. In *Stage Fright,* the twist is that it's the *right* man who is on the run.

Eve Gill (Jane Wyman), an aspiring young actress, shelters a fellow acting student, Jonathan Cooper (Richard Todd), from the police. He is suspected of murdering the husband of his mistress, Charlotte Inwood (Marlene Dietrich), a famous singer. Jonathan claims that he became implicated when he tried to help Charlotte destroy the evidence.

Eve's eccentric father, Commodore Gill (Alastair Sim), agrees to hide Jonathan in his house while she proves his innocence. To do this, Eve becomes Charlotte's temporary maid.

Eve's father devises a plan to force Charlotte to confess in front of the inspector investigating the case, Wilfred Smith (Michael Wilding). When the plan doesn't work, Eve tries blackmailing Charlotte into a confession while the police listen outside her dressing room. Charlotte agrees to pay, but insists that Jonathan is the real murderer.

Jonathan lures Eve into the basement of the theater where he admits not only to killing Charlotte's husband, but to another murder. He is ready to kill her, but Eve escapes. Jonathan is trapped onstage by police and killed by the falling fire curtain.

Smith and Eve, in love, leave together.

Some critics complained that the opening "false flashback" was dishonest. "I felt the flashback was justified," Hitchcock said, "because the scene is from the viewpoint of Eve Gill, who believes Jonathan's account of the crime."

"I was prepared for it," Richard Todd said, "having read the script and gone over it in depth. It didn't disturb me. Just part of the job.

"I didn't mind at all being the villain because it would be very boring to play a goody all the time. Fundamentally, he was a villain, but he didn't come over that way, until you realize what he was up to. In the beginning, he seemed rather a nice young man. Had to be, or the girl wouldn't have taken all that risk to help him.

"Dietrich was ruled by the stars. She didn't do anything without talking to her astrologer. When she realized I was newly married, she asked me to give her my wife's date of birth. About a week later, she said, 'You know, it's no good. You've married the wrong person.' She'd gotten in touch with her chap in America, and he'd looked it up, and it wasn't right at all.

"We proved her wrong—for twenty years.

"It was quite a pleasant film to make. It was good for my confidence, to feel I'd got through a movie with the great Hitchcock and hadn't made a mess of it. And he was very complimentary about it.

"This is what astonished me—only a year out of a repertory theater, and suddenly here I was with this world-famous great man, being entertained and having everything about the script explained at great length as if I was important, which I wasn't."

In the more than half century that has passed since the release of *Stage Fright,* Jane Wyman has consistently refrained from speaking ill of Hitchcock, but her praise of the director has been restrained. She said very simply, "He was a good guy."

When she went to England to film *Stage Fright,* she had just received the best actress Oscar for *Johnny Belinda,* and her hopes were high. The lack of special attention as an Oscar winner disappointed her. She felt Dietrich was being accorded greater respect. The picture was never one of Wyman's favorites.

Wilkie Cooper, photographic director for *Stage Fright,* told me that the greatest challenge was filming Marlene Dietrich's scenes. "Hitchcock gave me special instructions, which really surprised me, especially it being Mr. Hitchcock and all. He said that for any scenes with Miss Dietrich, I was able to listen to her instructions, and—this was the part that really took me aback—to do it the way she said. Needless to say, I didn't question Mr. Hitchcock's instructions, but I prepared myself for the worst. Perhaps seeing the expression on my face, he reassured me, saying, 'Miss Dietrich is quite expert and knows what she's talking about,' and he says, 'Don't argue about it with her. Just discreetly let me know.' No one knew more about his camera than he did. Mr. Hitchcock knew more about the camera than *I* did.

"Well, he was right about it. Miss Dietrich certainly did know a great deal, especially about camera lighting. Mr. Hitchcock had mentioned that she had learned from Josef von Sternberg. What she had to offer was very professional, and she knew what she was doing, especially for herself.

"What worried me was that she would look like she was in a different film. I needed to make it all match.

"The other problem was Miss Wyman. She could see that Miss Dietrich was getting all of this attention, which certainly must have seemed to her to be preferential. Well, it was. I can't say Miss Wyman was exactly a good sport about it, but she did her best not to complain.

"Miss Dietrich was pleasant enough to work with—as long as she got her way. She considered herself to be the director and the camera director for her scenes. I think Mr. Hitchcock must have made some kind of special agreement with her in order to get her for the picture. Though she didn't say it exactly, it was clear that there was only one concern she had, and that was that she look as young as possible. Actually, what she really wanted was to look younger than was possible for any camera or any lighting to achieve."

Hitchcock wanted Marlene Dietrich for the part, he told me, because she really was a great character, and he wanted her to bring that character with her to *Stage Fright*. He preferred actors who didn't require constant direction, and she certainly was one of those.

"Dietrich was very much herself," Hitchcock commented.

I told Hitchcock a story Douglas Fairbanks, Jr., had told me about Marlene Dietrich, with whom he had had a long affair. Fairbanks sculpted several nude figures of Dietrich during their time together, and when the romance ended, the friendship remained, and Fairbanks offered the figures to Dietrich. "You keep them to remember me by," she said. "I don't need them. I have myself."

Fairbanks kept them for years, and then he decapitated one and all, feeling that if anything happened to him, he didn't want people to find them and recognize Dietrich, even if the figures were impressionistic, and it was unlikely that they would have been identified, even *with* their heads.

When Marlene Dietrich reached the moment she had to recognize that no amount of camera lighting with perfect makeup and distracting costumes could camouflage the changes in her looks, she cared more about her public image than about her personal life. Her pride was great, and she chose to retire to Paris where she retreated into her avenue Montaigne flat. She not only retired from films and live performances, but also from eating in restaurants, seeing friends, or opening the door to receive her groceries. She dismissed her maid, and *became* her maid.

She answered the phone pretending to be her maid.

Her lifeline became the telephone. She loved to talk with friends, especially in America at three or four in the morning, which with six hours difference in time was a good moment for her. She liked to make the call, choosing the moment that suited her mood, rather than accepting a call. It was difficult even for close friends to guess the right moment.

When I called her in Paris, the phone was answered by a distinctive voice, speaking French, but with a German accent, immediately recognizable as that of Miss Dietrich. She said, "Miss Dietrich is out—out of the country. She will not be back for a very long time." The implication was that for *you* she would *never* be back.

I finally had the opportunity to ask Marlene Dietrich about *Stage Fright.* "Oh, which one was that, dear?" she said. When I reminded her that it was her Hitchcock picture, she laughed. She said that most people thought *Witness for the Prosecution,* in which she also starred, was her Hitchcock picture. I asked her how the two directors were different.

She explained that she never knew Mr. Hitchcock in the same way she knew Billy Wilder. "What a charming, funny, and kind man Billy was," she said. "Mr. Hitchcock was a very intelligent director, and he was a gentleman, an English gentleman, though I found him very

European. I never cooked chicken soup for Mr. Hitchcock the way I did for Billy Wilder. But I gave him some recipes. He was interested in cooking, but more in eating. I told him I always wore a hair net when I cooked. He did not have to worry about that, though, because he did not have so many hairs.

"We talked about food. He loved European restaurants, and luxe hotels. Mr. Hitchcock and Billy both knew French. Both men were gallant." They never "interfered" with her as she remembered.

"I was with Tyrone Power in the Wilder film and with Richard Todd in Mr. Hitchcock's picture. They looked alike. They were both very handsome men, and it is always a pleasure to look at a handsome man."

THE GOLDEN YEARS

❧

Strangers on a Train to *Psycho*

"I N THE EARLY 1950s, I was producing a radio and television show called *Twenty Questions*," publicist Gary Stevens told me. "It was sponsored by Ronson Lighters.

"One day the vice president of sales approached me and said blatantly, 'I know you know Alfred Hitchcock. Why can't you get a plug for Ronson Lighters in one of his movies? We don't have to get the name mentioned, because people seeing it will know it's a Ronson.'

"Hitchcock was preparing a picture at the time called *Strangers on a Train*. When I told him about it, he said, 'If this is important to you, I'll get it in some way. I'll work out something.'

"I thought he would throw it in on a table or something, but one of the thematic points in the entire movie was the lighter. Well, you're talking to the guy who planted that thing. Hitchcock made a picture about a lighter, and he did it for me as a favor.

"We had dinner one night, and he said, 'Gary, you better do a good job on this one, because I put your damn lighter in there.'

"After that, I was a very big man with the company, and they should have given me a few thousand dollars for it. I got a set of the lighter and a platter. It was worth $125, cost them $49."

HITCHCOCK WAS IMPRESSED by a novel he had just read, *Strangers on a Train,* by the then unknown Patricia Highsmith. Though anxious to buy the film rights, he instructed his representatives not to reveal the bidder. It had been his experience that not only would they have to pay an "unreasonable" sum, but that sometimes the agents might decide the property had such an exalted value that it would never be purchased at all. "Terrible," he said. "Writers can be difficult, but their agents, worse."

Hitchcock selected mystery writer Raymond Chandler to write the screenplay. As with Billy Wilder on *Double Indemnity,* Chandler was an incompatible collaborator. Though he was a fast worker, Chandler's first draft didn't please Hitchcock, and Ben Hecht was asked to work on it. Being unavailable, Hecht recommended his assistant, Czenzi Ormonde, who completed the script after shooting had begun.

Hitchcock originally had wanted William Holden for the part of Guy Haines, the professional tennis player who unwittingly becomes involved in a murder by a clever madman. Farley Granger won the part. For the insane Bruno Anthony, Hitchcock wanted Robert Walker, casting him against type. Pat Hitchcock was cast as Barbara, the younger sister of Ruth Roman, the tennis player's love interest. *Strangers* was the beginning of cinematographer Robert Burks's long association with Hitchcock.

The runaway merry-go-round, the cigarette lighter, and the thick eyeglasses were added for the film. Chandler had ended his version of the screenplay with Bruno straitjacketed in an asylum. Hitchcock remembered a runaway merry-go-round in an English novel called *The Moving Toy Shop.* In the novel *Strangers on a Train,* Guy, who is an architect, leaves a book in Bruno's train compartment, not a lighter.

This novel was for Hitchcock a "delicious" example of the kinds of characters he liked: the charming villain and a mixture of shades of gray in the hero, not just black and white, and the exchange-of-murders concept delighted him. The finished film was one of his favorites.

Farley Granger and I met for coffee and cake at the Petrossian Café in New York City after *Strangers* had played the night before on television. In 2003, except for his silver hair, he looked very much like Guy Haines in 1951, ready for a set of tennis. I asked him if, when he made that film, he had any idea people would be watching it a half century later on television?

He laughed. "I didn't even know how important *television* was going to be, and I certainly didn't know I'd be here to watch it!"

He described how he came to be in *Strangers on a Train*.

"I got a phone call to go to Hitch's house. I'd just come back from Europe. We sat out on the terrace of this wonderful little house he had for years and years and years. And he told me the whole story of *Strangers*.

"His telling it was as good as seeing it, because he was a wonderful storyteller. He said, 'Would you like to do it?' and I said, 'Of course I would.' And he said, 'All right.'

"He'd cast Robert Walker in the part of the murderer. A very interesting idea. Walker had a lot of trouble at this time. Drunkenness and everything, because he really did love Jennifer Jones, and he'd lost her to [David] Selznick. I said, 'Oh, I think that's terrific. He's just a wonderful, wonderful actor.' Hitch said, 'Yes. Wouldn't it be interesting if something happened during the movie.' I said, 'Hitch, that's *terrible* to say that,' and he laughed. I *think* he meant a scandal.

"Walker had always, up to that moment, played the boy next door in movies like *The Clock,* but Hitchcock cast him as evil, manipulative, a nut case. It started his career up again, you know.

"The last time I saw Robert Walker was at somebody's house. He said, 'We've got to get together. You know, we haven't seen each other for a long time.' I said, 'Sure, we will.' And he died, and we never did.

"Hitchcock had to take Ruth Roman because it was a Warner's movie, and no one else in the cast was under contract to Warner's. I thought she was good, but he didn't like her much, and she didn't go for him, because she felt he hadn't wanted her.

"He treated Pat [Hitchcock] as just one of the cast. And she behaved like that. They had evidently made a bargain, and they were totally professional."

"Were you really that good a tennis player?" I asked.

"No, but I played. A lot of it is me. I was proud of that. As soon as I knew I was doing it, they set me up taking lessons, but I'd been playing tennis for quite a while at Charlie Chaplin's house. So, I did know pretty well. Chaplin wanted people to come and play tennis, and I just got to know him and his wife Oona, who was the daughter of Eugene O'Neill."

"What was the most difficult scene for you?" I asked.

"The merry-go-round."

Hitchcock told me that this was the most personally frightening moment for him in any of his films. The man who crawled under the out-of-control carousel was not an actor or a stuntman, but a carousel operator who volunteered for the job. "If the man had raised his head even slightly," Hitchcock said, "it would have gone from being a suspense film into a horror film."

"Hitchcock was a genius," Granger continued. "You felt his mind always working under that calm exterior, which didn't show any strain. The technical people loved and respected him. He not only understood what they were doing, he had conceived it and created the effects, and he could explain it to them, how to achieve more than they thought they could, like with actors. A thing I loved was if you went up on a line or something wasn't right with what you did, he'd say, 'Let's do another one.' I'd say, 'Oh, damn it! I'm sorry, Hitch,' and he'd say, 'It's only a *moo*-vie.'

"I love that thing with our feet in the beginning, the contrast in the shoes we were wearing, and what it tells about us, and then how it's our shoes that meet first. And Hitchcock making his cameo carrying a double bass fiddle. He could poke a little fun at himself.

"Sometime at home, in front of guests, he'd say something terrible and outrageous. And Alma would say, 'Oh, Hitchie! Oh, Hitchie!'

"You know, when we were making this film, it was a thrill to work with the master, Hitchcock, and we thought the picture was really good, but we didn't know it was going to be one of the greats, and that half a century later, we'd appreciate it more, those of us who are around to appreciate it. I look so young, and I'm proud of my performance.

"Something that really impressed me was that he was so very formal and always wore a dark suit and tie, even when we were working outside on the tennis court, when it was nearly a hundred. Hitch never took off his jacket. He didn't even loosen his tie. I took it as an act of respect for the film.

"Hitch talked a lot with Robert Burks, the cinematographer. He seemed to think a lot of him."

This was the first of twelve films Burks would do for Hitchcock, the last of which would be *Marnie.* He missed *Psycho* because Hitchcock used his television crew.

Granger continued: "I remember Hitchcock said to me one night when we were shooting that he was bored because he knew how the story ended. I took it straight when he said it to me, because I was really new to everything, but I think he was really worried about getting the picture up there on the screen as good as the one he'd seen in his head.

"He had absolutely everything figured out and had this wonderful memory, so he never forgot anything. I wish I had his memory. Well, maybe not. Sometimes there are a few things you want to forget.

"I don't think I ever saw him get emotional so it showed, and some of the time he must have been frustrated. He seemed detached to some people, but I think he felt a great deal. He just had to keep this detachment, so he would always seem in perfect control. He was always very kind to me, and I liked him. Still do.

"We never discussed any homoerotic attraction Walker's character had for me, but I think Hitch did that with Walker, and he just wanted me to act kind of normal and not be aware of too much undercurrent. Of course, Hitch understood all of this, and he knew what he could do, and what we could do. He had a light touch. It was his way, and it worked because he got the best out of you.

"I'm asked more about *Strangers on a Train* than any of my other films. *Strangers* has a wonderful aura. The darkness of it, and then the brightness of the tennis. It's still so funny. I love it."

Tennis star Guy Haines (Farley Granger) meets a stranger on the Washington–to–New York train who offers to exchange murders. The stranger, Bruno Anthony (Robert Walker), will kill Guy's estranged wife if Guy will kill Bruno's hated father. Guy doesn't take Bruno seriously until his wife, Miriam (Laura Elliott), is found murdered in an amusement park.

Guy becomes the chief suspect, which threatens his tennis career, his romantic involvement with a U.S. senator's daughter, Anne Morton (Ruth Roman), his hopes for a political career, and even his life.

When it becomes evident to Bruno that Guy isn't going to kill his father, he tells Guy he intends to establish Guy's guilt conclusively by planting his monogrammed cigarette lighter on the island where Miriam was murdered.

With Anne's help, Guy is able to stop Bruno after rushing through an important tennis match and racing to the amusement park, where Bruno is killed in a chase on a runaway merry-go-round.

Bruno dies with the cigarette lighter in his hand, and Guy is cleared.

The British *Strangers on a Train* lasted two minutes longer than the American. The ending on a train with a minister unsuccessfully trying to have a conversation with Guy and Anne was cut for American audiences as well as in some British prints.

Hitchcock told me that the picture should have ended with Guy at the amusement park after he has been cleared of murdering his wife. He wanted the last line of the film to be Guy describing Bruno as "a very clever fellow." This ending, however, was not acceptable for Warner Brothers.

For the American ending, in which Anne and Barbara are waiting for Guy's call, Hitchcock had an oversized telephone built and put in the foreground, to emphasize the importance of the call they were expecting, while enabling the cameraman to keep the foreground and background in focus.

When the phone rings, Anne reaches for it and then answers a normal-sized phone. "I did that on one take," Hitchcock explained, "by moving in on Anne so that the big phone went out of the frame as she reached for it. Then a grip put a normal-sized phone on the table, where she picked it up."

One of the most memorable images in a Hitchcock film is the reflection in Miriam's fallen eyeglasses of Bruno strangling her.

"This scene is studied by film classes," Laura Elliott, who played Miriam, told me. "Bob Walker strangles me, and my glasses fall to the ground. To get the shot, the camera seems to shoot into the lens, and you see me floating down to the earth, Bob Walker standing up with his hands held out and his hat on and the leaves around him.

"We shot that on an absolutely empty soundstage, and Robert Walker was not even there.

"We shot the master in the exterior. Where he puts his hands around my throat, he was there, of course. Then the glasses fall off, I fall, and you cut to the shot on the soundstage. On the floor was a round, maybe three-foot-diameter kind of concave reflector, not a mirror, but a reflector, and the camera shot into that reflector.

"Mr. Hitchcock said, 'All right, Laura, now go stand with your back to the mirror,' and I said, 'Yes, sir.' He said, 'I want you to float backwards, all the way to the floor.'

"I looked at him. 'You want me to *float* to the floor?'

"'You know,' he said, 'like you were doing the limbo.'

"He said, 'Okay, action,' so I leaned back and back and back and back, and I get so far, I go *rap!* onto the cement floor. He would cut and say, 'Laura—*float* to the floor,'

"About the seventh take, I literally floated all the way down to the floor. Don't ask me how. All he said was 'Cut. Next shot.' He didn't say, 'Oh, that was wonderful,' or 'That was good.' It was just, 'Cut. Next shot.'"

Elliott, who enjoyed a long, successful career in films and on television, sometimes under her real name, Imogene or "Kasey" Rogers, recalled being cast as Miriam.

"I was under contract to Paramount, which is why the name Laura Elliott. They always gave you a movie star name, and I thought it was lovely, so I did twenty-eight films as Laura Elliott, and one of them, a loan-out to Warner Brothers, was, of course, *Strangers on a Train.*

"I remember there was another girl under contract to Paramount who three or four months before came in and said, 'Oh, I just read the most wonderful role, and you're perfect for it.' I looked at her, and thought, she and I are so different. She's a song-and-dance girl, I'm not, so I thought there's certainly nothing there for me. Then my agent called and said go and audition for this role. I told him, 'I don't think I'm gonna be right for it,' and he says, 'You go *anyway.*'

"I read this scene, and I thought, 'This is just wonderful. I just love this.' So I read with the casting director, he liked it, and he decided that I would test with six other girls. We all did the same scene in the music store there, same stage, same everything, same crew, and we had no direction. What we brought in is the way we interpreted the role. I had never met Mr. Hitchcock. I did the test, and I got chosen.

"I was elated. I mean, I was *thrilled* to work with Hitchcock, and it was an unusual role, because usually I'd do the little ingenue thing. I guess he liked what he saw in the tests, because he didn't change anything.

"I met him after I had been told I would get the role. I remember, I dressed very conservatively. I think I had a gray suit on, and a little hat. We wore hats in those days.

"He was very cordial, but he said, 'Why do you dress so severely?' because I had my hair pulled back.

"He said, 'I want you to get some glasses. I want you to wear glasses for this role. Just pick out any frame, anything you think would be fine.' He told me where to go, the place where they make the glasses, and we got six pair of glasses. We had two pair that were so thick that I literally could not see my hand in front of my face. These are the ones I wore in the movie.

"I could not see anything. So, when I'd look at Farley, I couldn't see him. When I tried to ring up a cash register sale, I couldn't see the cash register. To jump on the merry-go-round, I couldn't see the merry-go-round. He said, 'I want your eyes to look very little, pig-eyed, very small like little pigs.'

"We got two big lenses, two medium lenses, and we got two with clear glass that supposedly I could wear in the long shots. But I never had them on. When we got out at night to do the merry-go-round, all this stuff, the exteriors, he had me wear the same thick glasses. I don't know why. I was only twenty-something years old. I said, 'Yes, Mr. Hitchcock, yes, Mr. Hitchcock.'

"The next time you look at the film, you'll notice when I come out of the little booth chasing Farley, I run after him yelling, into a big close-up. I had already counted my steps to where the counter was. Then I turned and had my hand on the counter and ran along yelling at him, and when I came to the end of the counter, I stopped because I knew I had hit my marks. I was in place for the close-up, and that's where I yelled the last line, 'You can't throw me away like an old shoe,' or whatever.

"When the two boys come to pick me up, you'll notice all the time one'll always hold his hand out, and I trip down the stairs. Then one will help me up to the bus. It works wonderfully. I couldn't see the bus. I couldn't see the merry-go-round, but I liked the challenge.

"The traveling amusement park was one they brought to an exterior location. I think it was at Chatsworth Lake in the San Fernando Valley, but it's drained now. It was a thirty- or forty-minute drive from the studio.

"It was freezing cold out there. All the crew had on these big furry parkas, and as soon as they'd say 'Cut,' I'd say, 'Give me my jacket!'

"There are people who believe that you are the roles you play, that if you are playing a character who is bad, there must be bad in you.

"When it was in release, I remember making a great charity type of tour. It was a busload of celebrities, and of course nobody knew the name Laura Elliott.

"So I said to the guy who was producing it, 'You know, I'm just currently out of *Strangers on a Train*. I played Miriam.' He announced it next time, and the entire audience gasped and looked at me like, 'Oh, you terrible person.' And I loved it! Because I had convinced them. It's fun to be a bitch. That's a witch gone bad.

"After I got excellent reviews from the *Reporter* and *Variety,* Paramount didn't acknowledge anything, and they had me holding up color swatches for the camera crews to test color film.

"Hitchcock was always 'Mr. Hitchcock,' and if you saw him on his television show, that was who he was. One of the things he did, I think, was he saw in an actor or actress the qualities he wanted for a specific role. He usually picked people who had done more than I had, you know. I was a newcomer. But he would see what he wanted and cast them, and just let them do their thing. I didn't see him giving direction to Robert Walker or to Farley or to me. We just went into the scene, and he said, 'Walk here,' 'Walk there,' 'Okay.'

"He never said it to me, but I've always heard that he considered the most boring part of a film was the shooting of it, because he'd story-boarded, written, and done it in his mind, but I personally found that he was deeply interested in everything on the set. Believe me, he didn't miss a thing.

"Robert Walker was absolutely brilliant. If I were a guy and had the choice of roles, I would have taken his role. Farley did a lovely job, but you know, it's like a leading lady. If you're a beautiful leading lady, that's what you are, a beautiful leading lady, and everyone else gets the good roles."

Among others in the cast were Marion Lorne, who played Bruno's demented mother, and Norma Varden, who almost gets strangled by him at Senator Morton's party, and a few years later *is* murdered by Tyrone Power in Billy Wilder's *Witness for the Prosecution*. Laura Elliott later worked with Marion Lorne on the television show *Bewitched*.

"I was the boss's wife, and Marion Lorne was Aunt Clara. She was working in England, and Hitchcock knew her work. Actually, I didn't know her on *Strangers on a Train,* because I didn't have any scenes with her, but we worked together on *Bewitched* in a few episodes.

"You could see her quality of comedy in *Strangers on a Train.* She was brilliant as a comedian, absolutely brilliant. In fact, when I taught acting, I would always say to my students, 'If you want to study comedy, you go study Marion Lorne.' Her timing is perfect."

Food frequently appears in Hitchcock films, and even when it seems not to serve a purpose, it helps define the characters.

"Preferences in food characterize people," Hitchcock said. "I have always given it careful consideration, so that my characters never eat out of character.

"Bruno orders with gusto and an interest in what he is going to eat—lamb chops, French fries, and chocolate ice cream. A very good choice for train food. And the chocolate ice cream is probably what he thought about first. Bruno is rather a child. He is also something of a hedonist.

"Guy, on the other hand, shows little interest in eating the lunch, apparently having given it no advance thought, in contrast to Bruno, and he merely orders what seems his routine choice, a hamburger and coffee."

When Pat Hitchcock spoke with me, she said, "There's a story I want to tell you that's gone around, so would you please tell everyone what *really* happened. It was at the amusement park.

"My father said how much would I want to go up on the Ferris wheel? I said, 'I'm not going up. You know how scared I am of heights.' He said, 'I'll give you a hundred dollars,' and I said, 'Okay.' So, I went up with the two young men who were playing Laura's two boyfriends, and I have a picture of us waving.

"As a joke, some electricians turned off the lights and pretended they were walking away. Obviously, they weren't. I think we were probably up there two or three minutes at the outside.

"They turned the lights on, brought us down, and that's the story of the Ferris wheel. They said Daddy left me up there all alone in the dark for two or three hours, and that's the story that has persisted. They made a lot out of that because they were trying to make it a horror thing and make it fit my father's character, but my father wasn't ever sadistic. It just wasn't true. The only sadistic part was I never got the hundred dollars."

After *Strangers on a Train,* on a ship during a European holiday with her parents, Pat Hitchcock met the man she would marry, Joseph O'Connell.

Hitchcock told me that when he realized that she had grown up and was beginning her adult life, he was sorry that they had sent her away to boarding school. "It all went so fast," he said. "One day I was holding her hand while she learned to walk, and the next, she was getting married."

While she didn't like being away from her mother and father for such long periods of time, Pat had come to understand. "It's what British families do," she told me.

IN 1947, HITCHCOCK acquired the screen rights to a stage play he had seen in England, *Nos deux Consciences* ("Our Two Consciences"), written in 1902 by Paul Anthelme. Hitchcock set the project aside until 1952 when, after many revisions, it became *I Confess.*

When Warner Brothers was hesitant to make the film, Hitchcock offered to do another film for them without salary, working only for a percentage of the profits. The offer persuaded Warners, and that other film would be *The Wrong Man,* to be made later.

"Quebec was chosen as the location for *I Confess,*" Hitchcock said, "because it's the only place in North America where the clergy still wear cassocks, and that is important to the story."

> In Quebec City, Father Michael Logan (Montgomery Clift) is accused of killing a well-known lawyer. The priest knows the murderer, but he can't reveal his identity because the man confessed the crime to him in the confessional. The guilty person is Otto Keller (O. E. Hasse), the church sexton, who wore a priest's cassock to commit a robbery that led to murder.
>
> Police Inspector Larrue (Karl Malden) narrows his investigation to Logan, who had a motive for committing the crime. The lawyer was blackmailing Ruth Grandfort (Anne Baxter), wife of a prominent politician. He had threatened to make public a suspected liaison she had with Logan after he became a priest.
>
> Logan is arrested and tried for murder. The jury acquits him, but doubts remain as to his innocence. Following the trial, a

crowd in the street threatens Logan and Ruth. When Logan is
physically attacked, Keller's wife, Alma (Dolly Haas), tells the
crowd that her husband is the real murderer. Keller shoots her,
and then escapes into the Château Frontenac Hotel, where he
is trapped by police and shot. As he dies, he confesses again to
Father Logan.

In an early draft, Logan was found guilty and hanged before it is
determined he is innocent. There was also a draft in which he had
fathered an illegitimate child during his affair before he became a
priest.

O. E. Hasse had acted on the stage for Max Reinhardt and was an
extra for F. W. Murnau. Most of his career was spent in the German
cinema. Hitchcock cast him in one of his few English-language roles
as Keller, the ungrateful refugee.

Dolly Haas, the wife of artist Al Hirschfeld and a star of pre–Third
Reich German cinema, talked with me at her Upper East Side New
York City town house about *I Confess.* Like most actors, she was
happy to have had even a small part in a Hitchcock film. Anne Baxter,
however, was not happy after filming began.

Hitchcock had originally wanted the Swedish actress Anita Björk
for *I Confess.* Björk had just scored a big success in Alf Sjöberg's *Miss
Julie,* and seemed perfect for the part of Ruth Grandfort; but when
the unwed Swedish actress arrived in America with her lover and her
child, Hitchcock was forced by Warners to release her. Baxter, who
knew the Hitchcocks socially, replaced her.

"Anne believed that Hitchcock really hadn't wanted her," Haas
said, "because she wasn't blond enough, and she wasn't beautiful
enough. I told her it was just her imagination, but she was worried.

"Once, she asked Alma to go for a drive with her, and they got
back late for dinner. Hitchcock was silently furious. He hated eating
without Alma. He waited. Anne thought he blamed her, and she was
more certain Hitchcock didn't like her.

"Montgomery Clift didn't go anywhere without his acting coach, a woman named Mira Rostova. After every scene, he didn't look at Hitchcock for a reaction. He looked at Rostova. Hitchcock just hated that."

Clift prepared for the part by actually spending a week in a monastery, his friend, publicist John Springer, told me. The actor observed that because of the robes the clerics wore, they had a distinctive walk, pushing the fabric of their habits forward with their hands.

Karl Malden talked with me about his experience in *I Confess*.

"I got the part of Inspector Larrue by one of those lucky chances in my life. In the early 1950s, I was in New York City and ran into Monty Clift. Everybody knew he was going to be a big star, but it hadn't quite happened yet. Anyway, he was starting a new picture, being directed by Alfred Hitchcock. 'You lucky bastard,' I told him. Then, he said there might be a part in it that's just right for me. He didn't need to say more.

"Well, I got the part of Inspector Larrue, and I got to work with Hitchcock. It was everything I hoped it would be; more, but different from what I expected.

"I would describe Hitchcock as the ideal English gentleman. Every day he came to the set in a suit and a tie. I never once saw him take his jacket off or loosen his tie.

"He was the calmest director I ever saw, never ruffled, never any sign of being worried, never shouted, always in control. There was no unnecessary noise or talking or shouting on his set. It was a quiet set, because that's the way he wanted it.

"Hitchcock and his wife had dinner every night at the great hotel in Quebec, the Château Frontenac. He had a table for eight, so every night six of us would be invited to have dinner with them. I was pretty nervous at first, but I would have been a hell of a lot more nervous if they hadn't invited me.

"Hitchcock knew everything there was to know about food and

wine, and he made the meal greater than if you ate in the same restaurant on your own. The food and company were great, and there wasn't any shoptalk. He never talked about *I Confess* at dinner. It was as if it didn't exist.

"Hitchcock was the director for the dining room, too. Those six places were rotated every night, and all of us who were lucky enough to be included in the group looked forward to our turn.

"One night I got pretty relaxed. After dessert I felt confident enough to ask him the question I'd been thinking about. I said, 'You never tell us what you want. I know the blocking and the lines, but what I don't know is what you expect from me.'

"He never missed a beat. Very evenly, calmly, he said, 'You're a professional, and I'm a professional. I simply expect you to do your job.'

"Nothing else was ever said about it.

"I have this image in my mind of Alfred Hitchcock putting together a gigantic jigsaw puzzle and knowing where each piece goes. There wasn't anything he didn't understand about making film. His camera was always exactly where it should be. He was an intuitive genius.

"Hitchcock didn't like Method actors, but even when Monty had to stand and look out of the window while he found his character, Hitchcock didn't raise his voice or show emotions.

"I remember my own experience one night, taking Monty home when he was really drunk. My car didn't get over the experience for weeks, but I always remembered it was Monty who let me know about the film.

"I was looking forward to learning something from Alfred Hitchcock, but I really can't remember *anything* he said to me. The way I knew Hitchcock liked what I did was when I saw the picture and I saw how much he had favored me with screen time—angles, cutting, everything. And it sure wasn't because I was more beautiful than Monty."

"You had to like him," *I Confess* publicist Gary Stevens remembered. "He was doing the same thing in life as in those mini-cameos he did in the movies. He injected himself into situations which gave him an opportunity for a mini-cameo in life. He created himself his own way, and he got a big kick out of being Alfred Hitchcock."

"SOMEDAY," Hitchcock told me, "there will be three-dimensional wall video screens, and *Dial M for Murder* will come into its own. But at the time I was making that picture, I worried that 3-D might be a fad that would fade and that *Dial M* would go out as a 'flattie.'

"If one is going to make a 3-D movie, the most convenient medium to adapt it from is the stage. A play is seen in 3-D normally, and within the confines of a stage set it's much easier to control the added complications of shooting in 3-D. When I made *Dial M*, I was running for cover while waiting for the muse. A play is a safety net picture."

The actress he chose to star in his new film was the young Grace Kelly before her great fame, to which he would contribute. She was the perfect Hitchcockian heroine, the cool, elegant blonde with, as Hitchcock said, "fire seething within."

Edith Head told me that of all of the beautiful stars for whom she had designed clothes, Grace Kelly had the most perfect figure. "Grace had nothing to hide. She was perfect in her clothes because what was underneath was perfect."

Head said that most of her job was "hiding work," covering figure faults. "Even the beautiful stars who had to look perfect onscreen, they all had something to cover, all but Grace."

Jack Cardiff had recommended *Dial M for Murder* to Hitchcock. "I called Hitch to tell him I'd seen a play in London on television that I knew would make a great movie for him. I phoned a friend who was a producer and urged him to switch on his set and watch it. He agreed it would make an excellent film, but when he tried to buy the screen rights, it was too late. Alexander Korda had already bought them. Korda sold them, and *Dial M for Murder* was made, directed by Alfred Hitchcock."

The play, introduced on BBC television, had a long stage run in London's West End, followed by a success in America. Frederick Knott, who wrote the play, also wrote the screenplay.

The 3-D process required a much larger camera, essentially two synchronized cameras with two lenses and two strips of film. The larger camera unit made moving shots more difficult, almost returning to the immobile camera booths of early sound.

Special Polaroid glasses had to be passed out to each member of the audience for every showing of the film, and two projectors were needed to run simultaneously, in synchronization. Since most theaters *had* only two projectors, they either had to install two more or have intermissions between reels. The other option was to show the film in conventional format, which was usually the fate of *Dial M for Murder* after it left first-run theaters.

For 3-D, scenes were inserted specifically to exploit the illusion of depth. In the 3-D film *Man in the Dark,* an eye operation is seen from the viewpoint of the patient who has declined anesthesia, and scalpels seem to be poking the eyes of the screaming, empathetic audience. In *House of Wax,* a carnival barker bounces an elastic paddleball into the audience, and in *Kiss Me Kate,* a dancer seems to swing out over the audience.

Hitchcock's use of 3-D is restrained, with depth effects being reserved for important moments, such as when Margot reaches back for the scissors or when Inspector Hubbard holds out the incriminating key in 3-D close-up.

For the credits, Hitchcock wanted a close-up of a telephone dial. It wasn't possible to go in close enough on a real telephone dial using the 3-D process, so Hitchcock had an oversized prop telephone dial made. Later, when Ray Milland dials Grace Kelly from the club, the large dial is used with an oversized prop finger.

"3-D wasn't anything new," Hitchcock said. "They had it back in the '20s as a novelty, using red-and-green glasses. Skeletons threw their skulls at the audience, or bats filled the theater.

"Since I couldn't imagine Ray Milland or Grace Kelly behaving that way, I decided to redo the killing in *Blackmail,* when Anny Ondra reaches back to grab a bread knife to kill Cyril Ritchard. This time I would have Grace Kelly reaching back toward camera for something to defend herself, grabbing a pair of scissors. In 3-D, the scissors are in the foreground, and her hand seems to come back into the audience to grab them and kill the would-be strangler, who is in the background."

Former tennis star Tony Wendice (Ray Milland) plans to murder his wealthy wife, Margot (Grace Kelly), so he can inherit her money. He knows Margot is having an affair with mystery writer Mark Halliday (Robert Cummings), and she may leave him for her lover.

He has found a classmate from Cambridge, C. A. Swann (Anthony Dawson), who has a criminal record and needs money. Tony offers to pay Swann for killing Margot; Swann accepts. Swann is to enter the apartment with Margot's key; hidden for him by Tony under a stair carpet in the entrance hallway, and to strangle her.

Swann opens the door with the key, and before entering puts it back. Tony's elaborate plan fails when Swann is killed by Margot, who is defending herself. When Tony arrives, he puts the key he finds in Swann's pocket into Margot's purse.

Margot is accused of murder. Tony makes it appear that Swann was blackmailing her, threatening to expose her affair with Mark. Margot is found guilty and sentenced to hang.

Inspector Hubbard (John Williams) believes Margot is innocent. He discovers that the key in Margot's purse is Swann's own key.

Margot is allowed to leave prison temporarily to test whether
she knows about the key under the carpet. She does not, but
Tony does know where the key is, thus incriminating him.

At the beginning of the film, before a word is spoken, the relationship between the three main characters is clearly established when
Grace Kelly dutifully kisses her husband, Ray Milland, and then pas-
sionately kisses her lover, Robert Cummings. This is an example of
what Hitchcock described as "pure cinema." This scene was not in
the play, nor was the scene in which Ray Milland calls his wife from
his club during the attempted murder.

Grace Kelly told me that when she was standing on the set of *Dial
M for Murder,* a visitor was being introduced to Hitchcock by Ray
Milland. She heard Hitchcock say to the man, "Call me Hitch, with-
out a cock."

Milland and his friend laughed. Then, Hitchcock looked over in
her direction. "He was obviously embarrassed," Kelly said, "fearing
that I had heard.

"I walked up to him and said, 'I heard that.'

"Hitch started to apologize, but I stopped him.

"Don't worry. I went to a Catholic girls school, and by the time I
was thirteen, I'd heard everything." Kelly added, "And most of the
information was wrong."

Hitchcock, many years later, told me, "Grace Kelly had a wonderful sense of humor, if a bit bawdy."

Hitchcock said that he wanted Miss Kelly to be wearing as little as
possible when she is attacked, but he wasn't quite certain how he
should ask her to do this. He made a plan for her to wear a heavy red
robe. He hoped that at the last moment he could prevail upon her to
come out in "a nightgown that preserved some modesty, but not flan-
nel with a ruffle."

"When I mentioned the robe, she protested. 'Oh, no. My character, alone in her home at night, wouldn't stop to put on a heavy robe. It would be silly.'

"I said, 'What do you suggest?'

"She said, 'I have to come out in my nightgown.'

"Thus, it was Miss Kelly who chose that particularly flimsy nightgown, saying it was the style she, herself, would wear—if she wore one at all."

WHILE HITCHCOCK WAS working on *Dial M for Murder*, Lew Wasserman, was arranging a multi-picture deal for him with Paramount. Wasserman had been his agent since Myron Selznick died in 1944. Hitchcock would produce and direct five pictures that would eventually revert to him and four more pictures that would be Paramount's. The first picture of this deal was to be *Rear Window*, for which Hitchcock felt he had to have Grace Kelly.

When Hitchcock offered Grace Kelly the part of Lisa Fremont in *Rear Window*, she already had planned to accept the lead opposite Marlon Brando in Elia Kazan's *On the Waterfront*.

Then she heard from her agent that Hitchcock wanted her to be in Los Angeles for wardrobe fittings. "It was a big surprise," she said, "because I was just ready to accept another role in a major film. I read the script, and I knew that *Rear Window* was for me."

Rear Window was based on a short story by Cornell Woolrich, with a screenplay by John Michael Hayes; but there was a contributor not listed in the credits: Joshua Logan.

I was introduced to Joshua Logan by one of his closest friends, Henry Fonda. Logan, who lived at New York City's River House, was a collector of automatons, Swiss music boxes with performing French dolls.

After I was announced by the downstairs reception, Logan wound every music box and dimmed the lights. When I entered his living room, every doll would be performing—the magician doing magic tricks, the ballerina performing a pirouette, the fortune-teller proffering a fortune, the clown doing acrobatics, all competing for attention. My favorite was a small French doll with pouty closed lips who sat at her vanity, powdering her face.

Once when he was convalescing from an injured ankle, Logan told me he had amused himself by looking out of a courtyard window, watching his neighbors, "just like [James] Stewart in *Rear Window*. Do you know that I was responsible for Grace Kelly's character in that film?"

Leland Hayward, Logan's agent, had been trying to interest Hitchcock in stories by mystery writer Cornell Woolrich, one of which was "It Had to Be Murder."

"Leland asked me if I'd write a short treatment of it for the screen to help sell it to Hitchcock, so I read the story and made some changes. A few of them actually got into the movie, though I didn't get any credit. Or money.

"I started out with the audience knowing Jeff's leg is in a cast. In the short story, it's the last thing the reader learns, but my most important addition was the girlfriend. There wasn't any romance in the story, and I never saw a Hitchcock picture without it. Even *Lifeboat* has a love story. In Woolrich, there's only a male servant and a friend who's a police detective to help Jeffries [the Stewart character]. I kept them, changing the male servant into a female servant, and the girlfriend became his most important helper.

"Nedda [Logan's wife] had the idea for her to be an actress. In the movie, Grace Kelly is a fashion model. Close."

Hitchcock told me: "I always say *Shadow of a Doubt* was my personal favorite, but I am very proud of *Rear Window*.

"It's a movie about a peeping Tom, to be blunt. I think it's human nature. People love to peek, or they would if they weren't afraid of getting caught. The tabloids are a kind of peeking.

"A great advantage of the cinema is you can show a state of mind.

In *Rear Window* I wanted to show the claustrophobia of Stewart's situation and the extent of his boredom. It brings him to the point where the ordinary lives of his neighbors have to replace the intensity of his own adventurous life. His neighbors at least are in motion. His confinement must be conveyed, but not in such a way that the audience feels so bored it runs out of the theater. It must be heightened, dramatic boredom."

Confined to his Greenwich Village apartment, his leg in a cast, photojournalist "Jeff" Jeffries (James Stewart) peers at his backyard neighbors through a telephoto lens. He is visited daily by Stella (Thelma Ritter), a nurse, and by Lisa (Grace Kelly), a fashion model who wants him to settle down and marry her.

Each neighbor has a story. Jeff suspects that one of them, Thorwald (Raymond Burr), has killed his invalid wife. He tells a policeman friend, Doyle (Wendell Corey), who investigates but finds nothing.

A little dog is found killed. The day before, the dog had been digging in the garden. When Thorwald leaves his apartment, Lisa and Stella investigate. Lisa enters Thorwald's apartment.

Thorwald returns and finds Lisa there. He has her arrested. Thorwald sees Jeff watching.

When Stella leaves to post bail for Lisa, Thorwald appears at Jeff's door. Using flashbulbs to temporarily blind him, Jeff slows Thorwald, but finally the enraged man pushes him out of the window. Jeff's fall is broken by two policemen.

Thorwald confesses to having disposed of his wife's dismembered body parts in the river and in the garden.

Now with *both* legs in casts, Jeff dozes. Lisa lounges in blue jeans nearby, reading *Beyond the Himalayas*, demonstrating that she is ready to share his life as an international photojournalist. Seeing him asleep, she picks up *Harper's Bazaar.*

"At the end, Stewart is caught with his plaster down," Hitchcock said.

Grace Kelly was proud of "a character contribution" she had made to the plot. She told me that she had pointed out to Hitchcock the importance to a woman of her purse, which represents "her security, taking her private world with her wherever she goes." It was a prop that played an important part in pointing suspicion at the already suspicious-seeming husband who had his wife's purse, but not his wife. "Personally, I wouldn't go anywhere important without my own favorite Hermès black bag," Grace Kelly said. "I have my jewelry with me in case something happens and I suddenly have to dress up. For me, going out without that purse would seem almost like going out naked. Well, *almost*."

When the American Film Institute premiered the restored version of *Rear Window* in 1998, they wanted to invite the members of the cast, but they could locate only Georgine Darcy, who played Miss Torso, a dancer who was one of the neighbors James Stewart's character watches. Still looking very much Miss Torso, she talked with me in 2002 about *Rear Window*.

"I was in Las Vegas, doing an act there, and I received a letter from Paramount. They wanted me to come for a screen test. I was really a dancer, originally with the New York City Ballet, and I was not interested in the screen world. I didn't actually know who Hitchcock was. I had a three-month contract, and I didn't want to go to Los Angeles to do an audition. So I just didn't bother.

"Finally they sent me the script, and I read it. The truth of the matter was, I was finishing up my time in Vegas, anyway. So I came back to Los Angeles, and I went to see Mr. Hitchcock. I had never been on a soundstage before, and they were saying things like 'Kill the baby,' you know, the light, and I was looking around for a baby.

"Mr. Hitchcock was just watching me. It was almost like the beginning of *Rear Window*. He was watching every move I made.

Then he called me over and said, 'You have the job. Come into the office with me.' I still didn't know who Hitchcock was!

"I went into the office, and he said, 'Now, Georgina'—he called me Georgina—'do you have an agent?' I said no, and he said, 'There are a lot of men outside who would be *happy* to represent you. And you'll get a lot of money. If you don't have an agent, you're going to get scale.'

"With an agent, I would have made $750, which was considered a lot of money in those days for a very small part. But I told Hitchcock I couldn't do that, because I'd already told someone I'm going to give him 10 percent. Scale was $350, and that's what I was paid. I was seventeen. Funny how you think when you're little.

"I was dating a director, and we went out for dinner that night. I said, 'I got the part,' and he said, 'Who's directing?' I said, 'Gee, I don't know his name. A short little man, a bald-headed man with a cockney accent.'

"He looks at me and says, 'You don't mean Alfred Hitchcock, do you? He's only about the most famous director in the world! And don't ever call him "Hitch." You show him respect and call him "Mr. Hitchcock."' So, I never did call him Hitch.

"We were across the courtyard from him, and we all had little earpieces so he could direct you. The only time he ever came over was to personally direct someone. He'd ask you to put your earpiece in, and he'd talk to you.

"I remember one day he called me from the dressing room to watch a scene with the couple that lived on the fire escape, Frank Cady and Sara Berner. They slept on the fire escape, and they had their mattress out there. He asked Frank to put his earpiece in, and for Sara to take hers out. And he gave Frank instructions. Then he told Frank to take his out, and asked her to put hers in. And he gave her instructions. Then he said to me, 'Now watch this.'

"The cameras start to roll, and it starts to rain. He's pulling his mattress one way, she's pulling hers the other way, and they're fighting. You can hear them bickering. As it turns out, Frank fell into the window upside-down. And it was a perfect scene, just exactly what Mr. Hitchcock wanted, uncut.

"Well, the actress was furious when she found out that Mr. Hitchcock had given them different directions. But these are the kind of things that he did that I didn't see anything wrong in, or think it mean-spirited. There was a logic behind it. He was very much, in a strange way, into improvisation.

"I remember when he said to me, 'You're getting the only close-up in the entire movie.' It was when the little doggie was strangled. I said, 'I don't know how to do this. I don't know how to act. What am I supposed to do?' Now, there's no dog, no basket, nothing. Nothing to look at. He said, 'I want you to look over there and throw up.' That was his direction. I didn't need to throw up, but I guess I looked like I was going to throw up. And that's the kind of thing he would do.

"He loved Judith Evelyn, who was Miss Lonelyheart. He said, 'Now, watch this actress. She's really good.' Then, there were people he just didn't bother with. The worst thing that he could do was ignore you.

"He used to tell jokes, lots of cockney jokes. Some of them were off-color. He told them when he had Herbie [Herbert Coleman, the assistant director] and a lot of guys around, but no women. He called me, and he started this joke, and it was really endless! He went on and on and on. I hadn't a clue what he was talking about. They were all laughing their heads off. He finished with the punch line, and they were hysterical!

"And he looked at me. He said, 'Georgina. You didn't laugh. Didn't you think my joke was funny?' I said, 'I didn't get it.' He looked over to Herbie, and he said, 'Herbie, explain it to her.' And, of course, there was no joke.

"Once he asked me, 'What kind of pie do you like, Georgina?' I said, 'Oh, I guess apple pie, maybe cherry pie. But I hate pumpkin pie. Ugh!' He got pumpkin pie, and he did the scene several times. I had to eat this pumpkin pie, and I'd told him I hated it. But those were his little tricks, his private jokes.

"He was always kind of teasing me. I remember another time when I came back from lunch, and he said to me, 'Georgina, did you mast . . .' Just the beginning of the word, my eyes bulged out of my head. He said, 'Did you mas-ticate your food?'

"James Stewart was very sweet, nice to be around, but a very private man. I took a picture sitting on his lap, with his cast on, sitting in the wheelchair, and he said to the photographer, 'That's just for Georgine.'

"Grace [Kelly] wanted to be a ballet dancer, you know. She was always impressed with my ability as a dancer. I remember one day, Ross Bagdasarian, who wrote a lot of songs that he ultimately had published, came into my dressing room with Frank Cady. And he'd pound out these songs, and you'd hear all this noise coming from my dressing room. I remember Grace knocked on the door once and said, 'What's happening? Can I come inside and play?'

"Grace was very sweet. Without makeup, you wouldn't know it was Grace Kelly. She wore glasses, and she was a little pigeon-toed. Very unassuming, very much a lady. Very quiet.

"Afterwards, I ran into the killer, Raymond Burr. A darling man. I was doing a movie in New Orleans, and we were on the same plane. He was going to play King Bacchus at the Mardi Gras, and he asked me to call him at his hotel. He wanted to do a second *Rear Window*. Isn't that crazy?

"I think I worked six weeks on the movie, and we finished January 14th, the day of my birthday. I had my long hair in big curlers, and all my makeup off, and I was hot to trot. I had one foot out the door. And there's a knock on the door, and it's Herbie Coleman. He said, 'Mr. Hitchcock would like to see you on the set.' So I threw on my slacks and went over.

"And *everybody*—Grace Kelly, Jimmy Stewart, and all the rest—

they were all there to sing 'Happy Birthday' to me, and the photographers were there. Mr. Hitchcock called me over, and he said, 'Georgina, would you please go back into the dressing room and take the curlers out of your hair.' So I ran back and took the curlers out of my hair, but no makeup on at all. I looked like a sheet. And he had a cake made for me. It had the breasts, the torso—a headless torso. It was my eighteenth birthday and it said, 'Happy Birthday, Miss Torso.'

"I was like his mascot. He'd always call me to hear his jokes. He would pull little tricks on actors, and he'd want me to be there. He told me about his career, and I really liked him. I thought he was cute.

"After the movie, I called him at work, and we'd just chat. The secretary always put me through. When he was doing *Alfred Hitchcock Presents,* one time he asked me would I like to be in it.

"While we were doing the movie, he said to me, 'Georgina, if you would go over to Europe and study with [Michael] Chekhov for a couple of years, when you come back, I would make a big star of you.' I thought, 'Ha, ha, ha, isn't that funny.' I never took him seriously, but he actually meant it, I found out later on, because he really loved blondes, and he loved molding people. He didn't like 'actor' actors, he liked people like Tippi Hedren, people he could mold to do just what he wanted them to do. I wouldn't say not thinking for themselves, but almost.

"I was a kid; I didn't know, I didn't care, and he *knew* that. He asked me if I wanted to be in one of the television episodes. And what do you think I said? 'Oh, *no,* Mr. Hitchcock! I wouldn't want to embarrass you.' Well, I must have been really stupid. He really *wanted* to put me in a part.

"People came from all over the world to look at the *Rear Window* set. They dug the bottom of the floor out and dropped it so that they could have the Greenwich Village set down below and the apartment up higher. You didn't have to go anywhere."

Production manager C. O. "Doc" Erickson added: "It was all shot on Stage 18 at Paramount. "Mac" [Joseph MacMillan] Johnson built the set, and we had to rip up the floor and use the basement portion of the stage, which became the courtyard of the apartment building. It was my first job as production manager and the first time I worked on a Hitchcock picture. We didn't get credit in those days." Erickson worked as production manager on five Hitchcock films, from *Rear Window* to *North by Northwest*.

"We had three sets of lights," Darcy continued. "You just pull one switch and all the lights, the entire place changed. You had the day-time, the late afternoon, and night.

"It was one total set. You didn't have to go from room to room and break things down and put them up. I lived in my little apartment. I had a refrigerator that was plugged in. It was a complete little village. The only thing I didn't have was running water. It was an incredible set. It was his dollhouse, and we were his dolls.

"When they were restoring the film, I filled them in on a lot of the technical things, like the lighting, which no one really seemed to know about, which is extraordinary.

"It was funny, because they were asking me questions like, 'What color were Jimmy Stewart's pajamas?' That I couldn't tell you, but I certainly could tell you what color Grace's dresses were. And I still have the shorts from the movie. My little pink shorts. The men restoring the film turned the cuffs down, and you could see the orig-inal color. They kept them a long time because they were the key to the colors that had faded so badly on the film. It was wonderful the role my shorts played in restoring the film.

"Interviewers came here and talked with a lot of people, including myself for television. They kept trying to get me to say things about Hitchcock. 'Was he salacious? Was he mean? Was he gay?' You know, things like that, and I wouldn't do it. I knew what they wanted. You know, I'm not a little girl anymore.

"I thought, 'The man is dead. He was a genius. It's his hundredth birthday, and this is the way you celebrate his life? Looking for garbage?' I would not do it, and I ended up on the cutting room floor, with only two seconds of me. Tippi Hedren was the one who was quoted.

"I hate gossip. I saw him through the eyes of an eighteen-year-old. He never did anything that was out of line with me.

"He was unique. I mean, how many geniuses come along? And the junk that they're putting out. I mean, you go to the movies now, and it gives you a headache. *Rear Window* really has held up, hasn't it?"

"THE KISS IN THE HALLWAY is as if she unzipped his fly," Hitchcock said of *To Catch a Thief*. "The fireworks scene is the orgasm." He described Grace Kelly's character as "Ice that burns."

"Of all the pictures I've ever worked on, *To Catch a Thief* is my favorite," costume designer Edith Head told me. "And it was also the most difficult. From Grace Kelly's pièce de résistance gold ball gown to shopping for bathing trunks that would please Cary Grant, who was even more difficult to please than Hitch was. Cary knew exactly how he wanted to look, but he also wanted to be comfortable. He didn't want a tight elastic distracting him. He selected most of his clothes for his films. Grace was much easier to work with, but I never had a free moment to see the Côte d'Azur."

Hitchcock had specially requested, *insisted,* that Paramount send Head to Cannes to work on location with the wardrobe design and fittings, so important did he consider the costumes in this film.

"This was not the regular routine," Head went on, "but I was in costume designer's heaven. Can you imagine? Grace Kelly playing one of the richest women in America so she can afford the most elegant clothes and most fabulous jewels. Then, a fancy costume ball with hundreds of extras dressed as if they were in Marie Antoinette's court. Hitch told me to dress Grace 'like a princess,' and I did. Of course, I had no idea I was dressing a *real* princess-to-be!"

One of Grace Kelly's favorite anecdotes involved the gold ball gown.

"I was wearing the gold evening dress that was cut really tight, to show everything. Hitch walked up to me and sort of peeked down my dress and said, 'There's hills in them thar gold!'

"I found it especially amusing, because Hitch was always so decorous and dignified with me. He treated me like a porcelain doll."

Hitchcock was concerned that the settings for *To Catch a Thief* not appear *too* beautiful, according to assistant director Herbert Coleman. "While the screenplay was still being written, Hitch sent me and a group of us to Cannes to scout for locations along the Côte d'Azur. The last thing he said to me before we left was, 'I don't want picture postcard locations. I want people to see the French Riviera the way it really is.' The trouble is, that's the way it really *is*, the way it looks on picture postcards."

David Dodge's 1952 novel, *To Catch a Thief*, had been purchased by Hitchcock on publication. The screenplay was to be written by John Michael Hayes. Cary Grant and Grace Kelly were Hitchcock's first choices, his only choices, but he had to coax Grant out of a sort of retirement to take the part.

> John Robie (Cary Grant), retired cat burglar and ex-member of the French resistance, lives quietly on the Côte d'Azur until a series of jewel robberies focus attention on him. When he visits a fellow resistance member, Bertani (Charles Vanel), in his Monte Carlo restaurant, policemen arrive to arrest Robie. Danielle Foussard (Brigitte Auber), a waiter's daughter, helps him escape.
>
> Bertani arranges for Robie to work with insurance investigator H. H. Hughson (John Williams) to catch the real thief. Robie meets a likely victim, Mrs. Jessie Stevens (Jessie Royce Landis), an American millionairess, traveling with her beautiful daughter, Francie (Grace Kelly).
>
> Francie teasingly informs Robie that she knows he is the Cat. Her mother's jewels are stolen, but Mrs. Stevens believes in Robie's innocence.

Danielle's father tries to kill Robie, but is himself killed, and the police announce that Foussard was the Cat. Robie knows otherwise, because Foussard had a wooden leg.

During a costume ball, Hughson and Robie wear similar disguises, so that Hughson can take his place in the ballroom, while Robie investigates upstairs.

Robie captures the real cat burglar, Danielle, on a roof top, dangling her over the edge until she confesses to the police below.

Francie wins Robie, but her mother is part of the package.

Dodge's novel, supposedly based on a series of jewel robberies that took place on the French Riviera after World War II, was more complex than the film, which eliminated subplots, a necessity imposed by the medium. "The motion picture is more related to the short story than to the novel," Hitchcock said.

For *To Catch a Thief,* Hitchcock wanted a beautiful thrill-seeker with perfect confidence. "The Kelly character is disappointed that Grant's cat burglar character really *is* retired," Hitchcock explained. "It isn't as thrilling for her with him being innocent.

"Francie has a 'don't-muss-my-hair' quality," Hitchcock explained. "Ingrid [Bergman] had a 'muss-my-hair' quality. Francie doesn't have Ingrid's kind of vulnerability nor her warmth.

"She's accustomed to getting what she wants. She acts differently at the end when she *is* getting what she wants. She and her mother are ready to take over our hero's house and life."

In an earlier draft, Francie was married, but hopes to be divorced soon so she can return to Monte Carlo and marry Robie.

MANY ACTORS HAVE COMPLAINED that Hitchcock gave them little direction, while others have been grateful to be left alone to develop their own performance, as was Cary Grant. Hitchcock knew that Grant knew how to play Cary Grant better than anyone else. "I didn't have to direct him," Hitchcock said. "All I had to do was put him in front of a camera."

Grant told me he understood that he was sometimes regarded as being self-obsessed about his character's wardrobe and every detail of his performance. "I'm the only property I have, so I have to watch over it. You might say I have a vested interest."

Doc Erickson, the unit production manager, talked with me about what it was like working with Cary Grant.

"He could be a little obstreperous. Cary always wanted something, or he *didn't* want something, and he would let you know about it and become sort of a nuisance in that regard. Eventually, you just let it roll off your back.

"We'd brought down a new Lincoln limousine from London for him. I said, 'That's your car, Mr. Grant.' The chauffeur who came with the car was holding the rear door open for him.

"He acted like it was a big surprise and said, 'Now, that's really thoughtful of you, Doc. But you shouldn't have gone to all the trouble.'

"'The studio told me it's in your contract, Mr. Grant,' I said.

"'Please call me Cary, Doc. I want everybody to call me Cary.'

"A couple of weeks later, he came up to me and said, 'Doc, I don't like riding around in that limousine. Everybody gawks at me, and I don't like it. I'd rather have a little open car with a driver who doesn't look like someone out of a Mae West movie. This one won't take his cap off.'

"So, I got him a convertible and a younger driver without a chauffeur's uniform, and shipped the limousine back to London.

"A few weeks passed, then Cary said, 'Doc, I'm not happy with my car and driver. Why can't I have the limousine that's in my contract?'

"I had to bring the Lincoln back by air.

"I wondered what next. But for the rest of the shoot, he was just like the Cary Grant you see on the screen."

• • •

AT THE LONDON OPENING of the film, Alfred and Alma Hitchcock were presented to Queen Elizabeth and Prince Philip at the Tenth Royal Film Performance at the Odeon Theatre in Leicester Square, the same day Princess Margaret announced from Clarence House that she had decided not to marry Peter Townsend. Everyone knew this wasn't what Queen Elizabeth's younger sister had wanted. The news spread through the theater. By the time *To Catch a Thief* began, everyone in the audience knew that Princess Margaret had placed duty before love.

Hitchcock and Alma, being romantics, sympathized. They had been hoping Princess Margaret would marry the man she loved, and much of the audience shared their feeling. They wondered how this would affect the audience's response to the movie. Would they be too distracted?

The audience received the film enthusiastically.

"THE FIRST TROUBLE WE HAD with *The Trouble with Harry* was autumn 1954 in New England," production manager Doc Erickson told me. "We went to Vermont to get the fall foliage and so forth, but it was one of those years when the leaves didn't turn, and we had a lot of rain, so we had to shoot inside. We built our sets in a gymnasium in town, and then came back to Los Angeles to build a huge set on Stages 12 and 14 at Paramount with the backing and trees and foliage.

"So, we did the outdoor scenes on the stage and the indoor scenes on location."

Another "trouble" was when the huge Technicolor camera fell from its crane in the gymnasium of East Craftsbury, Vermont, grazing Hitchcock, but fortunately not causing any injury.

Yet another "trouble" was the unavailability of the actor who played

Harry, Philip Truex, whose body had to be replaced for some scenes with a stunt double.

The worst trouble with Harry was that it was the only Hitchcock Paramount film that didn't earn a profit. "It lost, I suppose, half a million dollars," Hitchcock told me. "So that's an expensive self-indulgence. I didn't think enough about the audience. Or the producers, for that matter. Here we come to the question of ethics—with other people's money.

"I think it was outside of what was expected of me. It was a little comedy of the macabre. I feel it is a true example of British humor, black humor, termed gallows humor. Do you know the old joke about a man being led to the gallows? When he saw it, he was alarmed. His reaction was, 'I say, is that thing safe?'

"*The Trouble with Harry* was taken from an English book by Jack Trevor, and for some reason, I moved it to *New* England. My approach remained typically English, and it didn't travel well. The English have always had a fascination for crime as such, and this was a story about a dead body. In truth, it didn't do all that well in England either. I should have paid more attention to Alma, who didn't find it amusing.

"The exhibitors—those people who distribute films and run the cinemas, my natural enemies—didn't find it amusing either, and they didn't think the public would. Then they made it true by not publicizing the picture and opening it in a few small theaters. It's easy to make the negative come true."

Young Arnie (Jerry Mathers), walking through the Vermont woods, hears some threats, and then gunshots. Investigating, he finds the body of Harry Worp (Philip Truex), and he thinks Harry has been murdered. He tells his mother, Jennifer Rogers (Shirley MacLaine), who recognizes the man as her ex-husband. She, along with the elderly Captain Wiles (Edmund Gwenn) and the spinster Ivy Gravely (Mildred Natwick), believe they will be prime suspects when Harry's body is found, so they conspire to bury it, with the help of artist Sam Marlowe (John Forsythe).

As questions arise concerning how Harry died, he is dug up and buried several times, arousing the suspicions of the deputy sheriff, Calvin Wiggs (Royal Dano). While trying to find out who killed Harry, Jennifer and Sam fall in love, as do Ivy and Captain Wiles. Finally, the town doctor, Dr. Greenbow (Dwight Marfield), determines that Harry wasn't killed at all, but died of natural causes.

In Alma's presence, Hitchcock had told me that one of the few things they didn't share was a similar sense of humor. "I had to curb his sense of humor," she told me, but in *The Trouble with Harry* she had let her husband go his own way, without her usual restraint.

Shirley MacLaine, who made her screen debut in this film, was discovered for the part of Jennifer by accident, *because* of an accident, while she was an understudy in *Pajama Game*.

"We were still looking for someone to play Jennifer, the young mother," Herbert Coleman, whom Hitchcock had promoted to co-producer, told me. Then, on a Broadway stage, I saw our Jennifer. She was playing the lead. As soon as the curtain came down, I told Doc [Erickson] we'd found our girl, Carol Haney.

"He opened up his program to show me Carol Haney had been replaced by Shirley MacLaine, who was in the chorus, and the understudy. Miss Haney had had an accident and Shirley was playing her part.

"She'd already caught the eye of Hal Wallis, who tested her. Hitch got hold of the test, then signed her."

In the stage-trained cast were Edmund Gwenn, Mildred Natwick, Mildred Dunnock, Royal Dano, and John Forsythe.

Forsythe's first meeting with Hitchcock was a tense one for him. Coleman recalled: "Hitch and I met John at '21.' Beforehand, John had explained to me that he would have to leave early because he had an appointment at two o'clock. Hitch took his usual care ordering the wine, then he got around to telling us how he wanted the dead body in *Harry* dressed. As always, he was pretty specific about how his characters should dress.

"'I want a dark blue blazer with silver buttons,' he said, 'a striped shirt with French cuffs and large silver cuff links, a wide hand-painted silk tie from Sulka, light blue trousers, blue and white plaid wool socks, and black shoes with tassels.'

"As the meal went on, I noticed that John seemed upset. He didn't leave early. He was still sitting there when Hitch and I left.

"Later, I asked him why, and he said, 'I couldn't get up from the table. I was dressed *exactly* like the dead body Mr. Hitchcock was telling you how to dress.' John didn't know that this was a joke, typical of Hitch's sense of humor."

When shooting began in Vermont, MacLaine had trouble understanding Hitchcock. Once, she thought she heard him say, "Dog's feet."

"I turned to Johnny Forsythe, and whispered, 'Dog's feet?'

"Johnny whispered back, 'He means pause.'" MacLaine was not yet acquainted with Hitchcock's fondness for cockney rhyming slang. "Dog's feet" were paws, so "dog's feet" meant pause. "Don't come a pig's tail" translated meant "Don't come twirly," which was "-Don't come too early."

While doing music for *To Catch a Thief*, composer Lyn Murray recommended his friend, Bernard Herrmann, for Hitchcock's next film. Herrmann scored *The Trouble with Harry* and would make an extraordinary contribution to the next eight Hitchcock films as well as to many of the *Alfred Hitchcock Presents* television programs.

Hitchcock's own favorite line in *The Trouble with Harry* occurs when Edmund Gwenn is pulling the body by the legs as though he's pulling a wheelbarrow, and the spinster lady happens along and says, "What happens to be the trouble, Captain?" Hitchcock liked understatement.

• • •

DURING THE FILMING of his next picture, *The Man Who Knew Too Much,* Hitchcock became an American citizen. Alma had become a citizen in 1950, but Hitchcock waited until 1955.

"I drove Hitch to the federal court building," Herbert Coleman told me. "He was nervous. He especially hated being in a crowd.

"Alma had often told me how much she wished he would become an American citizen. As we were driving, Hitch explained why he hadn't done it sooner.

"'The Hitchcock name is almost as old as the British Empire. It isn't easy for me to give all that up, so much British history and tradition. But Alma would never forgive me if I didn't go through with this.'"

During the post-production of *The Trouble with Harry,* Hitchcock decided to bring *The Man Who Knew Too Much* up to date. To help John Michael Hayes with the screenplay, he brought in Angus MacPhail, who had contributed, though uncredited, to the first *Man Who Knew Too Much,* and whom he had known for a long time.

> Americans Ben and Jo McKenna (James Stewart and Doris Day) are befriended by Louis Bernard (Daniel Gelin) in Marrakech. Later, Ben sees Bernard, disguised as an Arab, stabbed in a street market. As he dies, he tells Ben that a statesman is to be assassinated. "Tell London to find Ambrose Chappell."
>
> An English couple, the Draytons (Bernard Miles and Brenda de Banzie), disappear with the McKennas' eight-year-old son, Hank (Christopher Olsen). Ben is warned not to tell the police what Bernard told him. Hank's life depends on his silence.
>
> Following the kidnappers to London, the McKennas are greeted by Jo's fans, who know her as Jo Conway, a famous singer. Scotland Yard Inspector Buchanan (Ralph Truman) also awaits them, but Ben is afraid to say anything.

Investigating on their own, they go to Ambrose Chapel, not a person, but a church used by the kidnappers. Ben is captured after Jo goes to tell Buchanan, who has gone to Albert Hall.

At Albert Hall, Jo is confronted by a man she recognizes from Marrakech. He reminds her that Hank's life depends on her silence. He is Rien (Reggie Nalder), the hired assassin.

Ben escapes and rushes to Albert Hall where he and Jo search for the assassin as the concert begins.

At the music's climax, Jo sees Rien's gun and screams, spoiling his aim. The intended victim, an ambassador, is only wounded.

Jo and Ben are invited to the embassy, where Hank is being held by members of a government faction planning a coup. When Jo is invited to sing, Hank whistles along with her from where he is being held, and Ben rescues him.

Arthur Benjamin lengthened his "Storm Cloud Cantata" for the remake of *The Man Who Knew Too Much* by adding an orchestral prologue. Thus the Albert Hall musical sequence is twice as long as it was in 1934.

The second *Man Who Knew Too Much* was intended by Hitchcock as a remake by a mature artist of an effort from his youth. "I was an amateur when I did the first *Man Who Knew Too Much*," he told me, "but a talented one. I thought as a fully matured professional, I could make a better picture, but the second picture took on a life of its own."

"Some of it was better the second time, but some of it was better the first time. The only answer is, I suppose I'll have to make it a third time."

James Stewart as the hero gave Hitchcock exactly what he wanted, but those who have seen the first version cannot easily forget Peter Lorre's sinister geniality.

Stewart said, "I remember once I asked some question about my character, even though I knew that kind of question was a no-no for Hitch.

"I was sorry as soon as I said it. He shot me one of those pained, 'Oh, how-could-you, I-thought-better-of-you' looks of his. I'd seen others get that look, and I'd promised myself I was never going to put myself in the position of being at the receiving end of it. Enunciating not just the words, but each syllable, the way he did when he felt you'd played the fool and given a pretty good performance of being one, he said simply, only it wasn't really simple, and nothing Hitch ever said was a waste of words, 'Just be yourself.'

"Well, that's the toughest thing anyone could ever ask me to do. No cover. Go out there naked as James Stewart. I mean, what do you do with your hands?

"I remember when we were doing that scene in London's Albert Hall, and I was chasing Doris Day up the stairs while the London Symphony was playing, loud. It was a long speech which sort of cleared up a lot of the story. I'd worked hard on those words, and I was talking my head off while I chased after Doris.

"After we did the scene, Hitch said, 'Let's do it again. You were talking so loud, I couldn't hear the London Symphony. As a matter of fact, let's just cut the whole speech. Just follow Doris up the stairs and look tense.'

"Well, I considered the speech very important, but when you're working with Hitch, you don't try to do a scene two ways. You do it just one way. His. Hitch was always open to listening to an idea, if you had one. People say Hitch wasn't spontaneous, but he was. It's just that all of his spontaneity occurred on paper before he got to the set.

"Well, over the years I've watched that movie quite a few times, and every time, I've tried to remember that talky speech on the stairs I thought was so key. No matter how hard I try, I can't remember what it was I was talking about."

Not all of the Albert Hall sequence was actually shot there. As art director Henry Bumstead explained: "A lot of Albert Hall, the boxes and things, I had to do back here in Los Angeles, so that was a matter of measurements and photos, and I remember many nights I would be out making measurements and getting color samples."

The Man Who Knew Too Much was shot on location in London and French Morocco, and at the Paramount studios in Hollywood. "Down in Marrakech," Bumstead continued, "you'd come out of your hotel room in the morning, and you could hardly breathe, it was so hot. It was not only hot, but I'll tell you, it was scary.

"We had a bombing there. Hitch was directing out in the crowd from an old automobile. He sat in the front seat, with the driver, with the air-conditioning on, and it's the only time in all the time I worked with Hitch I saw him in a polo shirt. With short sleeves. It wasn't loose at the collar, it was buttoned, but no tie.

"I was riding in a jeep with a French officer, and I saw all these black carcasses hanging there in a meat market. He said, 'Watch this,' and he honked the horn. Then, all of a sudden, there's all this red meat. It was covered with flies.

"I remember going out to a restaurant with Doris Day and eating couscous. You know, you use so many fingers. But Hitch never did that. Doris Day wouldn't do it, either. She wouldn't eat anything people had their hands in.

"She had her husband and her little boy there. One day her husband, Marty Melcher, was photographing the set with a movie camera that was making noises. Hitch gave him a look, and we never saw that camera again."

Ray Evans told me how he and Jay Livingston came to write the Oscar–winning "Que Será Será."

"We were called in to meet with Alfred Hitchcock. He said, "Gentlemen, Doris Day is in the movie, and I need a song for her. I don't know what kind of song I want, but if it has a foreign title, that would be relevant, and it should be a song a mother would sing to a child.

"We had the title, 'Que Será,' in our file. When we played what we wrote for Mr. Hitchcock, he said, 'Gentlemen, when I met you, I didn't know what kind of song I wanted. *That's* the kind of song I wanted!'"

"Doris Day didn't particularly *like* the song because she didn't think it was commercial. The song became the biggest hit that *she* ever had."

IN 1955, shortly after *Alfred Hitchcock's Mystery Magazine* had been licensed, Lew Wasserman met with CBS television executives, and Hitchcock was offered a television series. He would be the host, an idea he particularly liked.

He once told me he had "the heart of a performer," but the more Hitchcock went public, the more he went private. "I was given a part to play, a public image to cover my nudity.

"But I keep my cameo appearances short because I am an actor of limitations. I can only play myself."

Hitchcock formed a television company, Shamley Productions, to produce a weekly series of half-hour shows for CBS. Joan Harrison became executive producer. Later, Norman Lloyd became an associate producer. At a Valentine's Day party in 2000 in the Hollywood home of director Curtis Harrington, Lloyd talked with me about *Alfred Hitchcock Presents*.

"What we wanted were stories with suspense, a twist, and an overlay of humor. In the early days of the show, we favored short stories that had already been published. When we liked a story, we had it synopsized and Hitch had the final say. Once the story was approved, we brought in a writer, developed the show, and hired a director. Hitch himself directed about twenty. I did quite a few. Some other directors were Robert Altman, Arthur Hiller, and Sydney Pollack.

"Most people think Hitch wrote his lead-ins or just made them up as he went, but they were all written by Jimmy Allardice, who found his niche writing Hitch's voice. He could only work under pressure, just in time for when we needed it.

"Sometimes he'd write something we *knew* Hitch wouldn't do. But when Hitch read it, he was delighted. Jimmy Allardice had a genius for capturing Hitch's unique sense of humor."

Arthur Hiller told me his favorite Hitchcock story.

"When his longtime friend and producer Joan Harrison married mystery writer Eric Ambler, Hitchcock gave a party at Chasen's. He found an old menu from 1892, and had Chasen's re-create the eighteen-course meal.

"Much of the food was flown from England. The fish was Dover sole. It was a long, long dinner. Hitchcock seemed to enjoy it immensely.

"Every course had a different wine, and he seemed to empty every glass.

"At the end of the meal, Hitch rose, or he tried to. He had a lot of trouble getting up out of the chair, but it would have been embarrassing to offer him help, not only for Hitchcock, but for the person offering.

"Finally, he got to his feet. He was holding a legal-sized pad of lined yellow paper. He had six or seven pages covered with notes. He began to speak. The words were formal, but the delivery wasn't. His speech was so thick, you could hardly understand him.

"'We are here to honor Joan and Eric. They first met in London, and we are wishing,' etc. As he spoke, Hitch's speech got thicker and thicker.

"We were all very nervous, sitting on the edge of our seats, leaning forward, terribly embarrassed for him. We kept hoping he would stop. He was swaying. He actually was pitching forward.

"Suddenly, he straightened up, looked at the audience, and in absolutely perfect British English, clearly enunciated, totally sober, without any hint that he had had one drop to drink, he said:

"'I do hope they'll be very happy.'"

• • •

THE HALF-HOUR SHOWS were so successful, the program was expanded to an hour in 1962 and retitled *The Alfred Hitchcock Hour.*

Lloyd said that one of Hitchcock's prime rules for directing television was, "'Remember, it's a close medium.'

"Hitch believed it, and I agree. In television, you get in close as fast as you can. Another rule he had was 'to write with the camera.' He hated, 'photographing dialogue,' as he considered most directing after the silent films. We tried to deliver those twist endings visually."

The program's musical theme, Charles Gounod's "Funeral March of a Marionette," was chosen by Hitchcock. He had heard it in one of his favorite pictures, F. W. Murnau's *Sunrise.* When a musical soundtrack was added to the silent film in 1928, composer William Axt included it in his score.

The shows, which were shot at Universal's Revue Studios, were aired on CBS and NBC during their ten-year run. Among the stars who appeared on the program were Robert Redford, Joseph Cotten, Claude Rains, Vera Miles, Barbara Bel Geddes, Steve McQueen, Peter Lorre, and Robert Morley.

The most important star who emerged from the series, however, was Hitchcock himself. He became an instantly recognizable celebrity all over the world. Pat Hitchcock recalled being in Tahiti with her parents about one year after the debut of *Alfred Hitchcock Presents.* "The recognition and reception was what you might expect for Elvis Presley." Television had given him a satisfaction that he would otherwise have been denied.

Pat Hitchcock remembered: "Actually, his fame with the average person didn't come really until after the television series. Then he couldn't go anywhere without being recognized, and he had to be very careful about the cameos after the television series. He had to put his appearance in the beginning of the story, because people would see him on the screen and say, 'Oh, there he is!' and that would break any mood, so he did it very early on in the movie.

"It was an experience for my daughters when they were out for a drive with their grandfather. Whenever they stopped at a light, people in cars next to them would wave, and daddy would turn to my daughters and say, 'You certainly have a lot of friends.'"

Pat appeared on ten of the programs. "It seemed a good idea," Norman Lloyd said, "to have three generations of Hitchcocks on one show. So, in 1960, Hitch, Pat, and Mary, Hitch's oldest granddaughter, appeared in the episode called "The Schartz-Metterklume Method."

Because his own company, Shamley, produced the shows, the value of the properties later allowed him to convert it to stock of Universal-MCA, thus becoming one of the largest stockholders of that company, and a very wealthy man.

IN AUGUST 1955, Hitchcock returned to Warner Brothers for one picture. It was the film he had agreed to do without salary, for only a percentage of the profits, in return for being able to make *I Confess*.

"My fear of the police was a help in making *The Wrong Man*," Hitchcock told me. "I could empathize totally with our falsely accused hero, who was in the hands of the police. He was in their power and no one believed him, a terrible position for anyone to find himself in."

The Wrong Man was based on a true case of mistaken identity followed by tragic consequences. In 1953, a musician named Manny Balestrero was arrested in New York City for armed robberies that he did not commit. Before he was cleared, he suffered the indignities of loss of freedom and personal humiliation, resulting in his wife's mental breakdown. After the story appeared in *Life* magazine, the writer, Herbert Bream, sold a film treatment to Warner Brothers.

"In a way, it was 'The Man Who Knew Too Little,'" Hitchcock said. "The hero is the man-on-the-spot."

He asked John Michael Hayes to work on the treatment and screenplay of *The Wrong Man,* also without fee, but for a percentage of the profits. Hayes declined, and their four-picture relationship ended. Playwright Maxwell Anderson accepted *The Wrong Man* assignment.

After the opening of *The Trouble with Harry,* the successful launching of *Alfred Hitchcock Presents* on television, and the completion of a Far East promotional tour for Paramount, Hitchcock turned his attention to *The Wrong Man.* Anderson's script was not going as Hitchcock envisioned it, though he respected Anderson and was proud to have worked with him. He brought in Angus MacPhail to provide a more starkly realistic quality. Hitchcock, along with MacPhail, did extensive research in New York City, where the film was set.

"When I worked with Hitchcock," Henry Fonda told me, "the backings were so real, you'd walk into them because you thought they were three-dimensional."

Christopher Emmanuel "Manny" Balestrero (Henry Fonda) is a musician at the Stork Club. When his wife, Rose (Vera Miles), needs expensive dental work, he hopes to raise money on his life insurance. At the insurance company office, he is mistaken for a criminal who held them up twice, getting away with $71. Arrested, he is identified as the suspect in other holdups, and he is treated as if guilty.

He finds an inexperienced lawyer (Anthony Quayle), who is willing to defend him. The trial goes badly for Manny, but life is worse for Rose, who has a mental breakdown and has to be hospitalized.

The judge declares a mistrial, and they must start over again. Meanwhile, the real robber (Richard Robbins) is recognized by a detective on the case, and Manny is set free.

His wife, so mentally disturbed, no longer cares what happens.
They go to Florida. Two years later, she recovers.

Hitchcock and Alma had seen Vera Miles in a television drama, and believed she could be a star, even a replacement for Grace Kelly. He signed her to an exclusive five-year contract.

"Rose Balestrero," Hitchcock said, "had done her fashion shopping in a local basement store, so we didn't need Edith Head. We would just buy her wardrobe where the real person shopped. So Miss Miles wouldn't feel too deprived, we had Edith create a wardrobe for her to use on her promotional tour."

About his work on *The Wrong Man,* Henry Fonda told me, "I didn't really know Hitchcock after that one experience. As a director, he obviously knew just what he wanted.

"Hitchcock had a light touch. He didn't say much, but I felt the part, and I could see in his eyes he was satisfied with what I did. It was a part I could really get into. Tragedy had touched my own life with the death of Jane's and Peter's mother.

"*The Wrong Man* was based on a true story, which made it much more moving. My character was found innocent and he'd managed to stand up to everything he'd had to go through, but his wife didn't make it. It was something I sure could identify with. She broke down from it all, and it was clear to me he wasn't ever going to have the happy family life he'd had before. His life was ruined.

"I had no criticism at all of the way Hitchcock worked, and I never heard any from anyone of the cast or crew. Of course, I was never one to get into that kind of thing. I was always too deep into my part.

"When I was offered the part, I liked it right away, and I was pleased to be in a Hitchcock film. *The Wrong Man* wasn't typical Hitchcock, but as soon as I read it, I knew it would be good.

"I think I'm an instinctive actor. Anyway, that's how I would describe myself, but I don't try to analyze myself. My daughter says,

'I'm a Method actor,' and I say, 'If you say so,' because if I don't, she can talk about the Method for hours.

"I'm not really a very interesting person myself. I haven't ever done anything except be other people: Clarence Darrow, Justice Snow, Manny Balestrero. I'm all the parts I ever played, so I guess I'm Manny, too."

Fonda considered himself like the subjects he preferred to paint—still-life. One of his favorites among his own works was a group of three Mason jars.

"Hitchcock was a good artist," Fonda said. "I would like to have talked about art with him. Drawing and painting always meant a great deal to me. But we never quite made it to a personal relationship.

"He was pretty reserved, and I guess I am, too. He didn't waste a lot of words. Neither one of us knew how to step over our shyness without being afraid of tripping.

"Alfred Hitchcock was always a gentleman, and I would like to have done another picture with him, and to have known him better, but our paths didn't cross again."

Hitchcock did not do his usual cameo appearance for *The Wrong Man*. It was a true story with an element of tragedy, so the humorous reaction his appearance would have elicited was deemed inappropriate. Instead, he spoke seriously in an introduction to the film.

"ROMANTIC OBSESSION has always obsessed me," Hitchcock said. "Obsessions of all kinds are interesting, but for me, romantic obsession is the most fascinating."

For Hitchcock, the ideal setting for a story of romantic obsession was San Francisco. "The first time my father saw San Francisco," Pat Hitchcock told me, "he fell in love with it, and throughout his life, he only fell more deeply in love with it. He thought it was very like Paris. He always wanted to make a picture in San Francisco." Until

Vertigo, however, the closest he had come was Santa Rosa for *Shadow of a Doubt* and the Monterey coast for *Rebecca.*

Whenever the Hitchcocks were in the vicinity of San Francisco, which was as often as they could manage, Alma indulged in the luxury of having her hair done, with a manicure, at the chic red-doored Elizabeth Arden salon. Afterward, she enjoyed having her husband meet her so she could see the look on his face as she walked out with her fresh coiffure.

While he waited, Hitchcock would look at Gump's, buy some cigars at Dunhill, and visit the nearby Williams-Sonoma store, which offered the ultimate in French cooking tools, pots and pans, and kitchen appliances. Hitchcock enjoyed searching for ways to enhance food preparation in their kitchen, and usually bought more than he had intended.

Since he enjoyed the immediate gratification of taking his purchases away with him rather than having them sent, he and Alma carried all of the pots and pans, copper and otherwise, they could manage.

Vertigo was based on the French novel, *d'Entre les Mortes* ("Between the Deaths") by Pierre Boileau and Thomas Narcejac. Their earlier novel, *Diabolique,* had been successfully done by Henri-Georges Clouzot in 1952, and was one of Hitchcock's favorite films. Both stories concern a man and his mistress conspiring to kill his wealthy wife in a way that doesn't appear to be murder.

The first title considered for *Vertigo* was "From Among the Dead," and the setting was changed from Paris and Marseilles to San Francisco.

When I spoke with Clouzot about Hitchcock, the French director said: "He is very attentive to logic, but it is the logic of his characters, which is not everyone's logic. I admire him very much and am flattered when anyone compares a film of mine to his."

Maxwell Anderson, who had written *The Wrong Man* screenplay, wrote a treatment of the Boileau and Narcejac novel that he called "Listen, Darkling." Hitch and Alma found it unsatisfactory and brought in Alec Coppel, who had written *The Captain's Paradise*. Coppel's treatment included the opening chase across San Francisco rooftops and the livery stable in the background of the final revolving seduction scene. Finally, Samuel A. Taylor, who had grown up in San Francisco, wrote the definitive screenplay. He had written the successful Broadway play *Sabrina Fair,* and collaborated with Billy Wilder and Ernest Lehman on the movie version, *Sabrina.*

The character of Scottie's old college girlfriend Midge was Taylor's idea. "She saved Stewart the embarrassment of having to talk to himself, and added some depth and detail to the character of Scottie," he said.

Billy Wilder, who had made *Sabrina* with Taylor, particularly liked the film *Vertigo.* While in his nineties and suffering from vertigo, he told me, "Vertigo without Kim Novak is no fun."

In the novel, the hero's acrophobia is less important, and he continues to believe that Madeleine has been reincarnated even after he understands her part in the conspiracy and is responsible for her real death.

"What fascinated me about *Vertigo,*" Hitchcock said, "was the idea that the man is obsessed with turning the girl into what she *is* and is trying *not* to be."

In the film, as in the novel, John "Scottie" Ferguson (James Stewart) had studied law, but chose the more physically active life of a police detective.

Following a traumatic experience involving him and a policeman who falls to his death from a high building, Scottie develops acrophobia and is unable to remain on the police force. Being "a man of independent means," he recuperates during an early retirement.

Gavin Elster (Tom Helmore), a wealthy shipbuilder who is an

acquaintance from college days, approaches Scottie and asks
him to follow his beautiful wife, Madeleine (Kim Novak). He
fears she is going insane, maybe even contemplating suicide,
because she believes she is possessed by a dead ancestor. Scottie is skeptical, but agrees after he sees the beautiful Madeleine.

Scottie falls obsessively in love with Madeleine after he saves
her from attempted suicide. When she does kill herself by leap-
ing from a high church bell tower, Scottie can only look on
helplessly because his acrophobia prevents him from climbing
the stairs to save her. Afterward, he has a mental breakdown.

Eventually recovering, Scottie is unable to accept Madeleine's
death. He searches for her until he finds Judy, a tawdry salesgirl,
who physically resembles Madeleine. He makes Judy over into
Madeleine in appearance, buying her the same clothes
Madeleine wore and changing her hairstyle. He tries to love her
as if Madeleine had returned from the dead. Then, a pendant
exposes her as Madeleine.

She was Elster's mistress, whom he disguised as his wealthy
wife. It was part of a murder plot staged to look like a suicide.
Judy dies just as Madeleine did, falling from the same church
bell tower.

Visitors to Mission San Juan Bautista are disappointed not to find
the *Vertigo* bell tower. It had been removed in 1949 because of dry rot.
The bell tower seen in the film is actually a process shot superim-
posed on the real building.

An additional ending, never used, was filmed in case the studio
insisted on Elster being brought to justice.

In her apartment, Midge is listening to a radio news report about
Elster's imminent capture in France. When Scottie enters, she turns
off the radio. Without speaking, he walks to the window while she
pours him a drink. As Scottie contemplates Russian Hill at night, she
brings him the drink, then moves away, understanding his mood.

Vera Miles was to have played Madeleine and Judy, but there was a delay in filming because of Hitchcock's gall bladder operation. When he was ready, Miles, who was having a baby, was not. Kim Novak was Hitchcock's second choice.

I talked with her after the premiere of the restored version of *Vertigo* at New York's Ziegfeld Theater in 1996.

Kim Novak was under contract to Columbia, and Harry Cohn was the head of Columbia. She remembered being called into his office.

"He threw a script at me. 'Alfred Hitchcock wants you on loan-out,' he said, 'and I've agreed. I thought it would be good for your career.' Then he added, 'It's a terrible, terrible script.'

"I took it home and read it that night. Well, I totally disagreed with Harry Cohn. The next morning, I went to see him, and I was happy he didn't give me a chance to speak. He just said, 'It was lousy, wasn't it?'" Novak was loaned to Paramount by Columbia in exchange for James Stewart appearing with her in *Bell Book and Candle*.

"I never agreed much with Harry Cohn about anything, though I didn't say much in the early days. He was really right about one thing when he said working with Alfred Hitchcock would be good for my career. It was great, working with Hitch and with Jimmy, and I knew it was a wonderful part and wonderful picture, but it didn't have the immediate success I expected. Now, it's not just a part of my life, but it seems to have become a part of so many people's lives."

Novak observed a difference in the attitude over the years of the fans who saw the film when it first opened and those who had seen it several times over the years. "People who had seen it when it first opened, and there were not so many of them, asked me simpler questions, about something in it they didn't understand. Now, they don't ask me, they *tell* me about it. They've seen it more times than I have.

"Once I made the mistake of asking Hitch about my character's motivation, and he looked at me solemnly and said, 'Let's not probe too deeply into these matters, Kim. It's only a movie.'

"I loved it. He allowed me to lose myself in the character, in *both* of the characters. He gave me the freedom to be creative. The only thing I couldn't do was move away from that tree!

"Jimmy [Stewart] was the best. I thought of him as Scottie, because we were both so much in our characters. I liked playing two characters and finding both of them within me. I liked knowing their secrets, but I identified more with Judy.

"And who wouldn't be great in that coat?" Though sometimes actors and actresses can keep the clothing they wear in films, she hadn't asked for the white coat she wore in *Vertigo*. "Now it's the most famous coat in the history of movies," she sighed.

When I visited Edith Head at her home, I told her how much I liked the coat. She said that I was one of many, and that she received more fan mail for that coat than for any other design of hers in her entire career. Then, she gave me the original drawing of it.

Hitchcock specified that Madeleine should wear a gray suit. Novak told Head gray was not her color, not flattering to blondes. Novak wore that gray suit, however, which helps to define the character. Scottie tried to transform Judy into Madeleine by changing her brighter, tighter, inexpensive clothes to Madeleine's classical, less obvious style.

"His pleasure," Hitchcock said, "was dressing rather than undressing his love. Dressing Judy was really *un*dressing her. But Scottie can't ever *really* possess the woman in his mind because she's *only* in his mind.

"When Jimmy Stewart's character undressed Madeleine, it's not necessary to show it happening. The imagination of the audience goes into play when they see her garments hanging up to dry.

"I would, however, have preferred to make the image of his undressing even clearer, not by showing it, but by showing more specific undergarments drying—a brassiere here, a pair of panties there—but it wasn't permitted."

Judy's loose hair contrasted with Madeleine's upswept whirlpool coiffure, which incorporated titles designer Saul Bass's swirling

Vertigo effect. These hairstyles, which played a major part in the film, were the creation of Hitchcock with Nellie Manley, who had done Vilma Banky's hair in the 1920s and was still working with Paramount.

Audrey Hepburn told me that a part she would like to have played was that of Madeleine and Judy. "It was very Pygmalion," she said, "like Liza Doolittle in *My Fair Lady,* a cockney ragamuffin who's taught to be a 'Lai-die.'"

"Women don't even *want* to be called 'ladies' anymore," Hitchcock observed. "Have you noticed? Nowadays a lady is a woman who waits until she's alone with you in the back seat of a taxi before she unbuttons your fly."

Bernard Herrmann considered music an essential part of the film. "But the music can't stand apart from the movie," he told me. "Its function is to set the mood and give continuity to the separate strips of film."

Hitchcock liked Elster's office so much, he asked Henry Bumstead to design and build a room just like it in his Bellagio Road home.

"He wanted to do this *Vertigo* den for all of his electronic equipment," Bumstead told me, "and I did it like the shipbuilder's office. I did it in pico pine, and we put a carpet in there that came from Marrakech from when we were there for *The Man Who Knew Too Much.* I hoped he was pleased with it, but he never said so.

"One morning I was going to work, and a horn honked. It was Alma outside the production office. She was sitting there in their little Ford Mustang, and she thanked me for how wonderful the room turned out. She said, 'Did Hitch ever say anything to you?'

"I said, 'He's never said a word.' Well, I won't tell you what she said.

"I said goodbye to her and got up to my office. The secretary said, 'Mr. Hitchcock wants to see you, immediately.'

"I went down to the office, and he laughed about it, and made a joke of it, more or less, and he said it turned out beautifully. And it did.

"Whenever I went to his place in Santa Cruz, he carried my bag up to the room. Can you imagine? But then, the minute I left and drove away, I was an employee again."

The interior of Ernie's, the San Francisco restaurant that is featured in *Vertigo,* was rebuilt at Paramount. "Ernie's was entirely a set," Bumstead said. "I was able to find the same wallpaper, and we had their dishes sent down from San Francisco. Even the Gotti brothers that owned Ernie's, they were in the picture.

"For two or three years after that, everybody came into Ernie's, and they wanted to sit where Kim Novak and Jimmy Stewart sat. No matter where they were put, they thought they were sitting at the same table."

After *Vertigo* was edited, Hitchcock was dissatisfied with an important shot in Ernie's. "Kim Novak passes Jimmy Stewart for the first time," associate producer Herbert Coleman told me. "She sort of glances at him as if she knows why he's there. That would've given the whole plot away. Hitch was going away on vacation, so he told me to reshoot it. This meant rebuilding the Ernie's set and bringing back Kim Novak and some background people in to reshoot the scene.

"Not all of the set was there, so I had to shoot in on a longer lens to hide what was missing in the background. When Hitch returned, he said, 'You shot it on the wrong lens.' He knew right away." The second shot of Novak at Ernie's was used in the film, but the first shot, with Novak smiling at the camera, can be seen in the original trailer.

A scene to which Hitchcock gave great consideration and one of the few about which he was ever indecisive was Judy's voice-over admission, that she is Madeleine and an accomplice to the murder of Elster's wife. Persuaded by Joan Harrison that the scene should be deleted in order to maintain the mystery until the end, Hitchcock ordered the film be released without it. An important theater chain owner, Barney Balaban, had seen the original version, and he liked it so well that he insisted the missing footage be restored. So did Alma, and the scene returned.

Henry Bumstead told me that Hitchcock specified Scottie's apartment should be in view of Coit Tower, a San Francisco landmark, both for interiors and exteriors. Bumstead designed it without asking any questions. Years later, when he was working on *Family Plot,* he asked Hitchcock why.

"Coit Tower is a phallic symbol," Hitchcock explained.

Hitchcock obtained composer Norman O'Neill's manuscript score from the original London stage production of *Mary Rose* and gave it to Bernard Herrmann as a guide to the emotional mood he wished to create through music in *Vertigo.* Both stories shared the theme of a beautiful woman apparently returning from the dead. *Vertigo* resembles the Orpheus legend, with the hero unable to resist looking back at his beloved Eurydice, even at the price of her second life.

When *Vertigo* opened, it received some unfavorable reviews and audience attendance was disappointing. The picture was not rereleased until 1984. By that time, the film had begun to deteriorate noticeably. Universal Pictures began a meticulous restoration project directed by James C. Katz and Robert A. Harris. They produced a new "mint" version of the film which cost more than $1 million to restore. Their contribution is so great that they head closing credits, wedding them to *Vertigo* forever.

Since its original release in 1958, *Vertigo* has, in a sense, itself returned from the dead, to become one of Hitchcock's most beloved films.

As work on *Vertigo* was being completed and promotion about to begin, and Hitchcock was thinking about *North by Northwest,* Alma was diagnosed with cervical cancer. Her chance of survival was viewed pessimistically by her doctors, and Hitchcock's world was in turmoil. The operation, however, was completely successful.

• • •

HAVING COMPLETED HIS five-picture deal with Paramount, Hitch-cock accepted an offer from M-G-M to develop a property they owned, *The Wreck of the Mary Deare*. Hitchcock, however, had other ideas.

Without informing M-G-M, Hitchcock and writer Ernest Lehman began working on what would become *North by Northwest*. When M-G-M found out, they were delighted. They believed they would be getting two Hitchcock pictures instead of one.

For years he had wanted to use Mount Rushmore as a setting, and *North by Northwest* was the picture that could accommodate it. Since he envisioned the climax as a chase across the carved faces of the presidents, the screenplay was at first called "The Man in Lincoln's Nose."

New York advertising executive Roger Thornhill (Cary Grant) is kidnapped by a gang of spies led by Philip Vandamm (James Mason), who believe Thornhill is CIA agent George Kaplan. Thornhill escapes, but must find Kaplan in order to clear himself of a murder it is believed he committed.

Following Kaplan to Chicago as a fugitive from justice, Thornhill is helped by beautiful Eve Kendall, who is really a member of Vandamm's gang. In Chicago, she delivers a message to Thornhill that almost costs him his life when he is chased across a cornfield by a crop-dusting plane.

Thornhill finds out from a CIA official (Leo G. Carroll) that Kaplan does not exist and Eve is a CIA agent. Thornhill has un-wittingly endangered her life. To save her, he goes to Rapid City, South Dakota, pretending to be Kaplan.

Before the spies flee the country with state secrets, a con-frontation in which Thornhill is shot by Eve is staged to prove her loyalty to Vandamm. Later, the trick is exposed by one of

Vandamm's henchmen (Martin Landau). Thornhill arrives in time
to rescue Eve in a chase over the presidents' faces on Mount
Rushmore.

The scene moves to Thornhill pulling Eve up into an upper
berth sleeper on their honeymoon as the train enters a tunnel.

This ending was considered pornographic to Hitchcock.

Hitchcock makes his cameo appearance at the end of the credits
when he rushes to catch a bus and misses it. The beginning of the
credits, designed by Saul Bass, is over a crisscrossing grid of lines that
become the glass skyscrapers of Manhattan. This was inspired by the
opening credits of F. W. Murnau's *Sunrise*, which begins with crisscrossing lines that become a European train station.

Mount Rushmore is located in the Black Hills of South Dakota.
The sixty-foot-high faces of Presidents Washington, Jefferson, Lincoln, and Theodore Roosevelt were carved from granite one and a
half billion years old, older than the Alps or the Himalayas. The carving took fourteen years with about four hundred workers led by the
artist Gutzon Borglum, who designed, promoted, supervised, and
sculpted this extraordinary work. His vision was made possible
because the idea had been born in the 1920s boom, when anything
seemed possible, and completed during the 1930s Depression when
nothing seemed possible, but the U.S. government was anxious to
provide money for public works projects that created jobs.

Himself a person of innate talent as both an artist and an engineer,
Hitchcock admired the massive sculpting achievement of Mount
Rushmore's faces and the prodigal engineering feat it involved. He
said that he particularly respected the concern for the safety of the
four hundred workers, with only two accidents resulting in minor
injuries during the entire fourteen years the work required.

Hitchcock's original plan was for Cary Grant to be chased up into
Lincoln's nostril. Then Grant would sneeze. Theoretically, this

would have been possible, since the nose is twenty feet long. "The humor was too full-blown for the studio executives," Hitchcock quipped.

The great success of *North by Northwest* caused renewed interest in Mount Rushmore, and brought millions of new visitors to the area. Many wanted to climb the presidents' faces, as had Cary Grant and Eva Marie Saint. They didn't realize that the actors had never climbed the carved faces in South Dakota, but rather a meticulously reconstructed scale-model Hollywood set. The Department of the Interior would not permit a chase on the real Mount Rushmore, not just because it could be interpreted as disrespectful, but because the faces had to be safeguarded from any possibility of damage.

Hitchcock was not disappointed; he always preferred the studio. Eva Marie Saint preferred the safety of the studio as well, and Cary Grant told me that he did, too, though adding, "I was grateful that it hadn't become necessary for me to take a stand for cowardice."

Saint recalled injuring her arm on M-G-M's Mount Rushmore.

"It was made of some kind of rubberized material that made it look like rock. It was very, very high, but I had no problem with heights. I went up to the top, and then I got a little nervous. I saw them putting these mattresses all around in a circle where we were climbing. I looked down. 'My God! One of us could fall.' So, boy, did I hold on to Cary Grant's hand! I still have a tiny, tiny little mark I got on my left arm.

"I'm always fascinated by what they're able to do in the studio. When I'm running away from that house on Mount Rushmore, and I think they're going to take me in the plane, I look back at the house, and it wasn't the house at all. It was just a scrim with a light."

"The first script I got was called 'The Man in Lincoln's Nose,'" Martin Landau told me. "Usually, the script comes to you with a letter that says, 'Check out this role.' This one just said, 'Read this. Alfred Hitchcock wants to have a meeting with you.' So, I read it, and

I knew it wasn't the Cary Grant part nor the James Mason part. It could have been one of the henchmen, but I had no idea what role I was going for when I went to see him.

"I went over to M-G-M. We had a chat, and he walked me around and showed me the storyboards of the movie. I literally saw the movie before I *did* it.

"Leonard was written as a henchman, but I chose to play him as a gay character, because Leonard felt the need to get rid of Eve Kendall. I felt it would be very interesting if he were jealous of her beyond just being a henchman. But this was 1958, so I played it very subtly.

"Hitchcock had seen me in a play, *Middle of the Night,* in which I played a very macho, egocentric jerk, and he cast me as Leonard. It's something that impressed me, and one day I drummed up the courage to say, 'How in the world did you see me in that play and think of me for this role?'

"He said, 'Martin, you have a circus going on inside of you. Obviously, if you can do that part in the theater, you can do this little trinket.'

"I remember going up to him after he whispered something to Cary Grant, and to Eva Marie, and to James, and he passed me by. I'd been working on the film for several weeks, and I walked up to him and said, 'Is there anything you want to tell me, Mr. Hitchcock?' In the theater, directors told you a lot. He had never said a word to me about my performance, and I felt a little left out. He said, 'I'll only tell you if I don't like what you're doing.'

"I felt he loved what I was doing. The only one who didn't love it was James Mason, who thought I was casting a kind of aspersion on his character.

"I never discussed it with anybody, but I chose to think that James's character was bisexual, and that my character was gay, but I think James didn't like what I did. There was a line that was added for me by Ernie Lehman. I say, 'Call it my woman's intuition.'

"At first, Hitchcock asked me to wear my own clothes for the picture. I said, 'The clothes *I* wear are not the clothes *Leonard* would wear.' To Hitchcock directly I said this. We got along very well.

"Then, Hitchcock wanted me to be better dressed than Cary's character, well tailored and neat. So, who does he take me to? A tailor on Wilshire Boulevard where he had the suits I wore in the film made to Cary's specifications, unbeknownst to Cary.

"We picked out fabric together. There was a blue suit. There was a gray suit.

"We're in Chicago, shooting the film, and I'm not working that day. I'm at the hotel. Hitch calls me from the La Salle Street Station, and he tells me he wants me to wear one of the suits to see how it looks in the environment. So, I put on the suit that I wear in the scene and go to the La Salle Street Station.

"There's a huge area of the station cordoned off. I wait my turn behind the barricade.

"I get tapped on the shoulder by Cary Grant's man, an English guy with a cockney accent. He says [cockney accent], 'Excuse me, but Mr. Grant would like to know where you got that suit.'

"I had not met Cary Grant up to now. He'd spotted this suit in the crowd. He said, 'There's only two tailors in the world that make a suit like that. One's in Beverly Hills and one's in Hong Kong.'

"Now, I'm aware of what's going on. He thinks I'm an extra from Chicago, and he spotted the suit. Obviously, no one in Chicago is as well dressed as Leonard.

"Shortly after that, I met Cary, who sort of looked at me, but looked at the suit with more clarity. Even the angle of the lapels, a little cutaway there, was made to his specifications.

"He would occasionally, when I wore a suit, say, 'Martin, let me try on your jacket. Let's see if it fits me.' Because I didn't have a thing in my contract saying that I would get the wardrobe, which he did. And I think he wanted my wardrobe as well. That suit fit him quite well, and obviously my character had more clothing changes than his character did.

"I never saw the suits after the film. I have a feeling they went a certain way. Whenever I met Cary, I never knew whether he was wearing one of my suits or not."

At the Beekman Place apartment in New York City of Milton Goldman, James Mason spoke with me about Alfred Hitchcock and his experience working on *North by Northwest.* "Hitchcock's efforts and genius went into preplanning and rapport with his technicians. We actors were typecast and chosen because of our track records that had shown him we could carry off the part he wanted delineated. He preferred that we not be overly creative, which meant anything that interfered with his camera and what he had in mind for it.

"He was even in any crisis. I remember at some critical moment with Eva's character, he said to her, 'My dear, it's only a moo-vie.'

"Occasionally, we would chat about the early British studios— Islington, Gainsborough. I knew quite a bit about that from my wife, Pamela, and Hitchcock enjoyed that subject.

"I remember this young actor, Martin Landau, who had an interesting, rather small part, though it's one people remember well. He had obviously worked a great deal on his lines, and he told me he felt he had the part down. He was rather a Method actor, which wasn't what Hitchcock preferred. Anyway, Hitchcock had something else up his sleeve. He shot everything out of order, leaving no room for any ad-libs, and there weren't any. But it *was* an exemplary performance by Landau, and it was obvious how much Hitchcock liked it.

"I have been asked many times about homosexual overtones and undertones between my character and Landau's Leonard. Well, of course. Obviously. But it was one-sided. Leonard had a crush on me which my character enjoyed, even his discomfiture, but my Vandamm had no homosexual tendencies, with eyes and whatever else, only for the Eva Marie Saint character, Eve.

"There is a scene in which Eve is supposed to board a plane, and

I'm supposed to follow her. I received the most direction I'd had for any scene I'd done for Hitchcock. He walked up beside me and spoke in that unique voice with its pear-shaped tones and his careful enunciation, a sort of posh cockney.

"'James,' he said, 'when she goes to board the plane, I want you to count to three, and then follow her.'

"I looked like I was trying to comprehend his meaning. My brow furrowed. I said, 'You mean three? But what if I don't have the right feeling on three, but rather I feel it on two? Or what if . . .' I saw the look on his face. I had him hooked. Absolutely hooked. Then he smiled. He'd realized I was putting him on.

"Cary was a very serious person, not the character he played. He would be there waiting, clutching his script as though his life depended on it until the last possible second. Then, he would step into his part, confident, flippant, and casual, appearing to be making it up as he went along."

Cary Grant had suggested Sophia Loren, with whom he had had an affair, as perfect for the part of Eve Kendall. Hitchcock didn't agree. "Miss Loren was not the right blonde."

"Hitchcock never liked to go on location," art director Robert Boyle told me. "But on *North by Northwest,* we actually used Grand Central Station rather than constructing it on the set. The amount of light we had to pour into that station almost broke M-G-M. It was usually easier to 'paint' a location on glass."

Bernard Herrmann called the film "a picaresque romp." As he told me, "The opening music, a fandango, anticipates the crazy dance Cary Grant is about to do across America. The final chase across Mount Rushmore was choreographed in the editing room to this fandango."

North by Northwest's most famous scene, that of the crop duster attack on Cary Grant, has no music at all. "Silence is a sound, too, for the composer, just as white is a color for the painter," Herrmann said.

It was Herrmann who introduced his friend Ernest Lehman to

Hitchcock. "Hitch was looking for a writer to work with him on *The Wreck of the Mary Deare*," Herrmann told me. "I thought they would hit it off very well."

Eva Marie laughed when I asked her if she thought Eve and Roger Thornhill had a happy life together after the film ended.

"Oh, definitely! Oh, yes! Or I wouldn't have *done* the film!

"I love where she explains herself in that scene where we have all the trees between us. Hitch wouldn't cut it when the studio said it was too long.

"If you cut it, you never would have known about Eve Kendall. It's the only place where she truly exposes herself.

"Cary was dear to work with. He said, 'Now, Eva Marie, you don't have to cry in this movie. No more "sink parts" for you. We're just going to have fun.' He said that the first day. I'd been doing serious films like *On the Waterfront* and *Hatful of Rain*."

Saint characterized James Mason as "wonderful, but so sinister in his part! His character was such a mean guy!

"Everybody got along so well. There wasn't a diva among us. Certainly not Hitchcock.

"During the final chase, when my scarf gets caught on a branch, that wasn't planned, just a mistake but we stuck with it. It was a good mistake.

"Something we had to change on the *20th Century* dining car was my line, which went from 'I never make love on an empty stomach' to 'I never discuss love on an empty stomach.' I had to 'loop' that. Can you imagine?

"I remember reading the script for the first time and thinking, 'I don't come in until page fifty-eight. What *is* this?' And then, I reread it. It's not *On the Waterfront*. It doesn't all have to make sense."

Between takes of the auction house scene, Hitchcock noticed Saint standing there in her elegant cocktail dress drinking coffee from a plastic cup. "Hitch was horrified, and I didn't know what I did wrong. He said, 'Eva Marie, there are so many people on the set. I don't want my leading lady wearing a beautiful $3,500 frock and drinking coffee out of a Styrofoam cup.' He had me put it down, and then had them put my coffee into a china cup on a china saucer. I thought, 'I should have known better.'" Hitchcock believed that she shouldn't break the illusion in front of other people, and not in front of herself, either.

When he was dissatisfied with some of the dresses M-G-M had designed for her, he said, "We must go to Bergdorf." He took her shopping at Bergdorf Goodman, New York's fashionable department store, where she tried on the most expensive outfits. "I told him that was the first and last time I had a sugar daddy.

"He picked out every piece of jewelry, every earring. He had a woman looking in Chicago for a stone to match a stone that I had.

"Sydney Guilaroff did the hair, and so many women through the years have said, 'Oh, it's such an easy bob.' It looks easy, but that's the whole idea. You think you can do it at home, but no. I said, 'I'll do anything to be this lady.' And so, he would do my hair during lunch, and we'd be eating our sandwiches over the hot iron.

"I loved it that Hitchcock cared so much—about Eve Kendall."

Not all of the clothes were bought at Bergdorf Goodman. The black dress with the red roses, that was Bergdorf. I loved that one. Everybody asks me if I kept it. But movie clothes were like maternity clothes for me. After you have the baby, that is *it!*

"Eve Kendall was the best money could buy, and her clothes had to reflect this.

"Hitch knew where you were going to sit, like in the auction scene. He knew I would be in the middle, Mason on one side, Cary on the other. You didn't wander around wondering. I never looked at a storyboard. We trusted him, and you felt you were the only person to play that part, because he saw you as that character.

"And he was always dressed up. You know, even the crew wore suits!"

There was a story of Saint blushing during her first scenes with

Cary Grant because as a girl the actor had been one of her idols. "No," she said, "I liked Claude Rains when I was a little girl. And Charles Boyer, and Fred Astaire. I hate when they make up things.

"About five years ago, they had the Hitchcock ladies interviewed together at a broadcasters convention in Pasadena, all of us who were around who had acted in his films. In the middle of it, I said, 'I really feel like we've all been married to the same man. We're the Hitchcock widows.'"

A young, very young, aspiring actress was taken shopping by Alfred Hitchcock. He wasn't, as Eva Marie Saint had joked, her sugar daddy, but rather, her real daddy. Pat Hitchcock recalled:

"Beginning when I was twelve or thirteen, my father took me shopping for my clothes, usually without my mother. He had very definite ideas for me, as he did for my mother and his leading ladies. I can't say I agreed with all of his selections for me. His taste for me was conservative. He had a tailored point of view, which I wasn't too mad about at the time. Skirts, blouses, and sweaters. He liked slacks, too, very much. I wasn't totally thrilled, but I wish I had all of those clothes now. He had a wonderful sense of what would look best on me, of what was appropriate to my personality, and comfortable."

Hitchcock admired Audrey Hepburn, and she was anxious to work with him. She had agreed to be in a film he was preparing, *No Bail for the Judge,* until she learned that she was going to be raped in a violent scene. Her character was a judge's daughter who pretends to be a prostitute in order to clear her father of murder.

"I had a responsibility to *The Nun's Story,* which I had just done," Hepburn told me, "and I owed it to Mr. [Fred] Zinnemann, who was a great director, not to do anything that would tarnish that film."

Samuel Taylor had written a screenplay and Laurence Harvey had been cast as her co-star. Then, she found out she was going to have a baby, and the project was abandoned.

• • •

"A WOMAN WROTE to me that she had a problem," Alfred Hitchcock told me. "Her daughter had seen the man murdered in the bathtub in *Diabolique.* So, she wouldn't take a bath. Then, she went to *Psycho,* and after that, she wouldn't take a shower. The woman asked me what she should do about her daughter.

"Well, I didn't waste a moment. I sent her a telegram saying, 'Send her to the dry cleaner.'"

"After Alfred Hitchcock, I became a 'psycho' for the rest of my life," Anthony Perkins told me. "Whenever I go into the store, or drive into a gas station, or walk on the streets, or go into a restaurant, I hear people saying, 'Look, there's Norman Bates.'

"Just one thing," he added. "When you write about me, could you please get it right? Tony Perkins, *not* Norman Bates."

Hitchcock said, "Anthony Perkins was marvelous, so perfect in the part that it may have damaged his career, and I may have done him harm."

Perkins had met Hitchcock only once before they began filming. "I signed before I ever saw a script," he told me. "I just wanted to work with Alfred Hitchcock. I was told I'd have the most important part, but I would have accepted *any* part to be in a Hitchcock film. When we met, Hitchcock told me, 'You *are* the film.' I didn't quite understand what he meant. I found out soon enough.

"I had heard something about the story, but not much. Everything was very hush-hush. I remember we all had to swear an oath that we wouldn't say anything to anyone about the story. Then, just before *Psycho* came out, one person was careless. Fortunately the picture was close to release, and it didn't do any harm. The person let it slip that I wore a dress in the film.

"Hitchcock was furious, though he kept his calm demeanor.

"I told Hitch I was tired of being a young romantic lead, and I wanted to do more interesting parts; but I was a little worried about playing a homicidal transvestite. It seemed to me that there was some risk to my career in taking on a part like that. I asked Hitch what he thought, and he just said, 'Why don't you give it a try? *I* would.'

"Martin Balsam and I had this scene together. We're talking it and rehearsing together, and we figured out that it would work much better if we overlapped our lines. Just as we were about to shoot the scene, I saw the storyboard, and realized we wouldn't be able to do it overlapping because we were both in close-ups. I'd been told that the storyboards were inviolate, and that he'd already made the movie in his head before he came to the set. But I thought I'd try anyway.

"I said, 'Hitch, Marty and I have been rehearsing our lines, and we thought it might go better if we overlapped our lines.'

"Hitch said, 'Try it.'

"He listened, and then he dropped the storyboard into a wastebasket. So much for anyone saying he wasn't open to suggestions."

"An example of where you need to storyboard," Hitchcock said, "is the man coming up the stairs to make sure that you get the contrast in the size of the image." He was referring to Martin Balsam's character, Arbogast, on his way to Mrs. Bates's bedroom, when the detective is seen from the front and from high above.

Hitchcock was open to other suggestions from Perkins. "It was my idea to be munching candy," Perkins continued. "Since my character has a line about eating like a bird, Hitch suggested candy corn.

"I told Hitch I really felt the character of Norman, and would it be all right if I wore my own clothes?

"He said, 'Fine.'"

Assistant director Hilton Green remembered Perkins as generally keeping to himself. "He was always private. Polite, pleasant, but kind of a loner. He asked me to have someone let him know five or ten minutes before he was to be called. Then, he'd go into his trailer, and when he came out, five or ten minutes later, he came out Norman Bates."

Anthony Perkins had a theory about why Alfred Hitchcock chose not to make *Psycho* in color.

"Hitch really loved Clouzot's *Diabolique*. I think it was one of the reasons he made *Psycho* in black and white."

Hitchcock had a different explanation.

"I do not like to see blood in life or on the screen. I made *Psycho* in black and white because I knew I did not want to show all of that red blood in the white bathroom."

Another reason was he wanted to keep costs down and to be able to use his TV production unit, which was accustomed to shooting in black and white.

Hitchcock continued. "It was important to have the biggest star we could have for the role of Marion Crane for the element of surprise, because no one would expect us to kill off our star so early in the film."

Janet Leigh was his first choice for Marion Crane. He told her that her part would be enlarged and made more sympathetic, if she agreed to do it.

"He explained to me that my death so early in the film was going to be a great shock to the audience," Leigh told me. "It was to me.

"It wasn't a very big part, but I was told it would be written up for me, if I took it. I grabbed it, and the part was made bigger.

"I knew right away that it was going to be a very good picture. Something special. But who could have imagined what it became?

"He said something to me before we did it. Then, he didn't say much of anything else during shooting. He said he would stop me if I did it wrong. He didn't want too little or too much, and he expected me to come up with nuances. We had a wonderful working relationship.

"I didn't need to ask what my motivation was. It was passion. That's a pretty good motivation, I'd say.

"He made me so aware of the power of imagination. I always took it for granted. There had to be something that the audience has to imagine in a characterization and they'll never forget what *they* put in.

"He only told me about 'position,' and if I was off-base. He said,

'You can do pretty much what you want.' There was a very nice meeting of the minds. There was this understanding that he appreciated what we were doing, and we knew what he was doing. We knew the rules, and we abided and we didn't argue, because it made sense.

"Saul Bass did a storyboard for the shower scene, and that was what was followed. It was perfectly planned, but it still took a week of standing in a shower. It was a drenching experience. The shower scene was a baptism to wash away Marion's crime."

Hilton Green recalled the shower scene from the other side of the curtain: "That was a tough scene for Janet. I mean, to be in the water for so long. Although she was covered, it was still not very pleasant.

"We shot, I think, five days. She was in the shower every day for most of it. Of course, the water was heated, but it wore on you after a while. She'd have time between shots, but it was very difficult."

Actually, neither Janet Leigh nor Anthony Perkins was there for the famous forty-five seconds of slashing. Leigh's body double took her place for the murder, and Perkins was in New York doing a play.

The scene had seventy-eight setups, some lasting less than a second. Though the body double was nude, nothing censorable was ever shown, and the knife was never seen to penetrate her body, though the illusion was that it had.

"If you allow the audience to imagine what's happening rather than see what's happening, that's what stays with them," Leigh continued. "That's what Alfred Hitchcock believed. The whole point being the manipulation of the audience, and that's what a magician does, and that's exactly what he did.

"After the film, we were friends, and we knew each other socially. We didn't double-date, we're not in the same generation, obviously, but we had rapport. If we went to dinner parties, they would always put us at the same table because it was mutually enjoyable.

"At his seventy-fifth birthday party that they had at Chasen's, everybody in town who was anybody was invited. There were the klieg lights and the red carpet, and there was a receiving line with the

Wassermans and the [Jules] Steins and the Hitchcocks. He'd spotted my husband, Bob, and me coming along, and as soon as he got to me, he leaned down and whispered to us the dirtiest story that we'd ever heard. We were in the aisles laughing, and people were trying to figure out what was happening. Everybody was craning their neck. 'What the hell is going on?' they were wondering."

Leigh characterized Hitchcock as "an imp, a mischievous pixie, and a genius." Her only regret was that she could never again appear in a Hitchcock film. "Hitch told me, 'Audiences will immediately think of *Psycho*, and that wouldn't be fair to the new picture or your character.'"

Psycho was Patricia Hitchcock's last feature film, though she continued to appear on television.

"I had mixed feelings when Pat chose marriage and family as her primary life, and her career and acting only as secondary," Hitchcock told me. "I thought she was a talented actress. I would never have cast her in three films and numerous television programs if I hadn't, but Mrs. H. was happy because she thought it would be a happier life for our daughter.

"The Madame was a romantic. Though I tried not to let it show, I suppose I am one, too. So it was natural our daughter would also be one of those.

"I did miss her when she left our house."

PSYCHO WAS BASED ON a novel by Robert Bloch, a contributor to the TV series. The novel was inspired by an actual Wisconsin serial killer, and the screenplay was written by Joseph Stefano.

> Marion Crane (Janet Leigh) steals $40,000 to start a new life with her lover, Sam Loomis (John Gavin). Then, in a remote motel, she is murdered in the shower after she had decided to return the money. The motel's owner, Norman Bates (Anthony Perkins), an amateur taxidermist, thinks his mentally ill mother

is responsible, so he puts everything, including the money, into Marion's car and sinks it in a nearby swamp.

When Marion's sister Lila (Vera Miles) and Sam search for Marion, private detective Milton Arbogast (Martin Balsam) appears. He has been hired to get the money back in exchange for all charges against her being dropped. He tells them Marion stayed at the Bates Motel.

Later, Arbogast is stabbed to death in the Bates house. Not hearing from him, Sam and Lila investigate. They believe Norman has the money. Lila searches the house, looking for his mother. When Lila sees Norman approaching, she hides in the fruit cellar. There, she finds Mrs. Bates—a mummified corpse embalmed by Norman.

A crazed Norman, dressed like his mother, rushes at her wielding a knife, but Sam disarms him.

A psychiatrist explains that Norman became both mother and son after he murdered his mother and her lover. Now, the mother side of him has taken over completely.

In a cell, Norman, now his mother, smiles a skull-like smile as she regards a fly on her hand and says, "Why, I wouldn't even harm a fly."

Draining the swamp, the police find other victims.

"For the opening love scenes," Janet Leigh said, "I wore a white bra and white half slip. After I stole the money and was off to Sam to show him what I'd done for him, I wore the black bra and black half slip. Mr. Hitchcock wanted to show Marion Crane as having both good and evil within her."

Leigh told me she would appreciate my making it clear that not only were these underclothes bought over-the-counter, because Hitchcock instructed it, but that it was also what *she* wanted. Someone wrote that she had wanted made-to-order lingerie, "which was ridiculous," Leigh said, "since I never wore made-to-order lingerie. Why would *that* be the moment I wanted to?

"Hitch was particularly anxious that I purchase a popular brand, so that women would recognize their own brassiere, and identify with me. It happened that my own brand was a *very* popular model."

The opening scene shows lovers Janet Leigh and John Gavin in bed, making love during her lunch break from the real estate office where she works.

"In real life, we knew each other casually," Leigh told me, "and there we were in our first scene, hopping into bed in front of a lot of people. Mr. Hitchcock did more takes than usual, so I knew we weren't giving him what he wanted.

"He called me over and very discreetly, so no one else heard, whispered to me, 'I think you and John could be more passionate. Would you please try it and see how it works out.'

"I went back and wondered what he had said when he spoke to John. I thought perhaps he'd put it somewhat differently in more specific terms when he coached him. I didn't know what to expect.

"I went back to bed with John, determined to give my all to ardor.

"It was only much later that I realized Hitchcock's mischief was at work, and I'd been had.

"When I asked John how Mr. Hitchcock had instructed him, and I said I didn't want him to leave out the lurid details, John told me Mr. Hitchcock hadn't said a word to him about our love scene.

"I understood immediately then that was how Mr. Hitchcock got what he wanted from me, which was to show that my character, Marion, wanted her lover more, very much more, than he wanted her. Mr. Hitchcock wanted me to be the one who was then more aggressive.

"At one point in bed, John said to me rather urgently, 'Janet, stop! You're getting me excited.'

"It was a pretty sensual scene, I think."

• • •

COMPOSER BERNARD HERRMANN said, "Originally Hitch told me, 'Write whatever you like, but please, no music for the shower.' He was adamant, but I felt music was needed.

"When the music was recorded, and we were dubbing the film and got to the murder scenes, we ran the scenes without music. Hitch was unhappy. I suggested he listen to the same scenes with music. He said, 'But I thought we had agreed not to have any.' I said, 'Sure, we can do it that way, but at least listen to what I've written.' So we ran it with the music, and he said, 'We must have the music, of course.'

"I said, 'But you said you were against it.'

"He said, 'A mere importuning, my dear boy,' which roughly translated meant he could admit when he was wrong."

Psycho was filmed at Revue television studios at Universal in five weeks during 1959 at a cost of $850,000. Three of the principal actors Hitchcock wanted to use were under contract to Paramount, the releasing company, and available for reasonable sums. Vera Miles, who played Marion Crane's sister, Lila, was still filling out her five-year contract with Hitchcock. Herrmann received his usual fee, but compensated by scoring the film for strings alone.

Assistant director Hilton Green described for me how Hitchcock merged television and feature film techniques to shoot *Psycho.*

"Mr. H. decided he wanted to make a low-budget feature with his television crew. The difference between working on television and a feature was like night and day. When he was doing a feature, everything was very precise. In television, he didn't have time. He had a great knack of being able to make very simple shots and get it done, rather than going into complicated camera movements and shots which he did on features.

"On *Psycho,* I would say 75 or 85 percent of everything was planned more carefully than you would for a television show. To prepare for a television show, you'd show up the day before, and we'd walk the sets together, making sure everything was okay. And that was it. Then, he'd come in and you'd shoot the two days or three days.

"He sent me to Phoenix, Arizona, for *Psycho*. That's where Marion Crane's office was. I had to meet people who worked in an office like hers and visit where she would live, and photograph closets of the clothes of young women who had jobs like hers. Then I drove the route she would take to go up to central California. I laid it all out and came back. I mean, that's how much research we would do. Altogether different from a television show.

"Mr. H. would cut in the camera. I mean, it wasn't any guesswork of lining it up. It made my job very easy.

"It was very difficult to do the scene when Mrs. Bates is discovered in the fruit cellar. The big problem was to cause a flare in the lens when she turned, with Vera Miles throwing out her arm and hitting the naked bulb, making it swing back and forth. This was what Mr. Hitchcock wanted, that effect, and it took a couple of retakes to get it, which he was very upset about. He wanted things to happen right away. We got it, the second day.

"Of course, the dummy was a dummy. The only time she really moved was in the basement when she turned. The prop man had to lie prone underneath her and do it upside down, really, to get that head to move right. It was quite an ordeal, but it just had to be worked out."

John Landis, a young director on the Universal lot during Hitchcock's last few years there, came to know him well.

"I first saw *Psycho* on television, and it made a huge impact on me," Landis told me. "I was fascinated by how funny it is. 'Mother's not herself today' is one of the lines.

"The ending is for me one of the great images of cinema. When he says, 'I wouldn't hurt a fly,' Tony Perkins looks insane, plus that subtle 'super' of the skull that comes on and off his face is just terrifying."

Psycho has been criticized for the effect it might have on impressionable minds. Hitchcock did not agree.

"I think it has an influence on sick minds," Hitchcock acknowledged, "but not on healthy minds. When I made *Psycho*, a man was arrested in Los Angeles for murdering three women. He was alleged to have said that he was inspired to murder the third woman after seeing *Psycho*. I was called by the media for a comment. I asked what film did he see before murdering the second woman? Maybe he drank a glass of milk before he murdered the first woman.

"A little boy came up to me once, he was about seven years old, and he asked me, 'Mr. Hitchcock, in *Psycho,* what did you use for blood? Chicken blood?

"I said, 'No. Chocolate sauce' And he said, 'Okay,' and went on his way, satisfied. He understood it was only a movie."

THE UNIVERSAL-
INTERNATIONAL YEARS

❦

The Birds to *Family Plot*

OUR SO-CALLED feathered friends are suddenly our feathered enemies," was how Hitchcock described *The Birds* for me.

When Lew Wasserman, longtime agent and friend of Alfred Hitchcock, and head of MCA, the powerful talent agency, acquired Universal Studios, he arranged for Hitchcock to trade his rights in the television series and *Psycho* for a major share in the ownership of Universal. Hitchcock moved to Universal where his first project was *The Birds*.

Watching television, Hitchcock and Alma had seen a commercial that featured an attractive blonde. It was Alma who noticed her and thought she could possibly become Hitchcock's new star. They both believed in the importance of first impressions.

Nathalie "Tippi" Hedren, the model in the commercial, was contacted, and she met with agents and executives at MCA. At first, she thought she was being considered for commercials, but then she was told she was being offered a seven-year contract by Alfred Hitchcock.

Hedren expected to be given parts on the television show. The salary was only about what she earned as a model, but it offered security, and Hedren was the mother of a four-year-old daughter, Melanie. (The child grew up to be actress Melanie Griffith.) By coincidence, Evan Hunter, who wrote the screenplay for *The Birds,* had given the name "Melanie" to the character Hedren would play in *The Birds* before he knew it was her daughter's name.

Hedren was given the news that she had been chosen to star in Hitchcock's new film at dinner at Chasen's, in the presence of Hitchcock and Alma, and Lew Wasserman. By her place at the table was a box from San Francisco's Gump's, one of Hitchcock's favorite stores. Inside was a gold pin of three birds.

Edith Head, who had created the wardrobe for Grace Kelly and Kim Novak, was to do the same for Hedren in her personal life as well as in her films. Hitchcock was preparing Hedren to be the next Grace Kelly. The problem was, Hedren said, she didn't want to be the next Grace Kelly. She wanted to be the first Tippi Hedren.

Georgine Darcy visited Hitchcock while he was directing Hedren.

"He was directing Tippi like a robot. He said to me, 'Now, watch this.' If he wanted her to deepen her voice when it would get too high or she was getting nervous, he'd have a signal for that."

Before *The Birds,* Hitchcock had planned to film *Marnie* with Grace Kelly. She had hoped to return to the screen, but quickly realized those hopes were in vain.

"My husband wanted the movie star without what went with it," Grace Kelly told me years later. "In *To Catch a Thief,* my screen presence was certainly larger than life. I think my husband fell in love with that character. I probably confused the roles myself. I read that I was going to be a fairy-tale princess, and I believed it. I became a princess, but 'They lived happily ever after' was much more complicated than in fairy tales.

"In a way, it was Hitch who gave the bride away, but I don't think he thought it was forever.

"When we married, my husband said, 'Being an actress wasn't a princess-like thing to do.' He was worried about how the citizens of Monaco would react to seeing me on the screen, but he said it would depend on the part.

"He wanted the girl I was, with her spirit, but he didn't want a *wife* with too much spirit.

"I'd always thought I wanted, as an actress, to play a wide assortment of parts, but in life, once I agreed to be a princess, I was typecast."

HITCHCOCK READ IN NEWSPAPERS of a bird attack around Santa Cruz, a large flock of seagulls, lost in the fog, that flew into streetlights and broke windows. It reminded him of *The Birds,* a short story by Daphne du Maurier that he had purchased for possible development.

The Birds told of a Cornish farmer's cottage inexplicably invaded by angry birds. Hitchcock decided that *The Birds,* relocated from Cornwall to northern California, would be his next film rather than *Marnie.*

Hitchcock selected novelist Evan Hunter to write the screenplay. Hunter had written *The Blackboard Jungle* as well as the short story "Vicious Circle" for *Alfred Hitchcock's Mystery Magazine,* which was adapted for the television program. He was also the writer of the *87th Precinct* series under the pseudonym of Ed McBain.

Hunter had the idea to contrast a "meet-cute" screwball comedy with the sudden horror of the bird attack. Hitchcock liked that, especially if Grace Kelly and Cary Grant could be the couple who "met-cute." Hitchcock encouraged Hunter to create more articulate and glamorous characters than the farmer and his wife in the short story.

Though Hitchcock was accustomed to solving impossible technical problems, *The Birds* proved to be more difficult than he had anticipated. He said that if he had judged accurately the technical difficulties involved, he would not have begun *The Birds*.

Art director Robert Boyle talked with me about some of the difficulties.

"Hitch asked me whether it would be technically possible to make the film. I read the short story, and it didn't give me too many clues except that there were going to be birds all over the place, pecking at the walls, coming down the chimneys, doing whatever they had to do to destroy the human race. That already seemed difficult enough, but I knew we would be involved in some technical procedures which were not new, but putting them all together would be new. It seemed rather chancy.

"The most difficult shot was the seagulls' point-of-view of the gas station explosion in *The Birds*. The overall design I had for the film from the very beginning was inspired by Edvard Munch's painting, *The Scream*, the sense of bleakness and madness in a kind of wilderness expressing an inner state. It was just what Hitchcock wanted. He insisted on a subjective approach, so that the audience would emotionally share in the characters' feelings as well as their fears of physical danger. The actors worked almost six months, but the artists and special effects people and those in the optical department worked more than a year.

"Hitchcock would push the technical aspect of any shot to any length *if* it satisfied that gut feeling of whatever he's trying to do— suspense, terror, whatever. He bonded reality to his purpose to get the real truth."

San Francisco socialite Melanie Daniels (Tippi Hedren) is fond of elaborate practical jokes. She plays one on lawyer Mitch Brenner (Rod Taylor), delivering lovebirds to his house in Bodega Bay, where he spends weekends with his mother, Lydia (Jessica Tandy), and his young sister, Cathy (Veronica Cartwright). Melanie lies, telling Mitch that she is in town to see an old friend, Annie Hayworth (Suzanne Pleshette). She has dinner with Mitch, and then stays with Annie, whom she has only just met.

At Cathy's birthday party, a flock of gulls attacks the group. A neighbor is found pecked to death. The next afternoon, birds attack the school children.

Birds cause an explosion in which people are killed, and this incident is followed by massive bird attacks. Some of the locals blame Melanie's presence for the birds' bizarre behavior.

Annie is killed and Melanie injured. As Melanie, Mitch, his mother, and sister flee, the birds watch . . .

For *The Birds,* Hitchcock decided to dispense entirely with music, replacing it with the sound of birds. German inventor-musician Remi Gassmann, who had designed a keyboard synthesizer capable of reproducing the sound of hordes of birds, "composed" the score. Bernard Herrmann was a consultant.

Hedren had to endure days of having live birds thrown at her. She had never anticipated this, and the ordeal took its toll on her, and on her relationship with Hitchcock.

"Hitchcock was more careful about how the birds were treated than he was about me," Hedren said. "I was just there to be pecked."

Ethel Griffies, the actress who played an ornithologist in the film, began her stage career in 1881 when she was three years old. Hitchcock had seen her on the London stage when he was a young man.

Some of the birds seen in the film were trained, some were mechanical, some were animated. Ub Iwerks, an animation pioneer, assisted Robert Boyle on the animated birds. One of the live bird actors, a talented crow, was so enthusiastic about his part that if there was more than one take, he would anticipate his cues.

"I was overwhelmed by birds who would not move to the right or close their beaks," Hitchcock said. "Much has been made of my comment, 'Actors should be treated like cattle.' Now I would say, 'They should be treated like birds.'

"Alma had never liked the original idea of doing *The Birds*. She didn't think there was enough story there. Well, she was right. Not enough story, too many birds." Initially, *The Birds* received mixed reviews and was disappointing at the box office, but later it came to be held in much higher esteem.

Hitchcock sent a gift to Hedren's six-year-old daughter, Melanie. It was a small doll dressed in a miniature of the green suit worn by her mother in *The Birds,* with her sleek blond hair coiffed in exactly the same manner as Hedren's had been. There could be no confusion about whom the doll represented, but the problem was that the box that contained the doll was not a routine cardboard doll box. Made of wood, Hedren perceived it as a coffin, and both she and her daughter have continued into the twenty-first century to be perfectly convinced of that.

Asked by a friend how she felt about Hitchcock, the adult Melanie Griffith said, "He was a motherfucker. And you can quote me."

"THERE WAS THIS continuous struggle on the set with regard to him holding it together, and there were people worrying about him," actress Diane Baker told me. "On *Marnie,* I think there was a sense of 'Hitch is disturbed' or 'He is not happy.' I felt he was a man troubled. They had people down from the Black Tower [Universal's executive office building] watching, to keep Hitchcock happy. There was a lot of worry about Tippi. I think Sean Connery had a very good time. He didn't let any of it bother him. He just did his part." Connery had been cast as Hedren's co-star.

Hitchcock liked Connery personally and found him good company. He was most impressed by his "professionalism." Hitchcock defined that term simply as "He came early, knew his lines, and hit his marks. I was pleasantly surprised. He directed himself and you could always find him." Connery was frequently there even when it wasn't necessary. "I was interested in seeing Hitch work, as well as in doing everything I could to make it easy for him," he told me.

Connery remembered having "a bloody good time" making *Marnie*. "Hitchcock and his wife were very generous to us, inviting us to their home, showing us southern California. He had his way of directing, as with every director. I saw he didn't wish to over-discuss things, and *any* discussion was 'over-discussing.'"

Since Hitchcock was comfortable with Evan Hunter, professionally and personally, while working on *The Birds,* he asked the novelist to adapt *Marnie* from the Winston Graham novel. "*Marnie* was *The Taming of the Shrew,*" Hitchcock told me, "but the public didn't notice. No one could tell a story like Shakespeare."

There was one scene in the novel that disturbed Hunter. As it turned out, the scene in question was the one to which Hitchcock was firmly attached.

After his marriage to Marnie, Mark, played by Connery, expects to enjoy a husband's conjugal rights, but he has underestimated the extent of his wife's psychological trauma. Patient with her rebuff on the first night of their honeymoon, later he is carried away by his passion.

In the opinion of Hunter, this "rape," as Hitchcock described it, would destroy all sympathy for and identification with the lead male character. Hitchcock described the scene he wanted in detail to Hunter and art director Robert Boyle, but Hunter was not persuaded. He offered two versions of the script, one version written as Hitchcock wanted, the other without the rape scene. Hunter believed that Marnie truly loved Mark, even though she couldn't really admit it to herself, and that Mark would be patient with her.

Hunter described Hitchcock's reaction to this suggestion: "He framed me up with his hands the way directors do, and said, 'Evan, when he sticks it in her, I want the camera right on her face!' And then he moved into a close-up of *my* face."

Years later, talking with writer Jay Presson Allen, Hunter was told, "That scene was his reason for making the movie. You just wrote your own ticket back to New York." Hunter was dismissed and given no writing credit.

Alfred Hitchcock had read the script of *The Prime of Miss Jean Brodie* before it was produced on the stage and thought the playwright, Jay Presson Allen, might be the right one to replace Hunter on *Marnie*. Allen, who lived in New York, went out to Los Angeles and met Hitchcock.

"We got along very, very well," Allen remembered. "The first day, instantaneously, we began to have a good time. I took the job. It was my first Hollywood job, and the Hitchcock family just kind of took me in." She had passed "The Alma Test," as Pat Hitchcock called it.

"Mostly we had dinner in their kitchen," Allen continued. "Alma cooked, and afterwards Hitch put on an apron and washed the dishes. When I offered to replace him at that job, he was insulted. He said that's what he did, and he did it better than anyone in the world. And I said, 'Well, I'm very good, too.' So he said, 'I'll give you a shot.' I did a little bit, and he said, 'Well, we can work together.'

"Alma was a superb cook. Very simple food. Hitch didn't eat anything fancy.

"Hitch and Alma, they were a pair. They practically read each other's minds.

"Alma was very, very, very bright. She kept everything going for him. Everything just moved according to what was good for what he wanted. She had a wonderful sense of humor. She was very unprepossessing-looking with reddish hair, very small.

"She was a great housekeeper. If you ordered up a perfect wife, she was it. Hitch was a perfectionist, and she's what he ordered up. She was a pro about everything.

"The house was very, very simple, not like a Hollywood house in any way.

"She wasn't around on the set, because that wasn't her style. She never, never, never spoke directly with me about what I was writing, although I'm sure she read every word.

"*Marnie* didn't turn out the way I hoped. I think Tippi was not up to it, and probably my script wasn't up to it. *Marnie was* written for her. It's not a terribly accomplished script. It was just the best he could do with the time he had with a first-time writer. I was never told there was another script.

"The film followed my script, but I never thought it was as good a movie as I could have done later. I'd never have gone out there for anybody but Hitch." In 1972, Allen's *Cabaret* screenplay was nominated for an Oscar.

"I'm a very swift writer. I don't think I could have worked on the script itself more than six weeks. I worked hard when I worked, but not long hours. And then, some of the time we played and called it work.

"He storyboarded everything. The storyboard was right up there in the office for anyone to see."

The scene that caused the breakup between Evan Hunter and Hitchcock, the honeymoon "rape," wasn't a problem for Allen. "I found out much later that it had been a problem, but not for me. I remember the rape scene now because it's what everybody wants to know about.

"The casting of Sean was amusing. We didn't know who to get for the part, an upper-class Southern man. I had changed the setting in the novel. One day he said, 'They're making one of those Bond books, and I hear the guy who's doing Bond is worth looking at. Let's get some footage.' So we got all this footage of this incredibly handsome young man with that thick Scottish accent. We looked at each other and just burst into laughter. 'Let's take him anyway.' We had no regrets about that. He was darling.

"On the set, Hitchcock was always absolutely, totally, completely in control. No upsets of any description."

Toward the end of *Marnie,* Hitchcock and Hedren were rumored not to be speaking directly to each other.

"I was there throughout all that time," Allen continued, "and the problem that 'Tippi people' have talked about over the years was not that overt. Not at all. Hitch was only trying to make a star of her. He may have had something like a crush on her, a *crise de coeur,* but there was nothing overt. Nothing. Nothing. He would never in one million years do anything to embarrass himself. He was a very Edwardian fellow. Hitch loved his family. I would say that he was possibly a little carried away by Tippi, how attractive she was, but that was all there was to it.

"Hitch was a fantasist. I think he might have had fantasy romances with his leading ladies, and, if so, Alma accepted this. It's kind of normal for a man, and they were, after all, fantasies.

"Hitchcock and I thought we would do a lot of scripts. We wanted to do *Mary Rose,* but Lew Wasserman just absolutely would not do it."

Margaret "Marnie" Edgar (Tippi Hedren) works as a secretary so she can steal money and move on. Her only ties are to her mother in Baltimore and to a beloved horse she boards.

Mark Rutland (Sean Connery) recognizes her from her previous position, but, even knowing that she is a thief, he hires her. He becomes so obsessed by Marnie that he insists she marry him even after he finds her stealing from his company. Mark's hobby is taming wild animals.

On their honeymoon, Mark forces Marnie to have sex, and she attempts suicide. He accepts a marriage in name only.

When Marnie is recognized by a former employer, Mark persuades him not to press charges.

Marnie's horse is injured and has to be shot, and Marnie leaves Mark; but she is unable to take money from the safe, even when Mark appears and offers it to her.

Mark discovers that her mother [Louise Latham] supported her illegitimate child by working as a prostitute. When a sailor (Bruce Dern) threatened her mother, it was young Marnie who killed him. Her mother, who had been crippled in the fight, ac-

cepted the blame, and was acquitted at the trial. This sup-
pressed memory led to Marnie's hatred of men.

Marnie is able to start a new life with Mark.

"Connery, like Mark," Hitchcock told me, "was the kind of man
who had always been handsome and had never seen anything but a
look of adoration in the eyes of women. They said 'Yes' before he
asked them, even if he didn't. If Mark found a woman who didn't
want him, it was a challenge, a red flag for a bull."

When Hedren had asked Hitchcock, "How could any woman be
frigid with a man like Sean Connery?" Hitchcock gave her his stock
answer:

"Fake it, Tippi."

Goldfinger, with Sean Connery as James Bond, was released at the
same time, and it out-drew and out-grossed Hitchcock's film. At the
Film Society of Lincoln Center gala tribute to Sean Connery, he told
me: "James Bond was a bigger draw than I ever was. I tried, but I
couldn't compete with him. Well, tonight they're honoring me
here—not Bond. At least I *hope* so."

In *Marnie,* Hitchcock once again uses a long, slow combination
dolly-crane shot that moves from a wide overhead view of a social
event to one small detail, the really important element in the whole
scene, as with the twitching eye of the drummer and the key in Ingrid
Bergman's hand. In *Marnie,* it is the face of Strutt, the man from
whom Marnie has stolen money.

The scene opens wide and high above the chandelier in the
entrance hall of the Rutland mansion. Guests are milling around as
others arrive. From a distance a butler can be seen opening and clos-
ing the front door each time new guests arrive. Near him, watching
with interest, is Lil. Diane Baker, who played that character,
described the scene for me.

"He moved the entire staircase. It just lifted up in the air, and the
camera zoomed down to the front door. He had to do that many,

many times, and that camera zoomed carefully right through the whole room, from high up, all the way from the second floor, through the second landing and then the stairs lifted up and everything parted, like the Red Sea, for him to move with his camera to the front door in a close-up of the Strutts. To watch this happen was fascinating, and many, many takes later, they got it. Sounds were creaking and things were moving. It was thrilling to be part of."

Baker described Hitchcock's directions to her for that complex scene in which she was a key player with no words.

"He said to me, 'Diane, you are to be sitting here talking, as the Strutts come in to the party, and you are just talking seriously. We're not going to be on you. We have no dialogue for you, just background chatter. But the camera will pan, and I want you to be smiling and having fun meeting these people, or chattering at the party. Then, the minute the door opens, and the Strutts walk through the door, and the camera's pulling back, I want you to be in a state. You see them, and it's a shock, even though you are the one that invited them to come.

"'You have to show the shock, the surprise. So, I want you to start off laughing, and I want you to end up with the smile draining from your face. You're dumbfounded.' He demonstrated for me how it should look, and he demonstrated the wrong way to do it, too. His face wasn't like mine, but he did it very well, and I got the idea perfectly.

"Then he said, 'There it is, and you don't have to do any faking. Otherwise, it would border on phony, false. You would overact and you would look like you were doing a horror movie, and we don't want that.' So, he was able to talk me through scenes.

"He said not to show too much, not to act. He once said to an actor who was overacting, 'There's so much writing on the face, I can't see your expression.'

"I was terribly nervous for the tea-pouring scene. I was afraid my hand would shake and the tea cup would rattle in the saucer or that I would spill the tea pouring it. I knew I'd been very nervous in rehearsal because I was being directed by Alfred Hitchcock, but Hitch was especially kind to me.

"Then once, after a very difficult scene, I looked to Hitch for a sign of encouragement. He turned away as if he wasn't paying attention to me. I was hurt. Later, I realized he did it to draw the right performance out of me. I was supposed to be a strong-willed young woman who was jealous and hurt.

"When I was listening at the window to what Marnie and Mark were saying, he would move my hair where he wanted it and put the curtain at a certain point in my face, where it covered my face just slightly so it gave a sense of the ominous or sinister. Then he would place the curtain exactly where he wanted it to hang, next to my face, so that it made me seem like someone listening secretly.

"He told me to think absolutely nothing. My face must register zero. It's very difficult to have absolutely no expression. I suppose it was for a close-up, but he knew frame by frame how he wanted to see it.

"He knew exactly what he was going to do, but he was prepared to make a change that suited the scene or if something happened.

"I liked him when I first met him. I'd been under contract to Fox for almost five years when Hitchcock asked for me. He had seen me on television. I was invited to his home, and I met with him and his wife.

"I immediately felt that Alma was as important in my involvement as was Hitchcock. It seemed as if they were of one mind. They were rather united and talked to me very nicely. I felt immediately upon my arrival that they were eager to have me. They liked my look, and they indicated that they thought I had a resemblance to Grace Kelly, and they started to bring out photographs of Grace and magazines to show me. I was sort of stunned that they would be looking at me and comparing me to her. In retrospect, I think it was maybe a conscious effort on their part to look at someone new who might fulfill a need that they had to find a Grace Kelly for their movies.

"Then it became much more difficult as the picture went on because of the turmoil. I felt he was struggling a great deal. He tended to fall asleep on the set after lunch when he was shooting. I began to understand that he and Tippi were having trouble.

"I knew there was trouble, because he was becoming very solicitous of my interests, talking with me, and he spent a lot of time ignoring Tippi and paying attention to me, which really did disturb me. He was not talking much with her. I noticed he would always begin talking with me in front of her or around her dressing room. Something wasn't quite right.

"I was caught right in the middle. After it became clear that Tippi wasn't going on with her contract after *Marnie,* I was invited to join the lunch group in his bungalow. I was very flattered. He profoundly affected me.

"But sometimes he would embarrass me. A man who was a friend of my father's dropped by to visit me on the set one day. He was head of transportation at Universal. When he left, Hitch said, 'Another one of your boyfriends?' so everybody could hear it. I was *so* embarrassed. I was angry."

Hitchcock's humor was better appreciated by Anny Ondra in 1929. During her sound test for *Blackmail,* he asked her in front of all if she had been "a bad woman" the night before. Ondra's response was to giggle and pretend mock shock.

"When I saw *Marnie,* I wasn't sure he fulfilled what he had in mind for our film," Baker continued. "I'm pleased with my own work in some parts of it. My character was to come in and create havoc, and I was rather nicely evil, and also playful. I was disappointed that there was no dot at the end of the character. It wasn't a fulfilled ending for my character. I just disappear.

"But who can say in the whole of life that you got a chance to work with Alfred Hitchcock?"

Hitchcock blamed himself for the film's failure, referring to his disappointment when he felt he had lost Grace Kelly for a second time. The first time he had lost her to Prince Rainier, who offered the real-life role as Her Royal Highness of Monaco, beyond anything Hitchcock felt he had to offer.

The second time, Hitchcock had regrets, because he believed "Miss Kelly" would have returned to star in another film for him, if he hadn't used "the bad judgment" to offer her the wrong part, that of the mentally disturbed thief, Marnie. He believed that particular role was deemed "inappropriate" by the Prince, a reaction that probably would have been shared by the principality.

In addition, there was a delay in the start of filming and the royal family had only one month in the year when they could be away from the palace for holiday. Any postponement meant there had to be a postponement until the next year. Grace Kelly might have accepted a postponement, but Princess Grace could not.

When it was certain that she would *not* be doing *Marnie,* Hitchcock wrote her a gracious note that she told me about in London, many years later. What particularly impressed her was the phrase, "Remember, Grace, it's only a movie."

"Because he handled it that way," she said, "we were still able to be friends and have dinners together."

Princess Grace said she missed acting and had wanted to return to films, especially after her first two children were born. She added rather wistfully, "Really, there never *was* a chance of it.

"Though Mr. Hitchcock wasn't considered an actor's director, as an actress, having worked with the best—George Seaton, Fred Zinnemann—I thought he was a wonderful director, as well as a dear man."

Marnie was Bernard Herrmann's last score for a Hitchcock picture, though he would go on to write music that was not used for *Torn Curtain.* "They wanted a lousy pop tune," Herrmann told me, "probably with bongo drums. Hitch was sensitive about the music being called 'old-fashioned' because, by implication, he felt the words might extend to him."

After *Marnie,* Hitchcock lost two of the dedicated technical people who had been so important to him and his films and who referred to themselves as "the Hitchcockians." Robert Burks died in a fire in his home, and editor George Tomasini died of a heart attack.

TOWARD THE END of *Marnie,* Hedren and Hitchcock were widely reported not to be speaking to each other. Assistant director Hilton Green was there on the set every day.

"On *Marnie,* I was close to Tippi Hedren. Nothing that was really bad happened. It's not true that Mr. Hitchcock and Tippi were not speaking to each other. You can't direct someone and not have them talk to each other.

"They weren't making polite small talk, but then, it wasn't Hitchcock's way to say much to actors on the set."

"Marnie," Hitchcock told me, "is about a girl who's a compulsive thief, but after every robbery, she goes to a farm in Maryland and uses some of the proceeds to support her horse. She loves to ride in the open air, with her hair blowing free, almost as though she were cleansing herself of the crime she's just committed.

"She runs up against a man who *knows* she's a thief, but he engages her in his company anyway. He courts her, but he's a little disturbed when he finds out she's robbed him, too. He's a late-Victorian, Edwardian type of hero, you know. That's a time I know and feel. It's a very intriguing yarn, very meaty stuff.

"It had wonderful possibilities, or so I thought. I thought I could mold Miss Hedren into the heroine of my imagination. I was wrong."

"It was a very painful experience I don't like to think about," Tippi Hedren told me. "I felt very sorry for Mr. Hitchcock.

"I trusted Hitchcock and he made me feel confident. But doing *The Birds* turned into a nightmare, when all those birds started pecking at me. He hadn't told me about that. I could have been blinded. But I was so very young, I did what I was told. I shouldn't have been put through that.

"I can't say I'm sorry I worked with Hitchcock, but I can't say I'm glad. I certainly wasn't happy about the way it all turned out. After *Marnie,* I was what they called hot, but he kept me under contract." She believed he prevented her from working with other directors who wanted her.

In 1967, with her contract ended, she was featured in Charlie Chaplin's *A Countess from Hong Kong.* Then, Hedren appeared in films, on television, and devoted herself to animal activist activities.

When I spoke with her in 2003, she said that she hadn't changed her opinion on Hitchcock, and that she felt exactly the same as she had after *Marnie.* Her tone indicated that, indeed, she did feel the same anger and disappointment.

Hedren felt that Hitchcock was obsessed with her, and then disappointed in her, professionally. "She didn't have the volcano" was how he summed it up. The film ended with an enduring bad relationship between the director and the star he had planned to create.

She blamed him. He blamed her. But if *Marnie* had been a success, it all might have been different.

Hitchcock sometimes may have fallen in love with one of his leading ladies, as she appeared onscreen, playing her part, a role that was partly his own creation. Then, when the film wrapped, so did his relationship to the character. Thus, Alma could say to me that she had never been jealous of any actress who appeared in her husband's films.

An actress, however, on occasion "betrayed" the character when, in Hitchcock's opinion, "She couldn't live up to her character. What it meant," he said, referring to Hedren's performance in *Marnie,* "it really was *my* fault. I couldn't bring her far enough."

Despite the troubled relationship, Hedren was there for Hitchcock when the American Film Institute honored him in 1979.

• • •

"I THINK THAT *Torn Curtain* was miscast," Hitchcock said. "I should have had a hero who was a singing scientist, to go with Julie Andrews.

"Casting is important, and it's very difficult to go against wrong casting. I had two stars, but they weren't right for their characters.

"At the beginning of shooting, [Paul] Newman sent me a several-page memo offering suggestions about his character. I took it quite personally and found it insulting. I didn't know it at the time, but it was not behavior uniquely designed for me. He was given to the practice with other directors. I gather they took it better than I did. Perhaps I suffered from a case of memo-itis, after my time served with Selznick."

Neither Andrews nor Newman was pleased by Hitchcock's light-touch style of directing actors. Andrews looked for more help and some encouragement. Newman wanted to try it more than one way to see how each performance played. Hitchcock felt he should do that at home.

"The Method actor may be all right in the theater," Hitchcock said. "He has a whole stage to move about on. But when it comes to film and you cut from the face to what he sees, the subjective camera, there must be discipline. I remember discussing this with a Method actor, not Newman, and he said, 'We're given an idea, and then we're supposed to interpret it any way we want.' And I said, 'That's not acting, that's writing.'

"My own appearances on the screen, the cameos, are always short, because I don't want to have to suffer the indignity of being an actor for too long. But I never improvise."

In a conversation with John Springer, Paul Newman's longtime publicist and friend, and me, Newman said that he'd been very pleased to be selected by Hitchcock to be in *Torn Curtain*.

Then, the rumor circulated around the set that Newman and Andrews had not been Hitchcock's first choices and that he wasn't pleased with "being forced to have us," Newman said. "We tried not to be affected by gossip. Hitchcock seemed cool to us personally and casual in his direction of us. I usually had input with my directors, but not with Hitchcock. Later, I found out that this was his style. It meant I was doing well, but nobody told me that.

"I think he owed it to us not to say we were miscast after he had approved us. We'd been signed and were doing our best. We were stars, and we brought in fans at the box office. We each said no to other scripts in order to say yes to him. I felt we were entitled to more respect.

"Afterwards, I saw a piece of the film. I don't make a practice of seeing my own films, but what I saw didn't look so bad to me. I never found out how Hitchcock really felt at the beginning, what was true and what wasn't, or how he felt after we made the film."

"THERE WAS AN ENDING written for *Torn Curtain*," Hitchcock said, "which wasn't used, but I rather liked it. No one agreed with me except my colleague at home [Alma]. Everyone told me you couldn't have a letdown ending after all that.

"Newman would have thrown the formula away. After what he has gone through, after everything we have endured with him, he just tosses it. It speaks to the futility of it all, and it's in keeping with the kind of naïveté of the character, who is no professional spy and who will certainly retire from that nefarious business."

Torn Curtain was inspired by the defection to the Soviet Union of British and American spies, notably that of Guy Burgess and Donald Maclean. Novelist Brian Moore was chosen to write the screenplay, but shooting began before Hitchcock was satisfied with the script, dictated by the limited availability of Andrews.

When U.S. nuclear scientist Michael Armstrong (Paul Newman) defects to East Germany, he is followed by his fiancée, Sarah Sherman (Julie Andrews), who doesn't know he is pretending to be a defector. His real mission is to steal a secret formula, and then return with it to the U.S. Accomplishing this mission, Armstrong's escape is complicated by Sarah's presence and by his having killed the agent assigned to watch him. After a wild bus chase, they are smuggled out of East Germany in the wardrobe baskets of a Czech ballet company traveling to Sweden.

The East German scientist who is tricked into revealing his country's nuclear secrets resembles Mr. Memory of *The 39 Steps*. Like Mr. Memory, Dr. Lindt (the name of Hitchcock's favorite chocolate) feels compelled to speak, in this case, to correct a fellow scientist, who also happens to be an American spy.

Hitchcock spoke about the drawn-out killing of Gromek, the East German agent, to show how "arduous" it is to kill a human being. "In my films, I believe, 'Thou shalt not kill—too many people.' Human life is too valuable. In my films, killing does not happen casually.

"It has been suggested that the killing of Gromek by putting his head into a gas oven was a reference to the Holocaust. Who knows? I was deeply affected by film footage of the prison camps I saw at the end of the war.

"*Torn Curtain* was a beige and gray picture. After Copenhagen, there was no more color. The hotel corridors were gray all the way, with one red fire extinguisher." Hitchcock personally planned all the color and costumes related to the sets and was very concerned with the lighting.

Bernard Herrmann took the same approach with the music, using an extremely unorthodox orchestra, mainly woodwind and brass, to create an oppressive atmosphere. After an argument with Hitchcock, the score was rejected and Herrmann was replaced by John Addison.

"Hitch was strong enough to have been able to do anything he wanted to do," Herrmann told me. "But he never liked to stir up things, to quarrel, and he didn't think my music was worth disturbing the calm for."

• • •

HITCHCOCK ATTEMPTED A project called *Kaleidoscope Frenzy,* and he shot some test footage in New York. The style of film he was contemplating was similar to that of Michelangelo Antonioni, whose *Blow-Up* he greatly admired. "Those Italian fellows are a hundred years ahead of us," he said.

Written by Hitchcock, *Kaleidoscope Frenzy* starts with a brutal murder by a killer who is moved to kill when he is close to any large body of water. The murderer is finally exposed by his mother. There were to be no stars, it was to be shot in New York and there would be nudity.

Hitchcock believed in it, but Universal said no, a word Hitchcock hadn't heard since his days with Selznick.

"I'M VERY ENTHUSIASTIC about my next picture," Hitchcock told Herbert Coleman. "Lew [Wasserman] has just bought Leon Uris's newest book for me, and Uris is writing the screenplay. I think it will be as picturesque as *The Man Who Knew Too Much* and as suspenseful as *Vertigo.*"

The screenplay Hitchcock received from Uris didn't please him, and he contacted Arthur Laurents, who read the book and declined to try his hand at it.

"He called up and asked me to come over," Laurents told me, "and for the first time ever, he asked *why* I didn't think it was good. He listened, but the old fervor was gone. I felt he wasn't Hitchcock anymore."

Samuel Taylor accepted the assignment, sometimes writing scenes just before they were shot. Art director Henry Bumstead felt the pressure.

"You know," he told me, "*Topaz* was a nightmare. I got high blood pressure on that picture. I'm still taking pills for it, and that's a long time ago.

"We started in Copenhagen, and we didn't know who the cast was. Hitch had a terrible time casting that picture.

"In Europe, I didn't have that much help. I was doing props and everything. I want to tell you, that was the toughest show I ever did. Doing all those sets, and European sets at that, the detail and the molding and everything is much more complicated. I was working every night.

"All the exteriors were done on location, and all the interiors at Universal. I had all the stages filled with sets. I was building furniture, and I had three assistants and three decorators.

"There were some good moments in the picture, but the thing is, there was no time to prepare, and they were writing the script as we started and were casting. Poor Edith Head! I remember she was going crazy, and I didn't know all the sets. There was just no time for prep, and I'll tell you, prep is the most important time on a picture."

In 1962, a defecting Soviet official reveals that something important is happening between Russia and Cuba. CIA agent Michael Nordstrom (John Forsythe) asks French agent André Devereaux (Frederick Stafford) to investigate, because France maintains diplomatic relations with Cuba. The French already know about a strategic agreement between Russia and Cuba.

During a visit of Cuban leader Rico Parra (John Vernon) to the U.N., Devereaux arranges to steal a copy of the secret treaty between Moscow and Havana. Traveling to Havana, he learns from his undercover agent and mistress, Juanita de Córdoba (Karin Dor), that the Soviets are building missile-launching sites there. After he leaves, she is exposed as a spy and shot by Parra, whose mistress she also was.

Devereaux, recalled to Paris and reprimanded for cooperating with the CIA, warns a senior official, Jacques Granville (Michel Piccoli), about Topaz, a French spy ring loyal to the Soviets.

When Devereaux's son-in-law (Michel Subor) is wounded while investigating French official Henri Jarre (Philippe Noiret), Nicole (Dany Robin), Devereaux's wife, admits that she was having an affair with Granville, whom she incriminates. Granville, exposed at a peace conference by Nordstrom, commits suicide.

Two other endings were filmed. In one, Devereaux and Granville have a duel in an empty Paris stadium, and Granville is shot from the stands by a sniper. In another, Devereaux sees Granville leaving on a plane for Russia at the Orly airport, and they exchange greetings. The ending finally used was an outtake of Philippe Noiret entering a house. Since his character walked with a cane, it was necessary to include only the last part of his going through the door before the off-screen gunshot signaling his suicide is heard. Audiences didn't respond well to the ending, but the studio had objected to any ending with the spy unpunished, and suicide offered a compromise.

Curtis Harrington, a young director at the Universal Studios during the shooting of *Topaz,* spent three days watching Hitchcock work.

"I asked if I could visit the set, because Hitchcock had a closed set, and didn't allow visitors. He said I could, and that's all I expected, to stand in the corner and be as invisible as possible. But what happened was, he took it upon himself, all the time, to come over and tell me what he was doing and why. He was extraordinarily kind to me.

"I got to watch him do one of those unique Hitchcock shots. *Topaz* has a scene in which the ostensible heroine is shot in an embrace by this man. This was one of those famous Hitchcock ideas, unique to him. He set up the camera so that as she fell to the ground, out of this man's arms, the camera up in the rafters looked directly down on the couple. As she fell to the ground, her skirt spread out and away from her, like a growing pool of blood.

"This was a very tricky shot, not something you can accomplish except with tricks. He had many members of the crew with monofilament threads tied to all the edges of her skirt. As she crumpled to the ground, they pulled the skirt away from her, and I think he shot it in slow motion, so it looked like the skirt just spread out magically around her, like a pool. Pure Hitchcock.

"*Topaz* has no stars. Ordinarily, Hitchcock worked with big stars. Directing these players, he would give them physical moves. He would say, 'Look up. Look down. Look to the right, then look back.' Now, he would *never* do that with Cary Grant or Ingrid Bergman, or any star. I asked him why he was giving those physical instructions.

"I'll never forget what he said: 'Well, Curtis, I have to try to bring them a very long way in one picture.'

"I remember at one point he fired an actor, and had the casting office send in five other actors. They all lined up, and he chose another one, and then proceeded shooting with that one. It was a small part, but he could not get what he wanted with the first player.

"He had a vision in his head, and that's what he had to create. When he had the players he really wanted, it must have been a great deal easier for him, because he didn't have to bring them anywhere.

"My own feeling about Hitchcock is that he was above all a romantic, and his vision is romantic. It's an idealized vision, even though he dealt with mystery and mayhem. It's the creation of the Hitchcockian world, and there isn't a shot that isn't thought about and created by Alfred Hitchcock.

"When I was doing *Mati Hari* with Sylvia Kristel, I gave her those physical instructions. I remembered what Hitchcock did, and I said I'm going to try to make her as good as possible in this, and I would give her beats. 'Look up, look down, look away, look back.' What was wonderful was that one of the French reviews said, 'She has an acting talent we have not seen before.'

"Astrologically, you know, Hitchcock had the same astrological configuration as Mae West. I think that's very significant, because they both had sex on the mind."

GERMAN ACTRESS Karin Dor, from the James Bond film *You Only Live Twice,* was cast in *Topaz* as Juanita de Córdoba. She told me how it happened.

"I was in Germany, and at four o'clock in the morning, my Hollywood agent called and said, 'Pack your suitcase. Mr. Hitchcock wants to see you.' So, I packed a little suitcase, not expecting to get the part, because I knew Mr. Hitchcock had already screen-tested over a hundred girls from all over the world.

"So, I arrived at Universal Studios and had lunch with Mr. Hitchcock in his office. He had a dining room there. We were sitting together, talking about everything. After about an hour, he said, 'Do you know Edith Head?' I said, 'Who doesn't.' He said, 'I think it would be a good idea if you go over and have your measurements taken.' That was his way to tell me I got the part. I said, 'I got the part?' He said, 'Yes!'

"So, I got my fittings with Miss Edith Head, which was, for me, very exciting, too.

"While we were talking in his dining room, he told me about the individual scenes, especially about the death scene, which he already had in his mind so clearly. He said, 'I want to have you in a purple dress. The dress has to spread out to look like she's sinking in a pool of blood.'

"But when I fell down the dress wouldn't spread out. The idea came. Nylon wire.

"They put nylon wire at the seams, and they tried it with a double. She did the fall several times. On every wire there was one person pulling it, about eight workers. Then, the wardrobe ladies came and put a big towel around her, and the girl got out of the dress. I came in a bathrobe, and they put the towel around me, and I slipped into my dress, so we could shoot it.

"We had one day when journalists from all over the world could ask questions. Mr. Hitchcock was there with all the actors. One journalist asked Mr. Hitchcock, 'Why did you take Miss Dor? She's dark-haired, and dark eyes, all your leading ladies are blond and blue-eyed.'

"He said '*Topaz* is based on a book by Leon Uris, and Juanita de Córdoba really existed. She was Cuban, so she had to be dark-haired and dark-eyed, but Miss Dor is blond inside.'

"One morning it was so ice-cold, and I was freezing. I said to Mr. Hitchcock, 'Is it only me who is freezing, or is it cold?' And he looked at me and said, 'It is only *you!* You are a coldhearted woman. You are a frigid woman. You are eating too many ice creams.' It was totally silent, because everybody wanted to hear what I said.

"I looked at him and I said, 'With the first two I agree. With the third one not. I hate ice cream.' And everybody knew how I loved ice cream. He was putting me on. From this moment, we really had a marvelous relationship, because he realized I opened my mouth and said something. He was famous for saying things like that to people and waiting for the reaction.

"Sometimes he spoke to me in German, and his German was quite good. For example, this scene where the police come into my house and search, the scene where I'm coming out of my bedroom and have to come down the stairs. We rehearsed. The first time I came out and I said, 'Mr. Hitchcock, do I go left or right from the camera when I come down the stairs?'

"He looked at me, and he said, 'You are going to the too-hot-washed sweater.'

"And I thought, 'My God, what can he mean by that?'

"Then I thought, what does a sweater do when it's washed with hot water? It shrinks, and the past tense of shrink is shrank. And the German word for armoire or cupboard is *Schrank.* So, there was an armoire, and I said, 'Ah, I know. I have to go to the armoire.' And he said, 'I *knew* you would get it.' This was his way of putting in some

German words sometimes, and trying to see if I would get it. But that was a toughie.

"If he was very pleased with me in a scene, he would say, 'Would you like to have dinner with Mrs. H. and me?' And we would go to Chasen's, their favorite, and I was always thrilled."

John Vernon, who played Rico Parra, felt he was playing someone like Fidel Castro's brother, Raúl. Vernon told me, "though it wasn't really anyone specific, and Mr. Hitchcock never said anything to me about it.

"I was asked to go to Edith Head's wardrobe department. 'Mr. Hitchcock wants to see you in dungarees.' I put on a pair of overalls or whatever the Cuban army's overalls were, and Edith Head said, 'My God, after all the films I've done here, all I can offer you is *this!*'

"He loved to joke a bit. He would say, 'Are you familiar with Cockney rhymes?' and I said, 'Not really.'

"'Well,' he said, 'there are too many dog's feet in your scene that you're doing.'

"'I don't know what you mean.'

"'Pauses, John.'

"And one other time, he'd just finished a scene, and I was still on the stage of the next day's shooting, pacing the set, and he said, 'What are you doing?'

"'I'm working at what I'm going to be confronted with tomorrow.'

"He says, 'What do you mean?'

"'I'm not quite sure how I should play this scene tomorrow.'

"He says, 'Oh, John—it's only a movie. Why don't you come into my trailer and we'll imbibe, and I'll tell you a few stories.'

"So, we sat in his trailer, and he says, 'Have you seen my film *Rear Window*?'

"'Yes.'

"'Do you remember the scene where Jimmy Stewart is staring out his window to the apartment across the courtyard? Well, I had Mr.

Stewart stare at a crack in a wall, and that's all he saw for three minutes. He looked at that crack in the wall, at the paint on the wall, seriously.

"'The great Russian director Pudovkin filmed a lady looking down at her lap. He said she should be staring at nothing, just staring down. The director then inserted two different things: an empty plate, which signified hunger, and then a dead baby, with the same look, staring at her lap, remorse, horrible remorse.'

"So, what Mr. Hitchcock was telling me was, if you've got a strong enough framework around you, the director is doing most of the work, so don't muck it up.

"There's a great scene where Rico Parra hears something from a woman holding her dying husband in her arms, and they're traitors. Rico comes into the room, and he says, 'What's going on?' She sort of mumbles. So he gets closer, and finally his ear goes practically into her mouth, and he gets the bad news that his lady friend is a traitor. Then, of course, he pulls back, and there's a shot of him taking it in.

"The next day Mr. Hitchcock says, 'John, we have to do that scene again.' Just after you hear the bad news. 'I was a little too far away from you. I shouldn't have cut you below the knees. I should have cut you *at* the knees.' So, talk about a mathematician or something!

"He fell asleep once during a long take, and no one dared wake him up. But we didn't want him to stay there the whole afternoon. Finally, he started to clear his throat. He quietly opened his eyes. He looked at me, and he said, 'Well, how was it John?' I didn't know what the hell to say. He started to laugh, and that was it.

"When I shoot Juanita, it was a love scene, really, holding her at arm's length, and looking down at her like that. Meanwhile, the gun is coming out of the holster, which you never see, and she's shot.

"There was another scene in a big conference room where the camera seemed to skim right along the table. There were stagehands on either side of the table, who pulled the chairs right out of the scene to allow the camera in. That was a ballet off-screen.

"Mr. Hitchcock was never late. Sometimes he'd say, 'We'll finish a little early. Come into my study,' his trailer, 'and we'll imbibe and tell stories.'

"When Mr. Hitchcock died, Pat and her husband received a lot of things, and one of them was a $6 million cache of wine, from all over the world. And Pat's husband, Joe was his name, said, 'John, you won't believe it. I got all this wine, and I've got twenty-five years AA.'"

IN ITS FRAGMENTED PLOT and documentary style, *Topaz* harks back to Hitchcock's 1944 World War II French shorts, *Bon Voyage* and *Aventure malgache.* Jeanne's murder by the Gestapo agent in *Bon Voyage* is similar to Juanita's death in *Topaz,* and in both, the pistols that kill the sympathetic women are not shown. Like *Topaz, Aventure malgache* is a complex story about politically duplicitous people with no really central characters. Like the French shorts, *Topaz* is set during a critical international moment, when the Cold War threatened to become a hot war.

Topaz was shot in Copenhagen, Wiesbaden, Paris, Washington, D.C., New York, and at Universal Studios in Hollywood. It was not successful financially or critically.

While in Europe making preparations for the filming of *Topaz,* Hitchcock visited Ingmar Bergman in Stockholm. Bergman suggested he use two Swedish actors, Per-Axel Arosenius and Sonja Kolthoff, for the Soviet defector and his wife. Then, Hitchcock traveled with Coleman and Taylor to Finland to scout locations for *The Short Night,* another Cold War novel he hoped to bring to the screen. His next film, however, was to be *Frenzy.*

The camera operator on *Frenzy,* Paul Wilson, spoke with me about Hitchcock.

"When I got to know him better, he was always asking after your family. He was a lovely man. He could be hard with people, actors in particular. He used to purposely fall asleep if he was fed up with the performance. I think he'd lay it on. He'd do a bit of pretense. And in pretending, he *did* fall asleep.

"He drew a lot of pictures, and when you put the camera near to what he wanted, it all fell in line. Uncanny. He'd made the picture in his head. He would tell me what I'd got in the camera, and it was right there on the ground glass exactly as he said.

"If there was a problem, it was always, 'We've got a problem with that shot,' not '*You've* got a problem,' or '*I've* got a problem.'"

Wilson also worked with Charlie Chaplin as the camera operator on *The Countess from Hong Kong.*

"They were extraordinary people, completely opposite. Charlie Chaplin hated to move the camera. I suggested on one occasion that we track into a wedding cake. And he said, 'I don't want any Hitchcock stuff in *my* picture.'

"Chaplin didn't just have his dolly marks chalked in, he had them *painted* in, because that was where the camera was going to stay. It was the same with the actors. During a rehearsal, Marlon Brando, having been standing in the same place for several pages of dialogue, said, 'Charlie, I feel I ought to move a little during all of this.'

"'Marlon,' Chaplin replied, 'when I want you to move, I'll tell you.'

"'Okay, Charlie,' said Brando, and that was it.

"With Hitchcock, it was totally different. There was nearly always a technically challenging shot in each film. In *Frenzy,* it was when we follow Barry Foster as he leads Anna Massey from the street up the stairs to his room, and then after they go in, we pull back down the stairs and back into Covent Garden and look up at the window where that room is. It had to appear as if it was shot continuously when it was actually two shots, half studio interior and half location, joined by a useful sack of beetroots. It gave me and my assistant, Gil Taylor, quite a workout."

Rusty Coppleman, the sound editor for *Frenzy*, appreciated Hitch-cock's sense of humor.

"In the scene where the hero thinks he's beating the villain about the head with an automobile crank, Hitch was a bit concerned, cen-sorship-wise, about the noise that we should apply on this. He said, "Go out and buy a couple of melons, and hit those and see what sound you get." The melon sounded extremely bloodthirsty, like brains being splattered. A cabbage didn't work, so I devised a sound.

"Then, I wrapped a bandage around my head, with a few streaks of red on it from a marking pen. We ran this scene with the sound I'd created, and Hitch said, 'That's very good.'

"I said, 'I hope that sounded authentic enough for you.'

"He saw the bandage, with the red on it, and said, 'Do you want an aspirin?'

Hitchcock chose a playwright rather than the novelist to adapt *Frenzy*, which was based on the book *Goodbye Piccadilly, Farewell Leicester Square*, by Arthur La Bern. The title of the novel was taken from the popular World War I song, "It's a Long Way to Tipperary."

"I would say the playwright rather than the novelist is generally the better for adapting for the screen," Hitchcock explained. "You need scenes that can 'play' as people from the theater can write them for you. Who was it who once said that drama is life with the dull bits cut out? Compression belongs to the playwright, not the novelist."

Covent Garden wholesale fruit merchant Bob Rusk (Barry Foster) is an impotent serial killer who strangles women with a necktie. One of his victims is Brenda Blaney (Barbara Leigh-Hunt), the ex-wife of his best friend, Richard Blaney (Jon Finch), who becomes a prime suspect. Fearing discovery, Rusk kills Blaney's girlfriend, a barmaid (Anna Massey), and Blaney is arrested.

Escaping from jail, Blaney is followed by the police to Rusk's flat, where Rusk has strangled another woman. Rusk is arrested, and Blaney cleared.

On New Year's Eve, just before 1970 became 1971, playwright Anthony Shaffer received what he considered one of the most memorable phone calls of his life. Amidst the banging sounds of cracker party favors, the popping of corks, and the buzz of celebratory conversations, Shaffer heard a strangely familiar voice, announcing himself as Alfred Hitchcock. The voice asked would he, Anthony Shaffer, be interested in writing a screenplay for his next film?

Shaffer assumed it must be a joke, because who, after all, would call anyone at a time like that to ask if he would like to write the screenplay for a Hitchcock film? He listened for a while, trying to detect which of his friends was trying to fool him. As he listened, it dawned on him that the caller might really *be* Alfred Hitchcock.

Peter Shaffer recalled how his twin brother, Anthony, became the screenplay writer for *Frenzy*. At the time, Anthony's play *Sleuth* was playing on the London stage to great acclaim.

"Hitchcock was interviewing Tony, and they were talking about Hitchcock's sort of credo, the MacGuffin, and all that, the willing suspension of disbelief, and so on. Hitchcock was saying that although his pictures are very often high melodrama and border on the improbable, there was absolutely nothing in them that was illogical or dependent on pure chance.

"'I challenge you, dear boy,' Hitchcock said. 'You'll never find anything like that in the plots of my films.'

"Tony said, 'Oh, really? I wonder if I can take you up on that?'

"They went to the little cinema by Hitchcock's office, and Tony said, 'Can we see *North by Northwest*?'

"There was the scene where Cary Grant is being chased by both the spies and the police in New York, and he ends up desperate and frightened in the concourse of Grand Central. He says to the man behind the grille of the ticket office, 'Give me a ticket to Chicago.' When the ticket seller hesitates because he recognizes him as a wanted man, Cary Grant leaves without a ticket and boards the *20th Century Limited*. Eva Marie Saint and the villains are already there.

"Tony asked, 'How did they know which train he was going to take?'

"Hitchcock responded, 'Daggers at dawn.'

"After a long silence, Hitchcock said, 'You've got the job, if you want it.'"

As he worked with Hitchcock, Shaffer found he was always hungry. Their daily lunch in Hitchcock's bungalow on the Universal lot was leaving him wishing for more food, and for some variety.

Hitchcock followed his daily regimen of steak, ground or filet, and during the first days, Shaffer ate the same and didn't say anything. He depended on the candy bar machine to sustain him.

One day, referring to the steak, potatoes, and salad lunch, Hitchcock said, "That was delicious."

Shaffer agreed. Then he ventured, "But I thought I might like to order something different one of these days."

"Of course, dear boy, of course," Hitchcock said. "Tomorrow."

The next day, Shaffer joined Hitchcock in his studio bungalow for lunch, expecting to be offered a wider range of choices from the Universal commissary menu. Instead, he was stunned to find the office filled with elaborate serving trays, chafing dishes, food warmers, and casseroles, succulent entrées, appetizing aromas, and an enticing dessert cart.

Hitchcock had ordered what Shaffer described as "a fifteen-course meal" from Chasen's, complete with a waiter from the restaurant to serve it. After lunch, Shaffer, far from being able to work more effectively, could scarely work at all. He could think only about a nap. The next day it was back to steak and potatoes.

Film and theatrical producer David Brown remembered once flying cross-country on the same flight with Hitchcock and Alma. "They were going to New York, and Hitchcock spent the whole trip talking about what restaurants they were going to and what he was going to order in each. In those days, it was Lutèce and Pavillon.

"During the luncheons at Universal that Dick Zanuck and I had with Hitch in his private dining room, he would expound on his theories of filmmaking. He told us he never shot anything that wouldn't be used in the film. Another theory was it's better if we know who the perpetrator is and the characters don't. That was one of his chief theories of suspense."

Curtis Harrington, in London at the time Hitchcock was filming *Frenzy,* spoke with him and Alma during their happy days there, before her stroke. Invited by friends to an elegant and very expensive restaurant, Harrington saw the Hitchcocks and Joan Harrison at another table.

"I discreetly waited until they finished their dessert and coffee before I went over to pay my respects," Harrington remembered. Mr. Hitchcock immediately recognized me, and he greeted me warmly. He introduced me to his wife and Miss Harrison, and at that moment, the captain arrived with the check. Mr. Hitchcock reached for his wallet. He couldn't find it. He looked up at me, very innocently.

"'Oh, Cur-tis,' he said, clearly enunciating my name, 'I seem to have come out without my wallet. I wonder, could you . . .'

"I nearly died. I didn't have that kind of money on me. Or off me. I was probably looking pale. He reached into his pocket again, and this time, he found his wallet. That was his sense of humor."

THOM MOUNT, formerly head of production at Universal, talked with me about Hitchcock's "bungalow" at Universal.

"One of the things that fascinated me as a young executive was the quality of a self-designed universe that was built for Mr. Hitchcock on the Universal lot. He had offices that were exactly the offices he wanted in the way he wanted them, meaning a very nice office, which he barely used, a little dining room, which he used a lot, a separate kitchen, areas for his assistants. Then, behind that in this sort of railroad car of a building, his cutting room, and behind that his screening room; and then, an additional room—bedroom, bath, a kind of wardrobe, so that if Mr. Hitchcock was working, if he wanted to, he could virtually live there.

"The commissary brought the food over. Mr. Hitchcock always ate the same thing every day: steak, mashed potatoes, and sliced tomatoes. And sometimes there was a dessert, if he felt he deserved it."

After some critical and box office disappointments, *Frenzy* restored Hitchcock's successful image. Costing $2 million to make, it brought back $16 million.

During the filming of *Frenzy,* Alma suffered a stroke. She wanted to stay at Claridge's, and when she felt better, she was flown back to Los Angeles. Hitchcock, who could not imagine a life without Alma, had to direct the rest of the film alone. Barry Foster told me that Hitchcock became listless and seemed uninterested in his picture, though he was always able to draw on a reserve of energy when needed.

"Hitchcock was so pleased when Alma was able to view *Frenzy* and she approved it enthusiastically," Foster said. "She had tears of happiness in her eyes."

ON APRIL 29, 1974, the Film Society of Lincoln Center honored Alfred Hitchcock, who arrived in the limousine with Alma and Princess Grace.

Among those who appeared at the gala tribute were François Truffaut, Janet Leigh, Joan Fontaine, Teresa Wright, Cyril Ritchard, and Samuel Taylor.

The Film Society's gala was still young, with Hitchcock being only their third honoree. Fred Astaire and Charles Chaplin had preceded him.

Martin E. Segal, the head of the Film Society of Lincoln Center, told me he noticed that Princess Grace had disappeared from the table where the special guests were eating, and she was nowhere to be seen. He went in search of her. He found her outside in the hallway, standing alone.

"Aren't you going to join us?" he asked her. "Please come and have something to eat."

Kelly declined. "Thank you, but I can't. Do you like my dress?"

"It's beautiful and you look beautiful in it."

"That's why I can't eat anything. My dress is so tightly fitted, I can't afford one bite, and if I go inside and watch everyone eating, I might be tempted."

"Then please let me bring you a chair."

"Thank you, but I can't sit down because I don't want to wrinkle my dress."

When Segal told Hitchcock what Kelly had said, the director nodded. "Yes," he said. "I understand."

At the tribute, Hitchcock commented, "They say that when a man drowns, his entire life flashes before his eyes. I am indeed fortunate for having just that same experience without even getting my feet wet."

He closed his acceptance speech in characteristic fashion:

"I'm sure you will agree that murder can be so much more charming and enjoyable even for the victim if the surroundings are pleasant and the people involved are ladies and gentlemen like yourselves.

"They tell me that a murder is committed every minute, so I don't want to waste any more of your time. I know you want to get to work."

THERE WAS GOSSIP during the filming of Hitchcock's next film, *Family Plot,* with people saying that he directed from a car rather than on the set because "he couldn't be bothered to get out," the implication being that he didn't care about the film.

He cared desperately, but by then he was in constant physical pain. His legs no longer supported him, and he was afraid of falling. He believed a director could not direct if he lost his dignity. "My dignity is a heavy burden to carry," he told me. The outside world, even most of the inside world, did not know the truth, because Universal was dedicated to protecting the director.

"I went to work for Mr. Wasserman in 1973," Thom Mount told me, "so I knew Mr. Hitchcock from then until he died. For *Family Plot,* a lot of the work was done on the soundstage, but Mr. Hitchcock had a very hard time standing up for any lengthy period of time.

"Walking was not his strong suit by that time, so we took an old Cadillac convertible and a welding torch, and we cut the sides, and the back off of it, fitted a flat platform on the back of the Cadillac, and on that flat platform we put a chair for a cinematographer, as if it were a crane that was mounted on a hydraulic lift. Mr. Hitchcock would sit in the chair and move himself around in any direction and see in all directions. The Cadillac was moved all around the soundstage, even though they were interiors, just backing it into place, wherever it needed to be. And so Mr. Hitchcock could move around.

"Of course, it had the dual purpose of being able to move to outdoor locations. Mr. Hitchcock would listen to the boom mike on a direct feed through a little earphone. He could hear everything that was going on, every little nuance of the actors' work and performance.

"Even if Hitchcock didn't necessarily love all actors, as long as each actor was part of the film Hitchcock was creating, that actor was important to him."

Before and during the shooting of *Family Plot,* Hitchcock's health was a problem, for him and for the film.

Hilton Green remembered: "Lew Wasserman would come by the set when Mr. H. was shooting every morning, and he would come over to me and say, 'How's he doing? Is everything all right?' Then he'd go talk to him."

Production was delayed by Hitchcock's health. After he complained of dizziness, a pacemaker was implanted. Then, there were operations for colitis and a kidney stone. Still, filming proceeded.

Family Plot, was based on *The Rainbird Pattern,* a novel by Victor

Canning. Hitchcock asked Anthony Shaffer if he would like to write the screenplay, but Shaffer declined. With some misgivings about the story, Ernest Lehman agreed. The locale of the novel was changed, and California replaced rural England.

> Spiritualist Blanche Tyler (Barbara Harris) is asked to locate a missing heir, whom she pursues with her cab driver boyfriend, George Lumley (Bruce Dern), an unemployed actor. The man they seek, Arthur Adamson (William Devane), is posing as a legitimate jeweler while kidnapping wealthy people for a ransom in diamonds. He is assisted by his wife, Fran (Karen Black).
>
> Following a false lead, they inadvertently become involved with the Adamsons, and Blanche and George are almost killed. Afterward, their paths cross frequently, causing Fran to believe in Blanche's powers.
>
> Adamson's next kidnapping is complicated by George and Blanche being accidental witnesses, and Blanche is held prisoner. George rescues her, foiling Adamson's plans and leading Blanche to the chandelier where the diamonds are hidden. Skeptical George now believes in Blanche's powers, but a wink from her to the audience implies otherwise.

Though Hitchcock didn't know it at the time, this last wink by Barbara Harris was to be his own last wink at his "public." Hitchcock told me he had wanted Jack Nicholson for the part of George Lumley, "but Mr. Nicholson was too busy flying over a cuckoo nest." Thom Mount said that Nicholson was not only busy, but too high-priced. The part went to Bruce Dern, who had played the sailor young Marnie kills.

"Hitch noticed me in *Marnie*," Dern said. "I had a small part in it, but I got the lead in *Family Plot*. Hitch was very different when he was directing *Marnie* from when he was doing *Plot*.

"With *Marnie*, he had everything storyboarded, and there wasn't room to ad-lib. You didn't get to know him at all. *Family Plot* was storyboarded, too, but if you wanted to try something, he was open, and if he liked it, he was ready to drop the storyboard and let you run with what you'd come up with.

"I thought it was because he got to know me better and trusted me, and I made him laugh. I told him jokes I can't repeat which he enjoyed and which pepped him up. A lot of actors were so in awe of him they couldn't do that. On *Plot* I found him friendly and always ready to listen to me, but maybe he'd just gotten weaker."

Shortly after shooting began, Roy Thinnes, who had been cast as Adamson, the villain, was replaced by William Devane. Thinnes never knew why.

"I'd just finished *The Hindenberg* with Robert Wise," Thinnes told me, "and he suggested me to Alfred Hitchcock. I was on top of the world.

"I met with Hitchcock in his office several times. He lifted his shirt and showed me his pacemaker. We tasted wine from his own cellar, had some amusing conversations, and talked a lot about my character. It doesn't get any better.

"Our first work was at the Grace Cathedral in San Francisco. Hitchcock believed that absolutely anything could happen in front of a congregation at high mass, and everyone would behave, because they were on their church behavior. The criminal, dressed as a verger, and his accomplice, disguised as an old woman, inject the bishop with a hypodermic needle in front of everyone during mass, and drag him away.

"Since my character wouldn't have wanted to leave fingerprints, I suggested using rubber gloves. I should have understood that you don't mess with something that's been storyboarded by Hitchcock. But he listened, and we shot with and without the gloves. But I sensed some tension about it.

"In the morning, my wife and I were invited to dine with the Hitchcocks at Ernie's that night. It couldn't get any better.

"Then, in the afternoon, we were dis-invited. This was after my suggestion of the gloves.

"At the end of each day, Peggy [Robertson], Hitchcock's assistant, told me, 'He just thinks you're wonderful.'

"I had promised my wife we were going to Ernie's that night, so we went to Ernie's. We had the special table, center stage. Then, my wife said, 'Look. In the corner.'

"It was Alma and Alfred, and the cast.

"During the evening, Alma came by, and she was so apologetic.

"Back in Los Angeles, my agent called, weeping, saying I had been fired.

"I'd worked three days with Hitchcock.

"About a month later, I was at Chasen's, and there he was. I nodded to him and to Mrs. Hitchcock. She said, 'He's sorry, dear. It's just that you're so very nice.' Hitchcock didn't say anything.

"I'd played the villain in a rather nice way because I wanted to develop his evil side so the audience could go along with my character. I could have, *would* have, played the part in a more sinister way if he'd told me.

"About a year later, Bruce Dern told me that on the last day of shooting, Hitchcock had asked him to come over to his bungalow to see the scenes he had shot with me.

"Hitch said, 'I made a terrible mistake, didn't I?'

"It made me feel a lot better. This great man had gone all the way out on a limb with my fellow actor to say, 'I made a mistake, didn't I?' He knew that Bruce would tell me.

"I was very upset when he [Hitchcock] died. I'd had the feeling that we would work together again."

Lillian Gish wanted to test for the part of Julia Rainbird, but it had been promised to Cathleen Nesbitt. "I had no idea what the movie was about," Gish told me, "only that the character was an elderly lady being directed by Alfred Hitchcock. It's taken me a long time to achieve the first qualification for the part. I started out with Mr. Griffith, so, I thought why not end with Mr. Hitchcock?" Despite Hitchcock's saying that his favorite chase film was D. W. Griffith's *Way Down East* starring Lillian Gish, she did not get the part.

Henry Bumstead found *Family Plot* a much simpler picture to design than *Topaz*. "It was mostly done around the studio, but, you know, everything you did with Hitch was demanding.

"There was that car chase up the mountains, and I found this area. When I took Hitch up there, he told the driver, 'Only a crazy art director would find this location.' But the location did work. The thing with Hitch was, it was hard to get him out to look at these locations. I tried as much as I could to take pictures and show him, so he had to trust me.

"We had a cemetery exterior, and we made a deal with the cemetery to let the weeds grow, and that we would clean it all up afterwards.

"You go out in the morning, and there's 150 people standing around the cemetery. They're serving breakfast, and everybody's got a sandwich, waiting for Hitch, and Hitch drives up. It is a little nerve-wracking.

"We're all standing around these tombstones, and Hitch is pouting. I'm pointing up to where the sun should be, but there's no sun. I had to go get a painter to paint the names on the tombstones so you could read the names without the sun."

"My youngest daughter, Pamela, when she was about twelve," Hilton Green told me, "wanted to come in and watch Mr. H. shoot. I said, 'No, he doesn't want kids.' But she insisted. And I said, 'Well, if you promise to stay in the back all the time, and not make a whimper.' So, I brought her in and stood her over in the corner in the dark watching. This was especially serious, because it was for a feature.

"I went over and talked with him. And he says, 'Who's the young lady that you won't let come in?' He knew everything.

"I told him she's my daughter, and he says, 'Why is she over there?'

"'Because I don't want her to disturb you.'

"'But that's your daughter. Bring her over here.' And he called the prop man and brought a chair, and Mr. H. had it put right beside him. I introduced them, and he says, 'Hilton, you can go.' And he sat there the rest of the day with her. He directed the movie and talked, and explained things to her. I just couldn't get over it."

THE FILM OPENED to mixed reviews on the negative side. Some were generous reviews by critics who respected and even revered Hitchcock. Most were routinely poor reviews. A few were excessively cruel. *Family Plot* was not a financial success.

Rumors circulated that Hitchcock was drinking too much at this time. Howard Kazanjian, who was working closely with him, wanted to refute these rumors.

"I never saw him drink, even wine. Only towards the very end, maybe six months before he passed on. In his top drawer, he would have a little bit of vodka, and he'd start that maybe at four in the afternoon, just about the time he went home. And that's what irritates me so much, when people say that he drank heavily. If Hitchcock had a drink, he had it late in the afternoon."

In spite of his physical problems, Hitchcock maintained his professional reserve, which extended to his dress code.

"Mr. H.'s dress code contrasted sharply with what we know now in Hollywood," Hilton Green recalled. "Many people took him by mistake as very stuck-up and felt he wouldn't talk, and that wasn't true.

"He was an introvert, very shy around new people. People would feel he was aloof, but he wasn't that. He was very reserved. He stuck with the same crews. If you did your job, he wanted you back."

"One cannot become too familiar with the people with whom one has to work," Hitchcock had told me. "One can't take the risk of exposing oneself as just an ordinary man."

"He was a gentleman," production manager Doc Erickson told me, "but he couldn't afford to be palsy-walsy with everyone, or he wouldn't have had time to make his pictures."

"What Hitchcock enjoyed most was planning his own films," Green continued. "When he wasn't doing that, he enjoyed seeing films in his own projection room. I would sit with him by the hour, running films. How he loved to run films! He saw everything that would come out."

One of the films Hitchcock enjoyed watching was *Animal House,* the work of a young director on the Universal lot, John Landis.

"Hitch loomed large in my psyche," Landis told me. It was almost like meeting a mythological figure. He was already elderly and walked with some difficulty. He wasn't very tall, but he was very large. He was heavy and had huge hands.

"I'd heard that he was a practical joker. My own experience with him was that he was absolutely charming, although he could be vulgar in a way that was unexpected. He had a saucy postcard sense of humor. He liked the risqué.

"The way I met him was, I was preparing a movie I ended up not making called *The Incredible Shrinking Woman.* I had an idea to do a teaser promo to go out in theaters, literally almost a year before the picture would. The idea was that you'd start with the famous silhouette and dissolve to Hitch sitting in a book-lined study, behind the desk, his hands folded on the table. He says, 'Good evening. I'm Alfred Hitchcock, and it is my great pleasure to announce to you that production has begun on perhaps the most important picture of all time, *The Incredible Shrinking Woman,* starring Miss Lily Tomlin.' Then, he would open his hand, and a three-inch Lily would wave.

"People at MCA liked the idea, but how do I get to Hitch? I can't just walk up to him. So I called Lew Wasserman and said, 'Lew, I'd really like to meet Hitch.' And Lew said, 'Sure. We eat lunch all the time. We'd love to have lunch with you.'

"I can't *tell* you how excited I was. I'm meeting Alfred Hitchcock!

"So I go to his bungalow, and he had this small dining room. It was probably built as an office, and it had a table which could sit maybe four or five people, a round table, and not much else.

"Framed on one wall in his office was a marvelous cartoon of two goats in a junkyard chewing on reels of film. One goat is saying to the other, 'I liked the book better.'

"He would have lunch there, every day, the same thing from the commissary, a small New York steak, French fries or mashed potatoes, and sliced tomatoes.

"He was very Buddha-like, and I was *awed* to be there. We were sitting, and he's looking at me with these sort of benign, calm, stern eyes.

"We were talking, and he said, 'I understand you want me to be in a promo. Tell me the idea.'

"I pitched the idea, and the first thing Hitchcock says is, 'Who is Lily Tomlin?'

"Well, Lily Tomlin's an actress and comedian, and quite a celebrity,' I said. That was at the height of her fame.

"Hitch said, 'Well, can we change her name?'

"'Well, Mr. Hitchcock, she's kind of—'

"That's when he said, 'Call me Hitch.'

"'Well, Hitch, she's very well known and established as Lily Tomlin.'

"'I've never heard of her.'

"I'm dying! I don't know what to do. I'm a deer in the headlights.

"He was teasing me. He was totally teasing me. But it must have been three minutes of torture. Then he laughed. We all laughed. He'd really fooled me. Of course he knew Lily Tomlin.

"Anyway, we didn't do the promo, but I ended up having lunch with him, maybe ten times in a year before he stopped coming to work."

Until he stopped going to his office at Universal, Hitchcock enjoyed inviting people to have lunch with him. When Elliott Gould called him to make a date, Hitchcock sang to him over the phone, "It won't be a stylish luncheon, we can't afford a muncheon" to the tune of "A Bicycle Built for Two." Gould remembered they had "Plebeian Steak."

When they met, he told Gould, "I'm perfect, from the waist up."

"At lunch," Gould said, "he commented that some people thought he was anti-actor, but it wasn't true; however, if one person thought he had to make himself more outstanding than the rest, it was distracting.

"'Take Beethoven's Ninth,' Mr. Hitchcock said. 'You realize one person wrote every note for each instrumentalist, but that they have to play all together in concert. That's how it is for me on the set to make a picture.'

"Hitchcock said that what counts is not how the actor feels, but how the audience feels. What he wanted from his actors, he said, was 'motion, not motivation.'"

David Brown detected in Hitchcock's extreme reserve a kind of suspicion of Hollywood. "Although well rewarded by Hollywood, he was an outsider in the Hollywood sense. I don't remember him milling around at Chasen's. He remained seated at his table, enjoying his dinner, and though he was in the front room through which everyone entered, he didn't make eye contact with the people passing through.

"I didn't see him at the usual functions. Of course, he was part of Hollywood, but he never felt, in my opinion, *really* part of Hollywood."

Tony Curtis, who knew Hitchcock socially with his then-wife, Janet Leigh, remembered when Hitchcock was told by his doctor to give up smoking.

"Mr. Hitchcock loved to smoke those handsome Monte Cristos. They looked like torpedoes. Beautiful. He knew I liked cigars then, and he gave me six boxes of them.

"I wanted to thank him. I like to draw, and I always liked to draw hands. I'm right-handed, so I've always drawn left hands, because I use my left hand as a model.

"I wanted to do something special, so I drew my left hand in the mirror, so it could pose as a right hand, and I had it making the A-OK sign with the thumb and forefinger. Then, since I had done the movie *Houdini,* I drew the right hand with a card popping out of it that said, 'Mr. Hitchcock—Tony Curtis.' I never called him Hitch.

"It was quite simple and, if I may be so bold, quite beautiful. I sent that to him, and he loved it. You know, I won't say it was abstract, but it was just abstract enough for him to enjoy it.

"He once told me a story, which I'm going to share with you.

"He says, 'There's a guy flying in an airplane with a pilot, and they're flying over a city. At one point, the guy opens the door and jumps out of the plane. He's got a parachute, and as he jumps out, he pulls the ripcord, and it opens. He floats delicately down into an area. He undoes his jumpsuit he's wearing, takes off the parachute, and there, underneath, is a tuxedo. He puts on white gloves and walks one block into the back door of a restaurant, goes in, and emerges as the maître d'.'

"I said, 'Okay, what?'

"He said, 'I haven't got the rest of it yet.'

"Anyway, he was a wonderful man. Charming, very erudite. I think that would be the word. Very articulate. His films are all, every one of them, intricately woven and beautifully done. You know that movie with Gregory Peck and the lines on the bed? Oooo! Wonderful. You know, one of my wives worked in one of them, *Psycho,* and it was an excellent film."

• • •

MARTIN LANDAU spoke with me just before his appearance at the commemoration of the seventy-fifth anniversary of CBS in 2003. He recalled the fiftieth anniversary, in 1978, when he and Hitchcock were there.

"At the fiftieth anniversary of CBS, Hitch and I spent an hour and a half talking, and that was the last time I had a lengthy conversation with him. We had a long talk about life. His wife had had a stroke, and we were talking about getting old. I mean, *he* was talking about it. He was very worried about her. She outlived him, but at that time it didn't look as if that was going to happen.

"The conversation was a lament in a way about the difficulty of doing things that were once simple. Everything had grown harder. The essence of it was—and I never had felt this before with him—I felt a very depressed man facing old age.

"But he was still talking about making films and he was going to his office at Universal."

IV.

THE LAST
YEARS

THE LAST YEARS

❧

The Short Night to The End

"I'M TOYING WITH a new film project now, but I don't know if the audience wants my fantasies anymore," Hitchcock told me in the late 1970s. His new project was *The Short Night,* a novel by Ronald Kirkbride that he had bought for the screen in 1968. After *Family Plot,* he was ready to start on it, with spirit and enthusiasm, though not with physical well-being.

"I'm a very lucky man," Hitchcock said, looking back on his life. "I began very early doing the thing I wanted to do. And I was able to continue doing it. I met the perfect companion for my life. We had the perfect child, our daughter, Pat. I wouldn't change anything about my life, except that it has to end.

"It all went so fast. I was a chubby little boy. I was going to the movies. Then, I was *making* them. Now, I don't know if I'll make any more. I'd like to.

"I've made many pictures for a long time. I'm proud of some of them. I'm not ashamed of any of them.

"Movies are my life, but even if I can't make any more, I would like to be alive—as long as the Madame is. I could never have a well day with her sick.

"Our life together is now as close as yesterday, as far away as tomorrow."

THE SHORT NIGHT is a film that never was. Hitchcock had wanted to make the film for ten years, and Universal did everything they could to make it possible. Thom Mount, who was assigned to help Hitchcock, found the director's working methods unconventional.

"I'm a young executive on the rise at Universal and having this relationship with Mr. Hitchcock for about a year, looking after him and his film and making certain that everything is as easy for him as possible. Then, the company is sending me to London to meet with a lot of our foreign sales and distribution people to bring them up to speed on the slate of pictures coming from the company next year. Mr. Hitchcock, hearing this over our customary lunch, looks at me for a long beat.

"He pulls a piece of paper out of his pocket. He writes down a name and number. He says, 'When you get to London, you call this gentleman, and it will be an educational experience.' I say, 'Great. Thank you.' I put it in my pocket, and go to London.

"I call this guy from the hotel. He says, 'Oh, yes. I understand that we're going to have lunch on Thursday.' I said, 'Great.' He says, 'Here's the address.'

"I don't know anything about London, so I get a car and driver. We get in the car and go, and we go and we go. Finally, I say, 'Where are we going?' And he says, 'Well, you know—this is Wormwood Scrubs, the prison.'

"I go to the prison, and the director of the prison is a friend of Mr. Hitchcock's. We have lunch in his office. And he describes to me the nature of the criminal mind. Over lunch!

"Mr. Hitchcock's sense of humor—just fabulous. I get in the car and go back to work.

"There was more to it, however, because Wormwood Scrubs was

an important setting for one of Hitchcock's favorite scenes in *The Short Night*. The film was to open with a prison break, and the prison was Wormwood Scrubs.

"*The Short Night* was the last screenplay that Mr. Hitchcock developed at Universal. We did a location scout in Helsinki, and we prepared generally to make the movie, knowing that Mr. Hitchcock's failing health might preclude his making it. But Mr. Hitchcock was game, and he prepared it, as he always had, knowing, in an unspoken way, that he probably couldn't make it. Mr. Wasserman's instructions were very simple.

"Mr. Hitchcock had been an enormous asset to this company and a great friend of Lew's, and we would treat him with dignity as long as he wanted to keep working. Even if the film has no potential for going forward, the company would support him in his work.

"It was fun, it was inspiring. We hoped. It was sad, too.

"Mr. Hitchcock worked on scripts like a madman. When we developed *The Short Night,* we did an Ernest Lehman draft. At this point, I had sort of graduated to being the executive in charge of everything, with Mr. Hitchcock. Every time I had lunch with him, which was about once a month and more often when we were on a script, I would make a report to Mr. Wasserman.

"Mr. Wasserman was *extremely* interested in Mr. Hitchcock's well-being. I would listen at these lunches to try and interpret Mr. Hitchcock's kind of left-handed sense of criticism.

"He would never say, 'This is awful.' He would say, 'Well, perhaps there's something lacking in that approach.'

"He was this fountain of wisdom about the art and craft, and yet, curiously, unapproachable. I know sometimes he was tough on me as a young idiot trying to be his servant.

"On the other hand, once you got past the protective membrane, which was the sort of cynicism and perverse delight in terrifying you, he became a very wise counselor, and his advice was always brilliant.

"For me, the central and most admirable thing about Mr. Hitchcock was his deeply passionate personal commitment to the work. Whatever his age, whatever his condition. He could barely walk at a certain point; it didn't matter, his mind was nimble as ever. His sense of humor was as astonishing as ever, and his angle of attack on material, always fresh.

"I've always been an avid reader of newspapers. I read several every day. I try to pay attention to the world around me. Mr. Hitchcock did the same thing. I'd walk in, and he'd say, 'Did you see the story about the teenager who cut her parents up with the buzz saw? She sealed the bodies in the family sedan while she drove to the prom. And all in the quiet San Fernando Valley.' He loved these aberrations, the unexpected nature of life and crime, and he would see a movie in these incidents."

Hitchcock had always liked to read. "One of the most enjoyable experiences Alma and I shared was reading separately, together," he told me. "We read in each other's presence. We each had a book, and an hour or more could go by without either of us saying a word. But I was totally conscious of her there, and her comforting presence. We did not need to speak.

"Usually, she read fiction, books from which we could make a film. I read mostly fiction books in my early days, and later nonfiction, especially about crime. I have always read the newspaper, particularly crime stories. which are the equal of fiction, or better. Even those which cannot be used in their entirety have wonderful kernels."

Ernest Lehman was selected as the writer for *The Short Night*, because, Mount explained, "We had him under contract at the time, they knew each other well, and Mr. Hitchcock liked him.

"*The Short Night* had been adapted from a book which had no third act. It had a wonderful opening, and an interesting second act.

Gavin Brandt, a double agent posing as a British spy but actually working for the Soviets, is helped to escape from Wormwood

Scrubs where he is imprisoned. He is to be driven through Europe
in the trunk of an automobile to his wife and children, who are
waiting for him in Finland, and then to the Soviet Union.

The young woman who is driving the escape vehicle resists
Brandt's advances, and she is killed in the struggle.

An American agent has been sent to Finland to intercept the
fugitive by watching Brandt's wife and children. He gets to know
the wife, and she, not realizing his mission, falls in love with him.
When she finds out who he is, she must decide whether to stay
with the American or go to Russia with her husband.

"Mr. Hitchcock had one scene in the book that he loved, the sort
of raison d'être for pursuing *The Short Night*. That was the sequence
he mapped out very clearly even before we got a first draft. The killer
is on this small island in Scandinavia.

"Our hero-victim is hiding there from the killer and submerges
himself in the water on the reed-lined banks of the island. He plucks
a dry reed and is breathing through the reed underwater. As the murderer is looking for this person, knowing he's somewhere in close
proximity, a wind comes up, and all of the reeds blow to the left. One
stands straight up. The killer looks at it for a beat, and we see the
reed; and we see the killer's eyes. He does not make the connection
and moves on.

"That sequence was the tone Hitchcock wanted for the entire
movie. Mr. Lehman turned in a draft, but it wasn't working yet."

Ernest Lehman saw a problem.

"Hitch was obsessed with the idea of the leading man raping and
killing a woman at the very beginning. What audience would have
any sympathy for the hero after that? I argued. But Hitch was
adamant until I convinced him that I could not go on with it that way,
even though I didn't want *Family Plot* to be his last picture."

"In 1978," Norman Lloyd told me, "Hilton Green, a person I
respected and liked, and whom I knew Hitch respected and liked,

who had worked with Hitch on TV and features, asked me about assisting Hitch on his new film.

"Hitch was determined to do *The Short Night* as a film, I think because he had no other project. This was in spite of the constant pain he was enduring from arthritis in his knees. His health was totally failing him.

"I was supposed to help especially with location shooting.

"When I arrived, there wasn't a script that satisfied Hitch. I didn't truly believe the picture would ever be made, and Hitch himself said to me, 'This picture isn't ever going to get made.' I asked why, and he said, 'Because it isn't necessary.'

"The story was a potboiler. Hitch had been dissatisfied with the first script. I knew that pre-production activity was what he always liked, with his retinue of friends and technicians. It was easier to get characters on your storyboard to do what you wanted than it was with live actors, although an actor might lend some brilliance.

"We were working on continuity when he said the moment had arrived to go to the screenplay. I asked who would write that screenplay, and Hitch said, 'You will.'

"'Not me.'

"Immediately I knew those were words I wished I could take back.

"Hitch became cool, and he really never forgave me. I tried to speak with him, but I wasn't able to get an appointment. Finally, I just walked into his office at Universal. He was there alone working on the script. He never liked the solitary life of a writer, and I don't think he actually liked writing. He liked drawing his stories.

"He never allowed me to take back my knee-jerk words, because I believe he heard the truth in them, that I didn't believe in his film. He took that as a betrayal.

"He did get someone to work on the screenplay, but the film was never made.

"I wished that I had gone on assisting him whatever way I could, though I don't think it would have resulted in another Hitchcock film. But I would have been faithful to our thirty-eight-year friend-ship.

"I wasn't allowed to change my mind because Hitch had too much pride for that. I knew I had wounded him.

"I believe he never let his guard down. Only with Alma. But it wasn't understood even by Hitch's closest friends how extremely sensitive he was or how personally he took everything. And for him everything was personal."

Mount looked for another writer. "I happened to find David Free-man, who had written something for me, so he went to work on this. During this period, Mr. Hitchcock started getting sicker and sicker, weaker and weaker.

"We did send a location scout off to Helsinki. We did continue to make the moves that he always made in preparation for a picture. We talked about a cameraman. We broke the thing down on the story-board and started talking about the cost, whether we really should shoot in Scandinavia or should duplicate the setting somewhere else.

"Mr. Hitchcock wanted to go to Helsinki. He wanted to shoot on these islands in the immediate region of the city. He had some other bits and bobs he wanted to do there, and we estimated that we could go there and shoot for three or four weeks, and then come back and finish the picture in the studio, which was very much his style. We began to talk about cast.

"Lew had spoken to Mr. Hitchcock's doctor and said, 'What can you do? Will it help if he doesn't have a steak every day?' and the doc-tor said, 'Well, it might have helped years ago, but it's not going to make any difference now.'

"So, we made the quiet corporate decision that we would proceed. If Mr. Hitchcock was well enough to get on a plane for Helsinki, we'll start the movie. Lew was very clear. 'If I have to lose a few mil-lion dollars making Hitch happy, it's the best money we've ever spent.' It was never a question.

"Mr. Hitchcock, however, was smarter than we are, as usual. He was well aware that he was getting to a point where it wasn't possible.

"One day, he sent me a draft of the script, marked up with comments on it, and a little card that said, 'Compliments of Alfred Hitchcock.' He wrote all his notes on this card. It said, 'If you think this project should be moved to another director, I give you my permission to do that.'

"Utterly unnecessary. We never spoke of it. That was the only thing that he said, and I simply called him on the phone.

"I said, 'Mr. Hitchcock, I simply want you to know the company is proceeding with the picture with you without any question.' He said, 'That's okay.' Period. But I thought it was an amazingly generous and unnecessary give on his part."

For Hitchcock, however, it was an admission that the end was near. It was important to him to believe that he was physically able to make another film, and although he was beginning to doubt he could, he still had his pride.

"I was in my office in the Black Tower when my phone rang," Hilton Green remembered. "It was Mr. H.'s secretary calling, frantic. She asked me to come to Mr. H.'s office as fast as I could. I had my tie in my pocket because I'd always worn a tie with him, as everyone did. She said, 'Don't bother about your tie.'

"I raced to his office and found him lying on the floor behind his desk. He'd fallen and couldn't get up. His secretary couldn't lift him. He was there waiting for me to help him up, because he didn't want anyone to know. He didn't want anyone to see him like that.

"I picked him up and put him in his chair. It just broke my heart."

Hitchcock faced the absence of Alma's advice and approval, on which he had depended for more than half a century. She was at home, but ill. "If Mr. H. said Alma liked it very much," Green said, "it was the greatest compliment Hitchcock could ever pay a writer." The only greater compliment was, "Alma loved it."

Mount recalled that when Alma was briefly feeling better, Hitchcock brought her the script of *The Short Night*. "She said she liked it, which really pleased Mr. Hitchcock, but that wasn't as important to him as that she had *read* it. After that, he was elated because he thought it could be like the good old days, at least for a while, having Alma's opinion and, even more important, to be able to show his work to her."

"My parents loved a beautifully set table," Pat recalled. "Even when only the two of them were having dinner together, my mother used a beautiful linen tablecloth, fine crystal glasses, lovely china, and good silver, and my father appreciated that."

When Alma became too ill to cook for her husband, he cooked for her. With the shift of nurses Alma needed, the Hitchcocks' small house couldn't afford to be crowded by the presence of another person, a cook.

One day, while Hitchcock was preparing the meal, he burned his arm badly with hot grease. In his words, "That made my short-order cooking short-lived."

HE CONTINUED TO appear at his Universal office. Green described the day that Hitchcock knew he couldn't go on:

"After Bob Boyle and I had scouted locations in England and Finland, and I shot some footage on a Polaroid camera to show what the locations looked like, I came back to Universal and laid it out for Mr. H. He said, 'Great.' I thought we were going ahead.

"Then, his secretary called me one day in my office, and she said, 'Mr. Hitchcock has to see you right away.'

"I went to his office. She said, 'You'd better go in.'

"He was sitting there behind his desk, and he said, 'I want you to do a favor for me. I want you to go see Lew Wasserman. And I want you to tell him that I'm all through, that I can't go on.'

"That was the saddest day of my life. I couldn't understand. I said, 'What's wrong?'

"He said, 'I can't make movies anymore the way I want to. I'm just not physically able.'

"I said, 'Of course you are. We can do this picture together. You know, you just tell us what you want, and we'll do it.'

"He said, 'No, I don't want to make movies that way.'

"I don't know if you know much about Lew Wasserman. Really a strong man. He cried. 'I knew this day was coming,' he said, and it was very sad.

"After that day, Mr. H. came in a couple of times. There was a tribute to him, the AFI. He got very weak." The American Film Institute lifetime achievement gala honoring Hitchcock was held in March 1979.

ON MAY 8, 1979, Hitchcock closed his office at Universal.

"Hitchcock's bungalow, which was the size of three railroad cars, was kept fully staffed, and nothing was changed," Mount said. "Mr. Hitchcock was sick, at home, and I let him and Alma know that the bungalow was standing. He sent word through Alma that we could close it. He wouldn't need it anymore.

"His was the last bungalow on what is called the front lot. It was put there deliberately, so that Mr. Hitchcock could walk about three hundred feet from his bungalow to the Black Tower should he want to see anyone.

"Afterwards, Lew had that little caricature from the television show painted on the side of the building, about twelve inches high, which was the only thing that identified it as Mr. Hitchcock's building. That building stayed there at least a year after Mr. Hitchcock's demise, untouched.

"The building has been moved from that location, and chopped up and turned into other bungalows. So, the building actually still exists, although it's in sections now, on different parts of the lot."

Hitchcock had told me, "As long as I have my health and energy, I would never retire," but even as he spoke, his health was rapidly declining. He had to bear considerable pain, but still, he did not want to retire. "I can't retire. I have no hobbies," he said. "What would I do?"

When the moment finally came, when Hitchcock decided not to keep his office at Universal, it meant he was admitting to Lew Wasserman, to everyone he knew, to all who knew him, to Alma, and especially to himself, that the Hitchcock body of work was complete. He had told King Vidor and me that the body of Alfred Hitchcock's work would be complete when the body of Alfred Hitchcock gave out.

The prospect of going to Helsinki for the filming of *The Short Night,* and leaving Alma, who was too ill to travel, had been difficult for him to contemplate, though he would have liked to have had another success in those last years, not so much for himself, as for the Madame. "If our health had held up," he said, "we would have done it again.

"I couldn't imagine being alive without Alma. I wouldn't want to be. I always thought I would go first. It never occurred to me that I would survive Alma. I'm older, you know. One day older."

Hitchcock said that Alma's vanity had vanished, and he missed it. She had taken great pride in her hair, wore light makeup, preferred high heels, and enjoyed having her clothes made by Edith Head. Herself only slightly taller than Alma, Head had known how to dress the petite woman.

Finally, Alma lost interest in her garden, which had always meant so much to her. "It was a terrible thing," Hitchcock said, "when she didn't care about being in the sun with her flowers."

In the last year, when Alma's health made it an effort to go out, the Hitchcocks received regular deliveries of dinners from Chasen's. It was no routine act for that restaurant, but the Hitchcocks were no ordinary patrons. For years, the Hitchcocks had given the restaurant their enduring support and affection, and the restaurant returned their feeling.

•   •   •

HITCHCOCK HAD ALWAYS appreciated and enjoyed honors. Never having received an Oscar as a director had troubled him. He had very much wanted that recognition from his peers.

In 1968, he had received the Irving Thalberg Award for his work as a producer. At the Academy Awards ceremony, he stepped up to the microphone and said, "Thank you." Just that. The audience was expecting more. So was he.

In the last few years of his life, Hitchcock heard there was talk of a possible knighthood. He would have liked such an honor, he told me, "Mostly so Mrs. Hitchcock might be addressed as Lady Hitchcock when visiting preserves on the ground floor at Fortnum & Mason. 'One bitter orange, one plum, Lady Hitchcock, and perhaps some digestive biscuits?' You know, that kind of thing, but too late for Fortnum's now."

A few years earlier, Alma had said that her husband's knighthood was a lingering hope she had for him. It meant much less to her, because she admired and had totally adjusted to "the classless system" of America, "but it would be nice for him," she said.

On December 31, 1979, Alfred Joseph Hitchcock became Sir Alfred. Not able to travel back to England, he was knighted by proxy a few days later by the British consul general in Los Angeles in the presence of Lew Wasserman, Cary Grant, Janet Leigh, and others.

Hitchcock had hoped that the honor would come to him, but by the time he received it, he had forgotten about hoping for it. He had lost an important element of happiness—being able to look forward—and there was little time remaining for Hitch and Alma to enjoy being Lord and Lady Hitchcock.

When a reporter asked Hitchcock why it had taken Queen Elizabeth so long to knight him, he responded: "It seems she forgot."

In early 1980, Hitchcock received the Man of the Year Award from the British-American Chamber of Commerce in Los Angeles. Ronald Neame presented the award to him. "He was very frail and in a wheelchair when I went up to him before the ceremony. 'Hitch,' I said, 'do you remember me? I'm Ronnie.' He smiled and placed a hand on my arm. 'Of course, I do, Ronnie. You're one of my boys.'"

UNABLE TO MAKE FILMS, lonely for Alma's companionship, Hitchcock lost interest in life. Food and wine no longer brought him pleasure. In almost constant pain, he lost his will to live.

"It's terribly embarrassing to be sick," he once told me. "And one's own death is so undignified."

On April 29, 1980, in the early morning, at his Bellagio Road home in Bel Air, Alfred Hitchcock died. The funeral service was held at the Church of the Good Shepherd in Beverly Hills. In accordance with his wishes, he was cremated, and his ashes scattered off the California coast in the Pacific Ocean.

On May 8, a mass was said for him at Westminster Cathedral in London.

Alma lived on more than two years after her husband. She stayed in their home, frail, with medical help, living in her private world, emotionally supported by the visits of their daughter, Pat, and her family.

Alma Reville Hitchcock died on July 6, 1982. Her funeral was at St. Paul the Apostle Church in Westwood, and her ashes were also scattered in the Pacific Ocean.

PAT HITCHCOCK talked with me at New York's Plaza Hotel just after Christmas in 2003. She and her three daughters had come from their homes in California for the holidays. In August, her granddaughter, Melissa, the only great-grandchild the Hitchcocks had known, had died at the age of twenty-four, and the family found it difficult to spend Christmas at home without her there.

Melissa, the daughter of their first grandchild, Mary, had been diagnosed with cystic fibrosis before the age of two.

When Pat told her father, he reacted characteristically. "We'll do something about it," he said, but his daughter explained there was nothing they *could* do. It was incurable.

Pat and her daughters, however, *have* tried to do something about it. In his spirit, they have created an Alfred Hitchcock cystic fibrosis charity.

"I AM AN OBSERVER OF LIFE," Hitchcock had told me shortly after I met him. "Personally I have preferred to live an ordinary, uncluttered life, doing my chores, which was making movies. The Chinese have a proverb to the effect that an interesting life is better not lived. I liked to make films *about* the man-on-the-spot, not to *be* him."

Near the end of his life, Hitchcock said that when he and Alma realized they couldn't travel anymore, it was then that they really felt old. "We could have traveled," he said, "but it would have been like trying to make movies when you really can't."

Hitchcock was a romantic, as was his wife. They had spoken about just one more trip to the Palace Hotel in St. Moritz, perhaps for Christmas, their favorite time to be there to celebrate their wedding anniversary.

"Neither of us wanted to disappoint the other," he said, "by admitting to not believing the possibility existed. Then, Alma and I stopped talking about our next trip to St. Moritz. Each of us had come to understand that it wasn't a place we wanted to return to, but rather, a time.

"The worst thing, you know, is when you cannot go back to a place where you have always been happy," he said, "because you are afraid that if you go back, you won't be happy—not because the place has changed, but because you have changed."

ALFRED HITCHCOCK— A COMPLETE FILMOGRAPHY

ABBREVIATIONS:
GB–Great Britain; G–Germany; US–United States.

FILMS

1920	(GB)	*The Great Day*	(designed intertitles)
1920	(GB)	*The Call of Youth*	(designed intertitles)
1921	(GB)	*The Princess of New York*	(designed intertitles)
1921	(GB)	*Appearances*	(designed intertitles)
1921	(GB)	*Dangerous Lies*	(designed intertitles)
1921	(GB)	*The Mystery Road*	(designed intertitles)
1921	(GB)	*Beside the Bonnie Briar Bush*	(designed intertitles)
1922	(GB)	*Three Live Ghosts*	(designed intertitles)
1922	(GB)	*Perpetua*	(designed intertitles)
1922	(GB)	*The Man from Home*	(designed intertitles)
1922	(GB)	*Spanish Jade*	(designed intertitles)
1922	(GB)	*Tell Your Children*	(designed intertitles)
1922	(GB)	*Number 13* (unfinished)	(director)
1923	(GB)	*Always Tell Your Wife*	(co-director)
1923	(GB)	*Woman to Woman*	(co-scriptwriter/assistant director/art director)
1924	(GB)	*The Prude's Fall* (incomplete)	(scriptwriter/assistant director/art director)
1924	(GB)	*The Passionate Adventure*	(co-scriptwriter/assistant director/art director)
1924	(GB)	*The White Shadow*	(art director/editor)

1925	(GB-G)	*The Blackguard*	(scriptwriter/assistant director/art director)
1926	(GB-G)	*The Pleasure Garden*	(director)
1926	(GB-G)	*The Mountain Eagle*	(director)
1926	(GB)	*The Lodger: A Story of the London Fog*	(director/co-scriptwriter/appearance)
1927	(GB)	*Downhill*	(director)
1927	(GB)	*Easy Virtue*	(director)
1927	(GB)	*The Ring*	(director/story/scriptwriter)
1928	(GB)	*The Farmer's Wife*	(director/scriptwriter)
1928	(GB)	*Champagne*	(director/adaptation)
1928	(GB)	*The Manxman*	(director)
1929	(GB)	*Blackmail* (silent version)	(director/adaptation/appearance)
1929	(GB)	*Blackmail* (sound version)	(director/adaptation/appearance)
1929	(GB)	*Juno and the Paycock*	(director/co-scriptwriter)
1930	(GB)	*An Elastic Affair* (short)	(director)
1930	(GB)	*Elstree Calling*	(segment-director)
1930	(GB)	*Harmony Heaven*	(segment-director)
1930	(GB)	*Murder!*	(director/co-adaptation/appearance)
1930	(GB)	*Mary* (German version of *Murder!*)	(director)
1931	(GB)	*The Skin Game*	(director/co-scriptwriter)
1931	(GB)	*Rich and Strange*	(director)
1932	(GB)	*Lord Camber's Ladies*	(producer)
1932	(GB)	*Number 17*	(director/co-scriptwriter)
1934	(GB)	*Waltzes from Vienna*	(director)

1934	(GB)	*The Man Who Knew Too Much*	(director)
1935	(GB)	*The 39 Steps*	(director/appearance)
1936	(GB)	*Secret Agent*	(director)
1936	(GB)	*Sabotage*	(director)
1937	(GB)	*Young and Innocent*	(director/appearance)
1938	(GB)	*The Lady Vanishes*	(director/appearance)
1939	(GB)	*Jamaica Inn*	(director)
1940	(US)	*Rebecca*	(director/appearance)
1940	(US)	*Foreign Correspondent*	(director/appearance)
1940	(US)	*The House Across the Bay*	(shot additional scenes)
1941	(US)	*Mr. and Mrs. Smith*	(director/appearance)
1941	(US)	*Suspicion*	(director)
1942	(US)	*Saboteur*	(director/appearance)
1942	(US)	*Shadow of a Doubt*	(director/appearance)
1943	(US)	War bonds short	(director)
1944	(US)	*Lifeboat*	(director/appearance)
1944	(GB)	*Bon Voyage*	(director)
1944	(GB)	*Aventure malgache*	(director)
1945	(US)	*Spellbound*	(director/appearance)
1945	(GB)	*F3080 (Memory of the Camps,* later *A Painful Reminder)*	(advisor)
1946	(US)	*Notorious*	(director/story/ appearance)
1947	(US)	*The Paradine Case*	(director/appearance)
1948	(US)	*Rope*	(director/appearance)
1949	(GB)	*Under Capricorn*	(director)
1949	(GB)	*Stage Fright*	(director/appearance)
1951	(US)	*Strangers on a Train*	(director/appearance)
1953	(US)	*I Confess*	(director/appearance)
1954	(US)	*Dial M for Murder*	(director/appearance)
1954	(US)	*Rear Window*	(director/appearance)
1954	(US)	*To Catch a Thief*	(director/appearance)
1954	(US)	*The Trouble with Harry*	(director/appearance)

1954	(US)	Safe-driving campaign trailer	(appearance)
1955	(US)	*The Man Who Knew Too Much*	(director/appearance)
1956	(US)	*The Wrong Man*	(director/appearance)
1957	(US)	*Vertigo*	(director/appearance)
1959	(US)	*North by Northwest*	(director/appearance)
1960	(US)	*The Gazebo*	(voice on telephone)
1960	(US)	Ford Motor Company promotion	(host)
1960	(US)	*Psycho*	(director/appearance)
1963	(US)	*The Birds*	(director/appearance)
1964	(US)	*Marnie*	(director/appearance)
1965	(US)	*The Dark Intruder* (TV pilot)	(producer)
1966	(US)	*Torn Curtain*	(director/appearance)
1969	(US)	*Topaz*	(director/appearance)
1970	(US)	*Makin' It*	(appearance from 1930s)
1972	(GB)	*Frenzy*	(director/appearance)
1976	(US)	*Family Plot*	(director/appearance)

TELEVISION (director credits only)

Alfred Hitchcock Presents

1955	*Breakdown*	(director/introduction/producer)
1955	*The Revenge*	(director/introduction/producer)
1955	*The Case of Mr. Pelham*	(director/introduction/producer)
1956	*Back for Christmas*	(director/introduction/producer)
1956	*Wet Saturday*	(director/introduction/producer)
1957	*One More Mile to Go*	(director/introduction/producer)
1957	*Perfect Crime*	(director/introduction/producer)
1958	*A Dip in the Pool*	(director/introduction/producer)
1958	*Poison*	(director/introduction/producer)
1958	*Lamb to the Slaughter*	(director/introduction/producer)
1959	*Banquo's Chair*	(director/introduction/producer)
1959	*Arthur*	(director/introduction/producer)
1959	*Crystal Trench*	(director/introduction/producer)

1960 *Mrs. Bixby and the Colonel's*
      Coat   (director/introduction/producer)
1961 *The Horseplayer*   (director/introduction/producer)
1961 *Bang! You're Dead*   (director/introduction/producer)

Other Television

1957 *Four O'Clock*   (director/producer)
      (*Suspicion*)
1960 *Incident at the Corner*
      (*Ford Startime*)   (director)
1962 *I Saw the Whole Thing*
      (*The Alfred Hitchcock Hour*)   (director/introduction)

INDEX

337